IN THE DARKNESS OF THE
CINEMA

PITT LATIN AMERICAN SERIES
CATHERINE M. CONAGHAN, EDITOR

UNIVERSITY OF PITTSBURGH PRESS

IN THE DARKNESS OF THE CINEMA

GENDER AND MOVIEGOING
IN EARLY TWENTIETH-CENTURY
URBAN BRAZIL

LENA OAK SUK

Published by the University of Pittsburgh Press, Pittsburgh, Pa., 15260
Copyright © 2025, University of Pittsburgh Press
All rights reserved
Manufactured in the United States of America
Printed on acid-free paper
10 9 8 7 6 5 4 3 2 1

Cataloging-in-Publication data is available from the Library of Congress

Hardcover: 978-0-8229-4864-3
Paperback: 978-0-8229-6784-2

Cover art: A cinema program in both German and Portuguese. "Varieté," Cine República program, n.d., Cinemateca Brasileira São Paulo, 1481-31.

Cover design: Alex Wolfe

Publisher: University of Pittsburgh Press, 7500 Thomas Blvd., 4th floor, Pittsburgh, PA 15260, United States, www.upittpress.org

EU Authorized Representative: Easy Access System Europe, Mustamäe tee 50, 10621 Tallinn, Estonia, gpsr.requests@easproject.com

CONTENTS

Acknowledgments
vii

Introduction
A Night Out at the Movies
3

1. Melindrosas and Movie-Struck Girls in Brazilian Print Culture
27

2. Region and Race, Gender and Urbanization in Brazilian Silent Cinema
51

3. Making Cinemas Safe for Senhoras in 1920s Rio de Janeiro and São Paulo
85

4. Class, Race, and Desire at the Movies
107

5. Dreams and Memories of a Respectable City
141

Conclusion
Seductions in the Street and Gendered Visions of Urban Life
175

Notes
181

Bibliography
203

Index
219

ACKNOWLEDGMENTS

Thank you to the many people who motivated me, encouraged me, and supported me to write this book. Even if we only met or conversed once, hearing you take an interest in my scholarly work reminded me that this project was worth finishing.

I began this book project as a graduate student at Emory University, and I thank my advisor, Jeffrey Lesser, for his years of support and advice. I also thank Thomas Rogers, Yanna Yannakakis, and Matthew Bernstein for their input on this project in its early years. Leonardo Marques, Debjani Bhattacharyya, Cari Maes, and Isabella Goulart have been friends through so many stages of this project. Leo, Giselle Candido, and Isa—thank you for welcoming me back to Brazil after so many years away, after I had finally submitted revisions for this book.

I thank Eduardo Morettin for many years of support, and the research group História e Audiovisual at the University of São Paulo, who welcomed me to their meetings and pushed me to be more rigorous in my research. I also thank José Inácio de Melo Souza for his generosity and foundational research. Sheila Schvarzman's work and advice have also been key. To all the attendees I met at the Colóquio Internacional de Cinema e História, I wish I could attend more often to benefit from the incredible scholarship emerging out of this group. Aiala Levy, Courtney Campbell, Julio Moraes, and especially Rielle Navitski were helpful colleagues who shared sources and knowledge during the research phase and beyond.

I owe immense gratitude to Heloísa Buarque de Almeida, who generously shared her collection of rich oral histories. To Carol Mishima, Kristofer Krantz, Robert Rosenquist, and Mariana Felix, I give a hearty hug for their friendship and their support. I thank all of the *tias* and *avós* who spoke to me and told me about their lives, especially my neighbors and family friends.

Archivists and attendants at Brazilian archives were essential to the development of this book. First, I thank the staff at the Cinemateca Brasileira of São Paulo. During times when I wanted to give this project up, I was motivated to finish so that I could contribute to the library and community at the Cinemateca, even if just a little. I also thank Ricardo Mendes and the staff at the Arquivo Histórico de São Paulo; Ricardo provided me with digital documents and shared his vast knowledge of São Paulo history and the archive's collections. Alexandre Miyazato, Victor Martins de Souza, Rodrigo Archangelo, and the staff at the Cinemateca Brasileira in São Paulo were excellent guides and resources. I also thank Daniel and Gabriella at Project Gutenberg for allowing me to join the *cafezinho* at the Cine Maior Idade program, where I had so many fun conversations about moviegoing. Jacira and the students at the Oficina do Cérebro also welcomed me into their classroom, shared memories, and helped me on Portuguese crossword puzzles. I thank the staff at the Arquivo Multimeios of the Centro Cultural São Paulo (CCSP), the Centro de Documentação e Informação Científica at the Pontifícia Universidade Católica de São Paulo (PUC-CEDIC), the São Paulo State Public Archive, Museu Lasar Segall, the Biblioteca Nacional, the Arquivo Nacional, and the private collection of the Liga das Senhoras Católicas. Although not all the collections I viewed became a part of the book, they were still formative to my thinking about gender and film history in Brazil.

Research was facilitated with the financial and professional support of the US Fulbright Student Program, the CLIR Mellon Dissertation Fellowship in Original Sources, and the James H. Guilbeau Jr. and Thelma Cummings Guilbeau Endowment in History. Early trips to Brazil were made possible by a CLAH Scobie Award, a BRASA Brazilian Initiation Scholarship, funding from Emory University, and an NEH Summer Seminar in São Paulo led by the late David William Foster, another excellent advisor.

I thank Josh Shanholtzer at the University of Pittsburgh Press, who was incredibly patient in waiting for this book's revisions. I thank the anonymous reviewers who provided the best kind of reviews—encouraging, judicious, and full of specific suggestions for improvement, especially "Reader 2," who read this manuscript twice and helped it immensely both times.

I thank my friends Sara Ritchey and John Troutman for welcoming me to Louisiana, and then for helping me to explore new opportunities. I also thank Ian Beamish, Liz Skilton, D'Weston Haywood, Hilton Cordoba, Cheylon Woods, Katie Edwards, Leslie Bary, and Rich Frankel, who wrote with me or read this manuscript in its early stages. Thanks to the students at UL Lafayette who taught me so much. At the University of Texas at Austin, I thank Seth Garfield, Adele Nelson, Sonia Roncador, the Institute for Historical Studies, the Critical Archives Reading Group, and UT Libraries. I also thank colleagues like Laura Caloudas, Laurie Young, Sarayu Adeni, and Margaret Rieley, who have inspired me with their professionalism and love for adventure. Thank you to the scholars who offered professional advice or scholarly support at different points over the years, including Anne Rubenstein, Matthew Karush, David Eltis, Carmen Alvaro Jarrín, Roney Cytrynowicz, David Lynn, Alex Borucki, Alicia Monroe, Fabricio Prado, Uri Rosenheck, Ariel Svarch, Jennifer Schaefer, Mollie Lewis, Alice Trusz, Paula Santoro, Nina Giacomo, Tony Rosenthal, Alessandro de Oliveira dos Santos, Arthur Knight, Iris Kochen, Nikki Ferraiolo, Leena Batra, Amy Lucko at CLIR, Kelly Besecke, Lauren Coats and the NEH Institute on "Textual Data and Digital Texts," and the scholars of the NEH Summer Seminar "Brazilian Literature: Twentieth Century Urban Fiction."

To the writers and the writing group that helped me finally finish this project—Pablo Palomino, Melisa Casumbal, Mary Battle, Stephanie George, and Dinah Hannaford—what can I say but that I couldn't have done this without you. Special thanks to my friend Dinah, who always knows the exact dosage of tough love and practicality to get me moving.

I thank my parents, Elijah Suk and Agnes Suk, who always believed that I could accomplish whatever goal I set and gave me strength when I needed it most. To my big, jolly Korean family, including Danny Suk, Jisun Yang, Lois Suk, Coby Suk, Theresa Lee, Harabuji, Halmoni, all my uncles, my aunts, the Kim cousins, and the Suk cousins, thank you for all of the love and encouragement that you have provided me throughout the years. I thank my husband and partner, George Kientzy, who has been a deep well of patience, support, and chocolate. Thank you for keeping up the morale. Finally, to Moses George Kientzy, Jun Zephirin Kientzy, and Vera Iseul Kientzy—I've been working on this book your entire lives. You've been so patient and encouraging, thanks and love you always.

… IN THE DARKNESS OF THE
CINEMA

INTRODUCTION

A NIGHT OUT AT THE MOVIES

On a night out at the Cine República in 1920s São Paulo, Brazil,[1] moviegoers crowded the street as they waited in line for tickets, though ushers and a metal barricade stood to prevent the crushing of bodies.[2] They listened and danced to a live jazz band in the lobby before they entered the screening room, bottlenecking at the doors.[3] Women, demonstrating their respectability, sat with chaperones in the first few rows on the ground floor. Unknown persons and those presumed up to no good filed into the darkest corners in the back. The most elite *senhoras*—or "ladies," a title marked by a combination of class and respectability—filled the private boxes that wealthy families rented by the month. There they sat "in the front with their heads tilted, and men stand on foot behind them."[4] Even as they sat decorously in their private boxes, the young ladies had chances to read and hum the sexualized lyrics of the *sambas cariocas* (popular music from Rio de Janeiro)[5] printed in the multipage cinema program: "I kissed my girl / without anyone seeing us / the moon saw, smiled, and heard, everything that I said . . . what a delicate taste / the kiss of a *morena* [brown-skinned woman] / I don't deserve it / and I suffer for it / to the point of pain."[6] These lyrics were printed among advertisements for German pianos and "Ambra soap," the "perfume of the aristocracy."[7] To the scandal of the ladies, other young boys avoided the bottleneck in the center aisle by running through the private boxes and then jumping over the short wall into the seats below.[8] The hundreds of moviegoers who had bought the cheapest tickets climbed three flights up a narrow staircase to the third-floor balcony. The cinema held two thousand moviegoers, and it took time for all to find their seats and settle down.

There were loud shushes as the lights dimmed, but people continued to chat when the first film, a short documentary, showed the "marvels" of the Brazilian countryside and panoramic shots of distant cities. The more prudish portion of the audience grimaced at the sight of scantily clad Indigenous people or Afro-Brazilian women market sellers on screen, but whether they admitted it or not, many others had come just to see such pleasurable, sensational sights. Filmmakers and viewers made permissible the images of Brazil's "uncivilized" interior, the exhibition of brown, naked bodies, under the guise of anthropological education, which they packaged within the modern medium of cinema and the elegant furnishings of the movie theater.

The shushes grew louder as the feature film began, usually a Hollywood drama, a European import, and occasionally, the grand premiere of a Brazilian production. Even those who outwardly disapproved of the less respectable members of the audience could still be held rapt by images that were foreign, exotic, sexy: Rudolph Valentino as a Middle Eastern sheik, Pola Negri as an Egyptian dancer, and Mary Pickford as a geisha and as an Indian woman, face darkened by dirt. To the annoyance of those engrossed in the story, a group of young boys loudly cracked jokes during the most dramatic moments.[9] The amateur film critics in the audience sneered at both groups, the boys who disrespected the film and the tasteless fans who knew nothing of cinema as art, but instead enjoyed anything with a handsome actor.

In between each film, the lights flashed on, forcing anyone in a close embrace to suddenly withdraw. Others took advantage of the light to admire the handsome men with pomaded hair and women with short hair and even shorter skirts. When the film ended, the two thousand patrons filed slowly out of the cinema, bottlenecking again at the main entrance. As moviegoers slowly spilled onto the streets, they criticized the films and made jokes about whom and what they saw. The same boys who had shouted obscenities during the film's most dramatic moments sang the lyrics of another *samba* printed in the cinema program so that the exiting ladies could hear them. The song was about a young guy "crazed" for "fried fish," and when exiting a streetcar, he grabs the leg of a young woman, apologizing, "I thought it was the horn!" The chorus followed:

> "How good it is,
> In a honk-honk-honk-honk
> Walking slowly in the dark
> Honking with satisfaction."[10]

The sexual innuendo of "honking with satisfaction" was not lost on those leaving the movie theater, whether they too were boarding a streetcar or stepping into a flashy automobile. Just as the rumbling and honking of the city, represented by the streetcar, infiltrated the movie theater via the song "Fried Fish," the sounds, songs, jokes, and emotions from the cinema spilled out onto the sidewalk.

Songs about kissing in the moonlight, couples embracing in the darkness, women with short hair dressed as *melindrosas*, a type of Brazilian "modern girl"—these images and figures were not contained within the walls of the movie theater, but were part of a new urban landscape in Brazil. Both real and imagined, these visualizations of gendered and sexual practices were present in city streets and in the blooming popular production of film, literature, magazines, and memories. In the expanding print and visual culture of the time period, artists, intellectuals, filmmakers, and moviegoers imagined how shifting gender norms were part of Brazil's ever-changing urban environments. Did women's expanded spatial mobility, their looming presence in spaces of leisure and consumption like movie theaters, portend the liberalization of gender norms? Could Brazilian cities accommodate these new types of femininity and rituals of romance while maintaining the moral sanctity of the "traditional" Brazilian family? On and off the silver screen, what would a "modern" city look like, what was women's place within it, and what would these entangled concepts mean for the future of Brazil?

In the Darkness of the Cinema argues that sexual morality, gender, and urban space were mutually constitutive in the early twentieth century and beyond. Artists, intellectuals, filmmakers, and moviegoers imagined how women and gender norms were essential to determining the shape and moral fiber of Brazilian cities and Brazilian society writ large. They viewed movie theaters as bellwethers for how urbanization catalyzed changing gender norms and vice versa. Whether women could participate in urban consumption and leisure while upholding traditional expectations for family and motherhood was a key question as to what urbanization meant for Brazil. In a study of moviegoing and film culture, we see how sexual morality and gender were central to determining individual social status, and also were intertwined with the potential of urban life. Such an examination not only enriches our knowledge of women's everyday experiences and expectations for gendered propriety, but also illuminates the role of gender in constructing visions of the modern city. Intersecting with race and class, ideologies of gender were pivotal in the construction and representation of cities like Rio de Janeiro and São Paulo. From intellectuals' hand-wringing in the 1920s to moviegoers' nostalgic memories in the late twentieth century, Brazilians looked to movie theaters—and the social activities within them—as an arena for the changing rules governing sexual morality. And their judgments of women's behavior were entangled with their hopes, dreams, and memories of urban Brazil.

A night at the movies was not limited to watching the films on screen. Rather, moviegoing was the site of multiple activities, media, and interpretations. Beyond the exhibition and reception of films, moviegoing included the social practices of audience members, the built space of the theater, the advertisements for aspirational commodities, the whispers floating amid the music, and the scandals that moviegoers witnessed or imagined to occur in dark corners and seats. Moviegoing was an experience at once visual, visceral, commercial, and spatial. As a place that was both private and public, global and local, elite and popular, the movie theater was a microcosm of the turbulent early twentieth century in Brazil. Cinema was a locus for the transnational flow of US, European, and Latin American films. Through media like Rio de Janeiro's sambas, printed in São Paulo film programs, or a São Paulo film critic's review of a film from Recife, cinema was also a hub for regional and national circulations of popular culture. Cinema's reach was wide, touching various sectors of the population. Film intellectuals and filmmakers, municipal officials and engineers, public health professionals, artists and writers, movie theater owners, and of course the moviegoers themselves used movie theaters and thought about the meanings of cinema. Their diverse perspectives across a vast array of historical sources provide a rich portrait of the early twentieth century and beyond, and underline the role of gender and sexuality in shaping a dynamic time period.

In 1925 an essay entitled "Cinema in the Light and the Dark" appeared in *Vida Doméstica*, a Brazilian women's magazine. Playing on the various meanings of "light" and "dark," the essay detailed how the lights would flicker on between films during a night at the movies. The acts that occurred in the movie theater included sexual assault, adultery, and other forms of deviance, which according to the essay affronted traditional family relationships. In the darkness, *bolinas*—a term for men who groped women in movie theaters—not only victimized women but "tormented zealous husbands and fathers." Yet when the lights came on, the bolinas were the first to uphold these hierarchies and to condemn "the rare confrere that gets caught with his hand in the cookie jar."[11] In the brightness, a woman screamed, not because she was being assaulted, but because she spied her husband in the arms of another woman. Upon being found out, the husband fled, "leaving his mistress to brave the four winds." The cinema in the "dark" and the "light" was simultaneously a space for private sexual acts and for the condemnation of them.

As evidenced in the story, the movie theater was a double-edged sword. On the one hand, it provided a venue for forbidden sex acts—a threat to the gendered order. In the darkness of the cinema, women were subject to harassment, husbands cheated on wives, and marriage, chastity, and moral values were all at stake. But when the lights came on, the movie theater was also a space to expose these acts, condemn bad practices, and reinforce (even if hypocritically) standards of sexual morality. The surreptitious bolina openly criticizes his "confrere," and a jilted wife asserts her family position over the hidden mistress. The anecdote serves to illustrate wider anxieties regarding the instability of gender and sexual norms. And movie theaters were not just a suspicious cause of these ills, but the perfect stage to both perpetrate and condemn such crimes. On a metatextual level, the story of the "dark" and the "light" is also an example of how observers of the moviegoing experience brought these acts to light for a wider audience, amplifying such stories across multiple media.

However, between the dark and the light, there are inevitably shades of gray, and here too is where cinema provides a revelatory platform. Although the essay above points out egregious examples of assault and adultery, what about the semilicit acts that characterized the moviegoing experience? The romance, the flirtations, the pleasurable enjoyment of watching alluring movie stars on a big screen? In these small gestures, affects, and emotions, we see a more nuanced way in which cinema was a destabilizing force in Brazilian society. Moral panic and hand-wringing portrayed cinema as throwing all good morals into disarray, but moviegoing illuminates how concepts of sexual morality and gendered propriety were constantly evolving. Moviegoers simultaneously constructed and negotiated the boundaries between forbidden pleasure versus semilicit romance or even a newly acceptable form of dating. The limits and rules of such behavior were dynamic, and cinema provided an arena for commentators of the time period to explore and determine where exactly these limits lay.

Gender, Honor, and Early Twentieth-Century Brazil

The largest country of South America, larger than the continental United States, Brazil is a vast nation made up of a diverse populace and distinct regional identities. In the early twentieth century, Brazil was a profoundly hierarchical yet also flexible society. Beginning in the late nineteenth century and post-abolition time period, immigration, industrialization, and urbanization threw many Brazilians' social status into flux. While the destinies of the "intractable poor"—those who remained in poverty even as they drifted between various social and legal statuses—and the oligarchic "traditional families" were more certain, geographic and social mobility characterized the lives of the millions who participated in mass migrations to Brazilian cities or who joined new sectors of work.[12] A descendant of rural enslaved people might become a factory worker in the city; a shopkeeper might become downwardly mobile amid a growing class of urban professionals.[13]

In previous centuries, Brazil had been the largest recipient of enslaved people from the trans-Atlantic slave trade, and it was also the last nation in the Americas to abolish slavery in 1888. At the time of abolition, Brazil's total population was about 14 million, and by 1920, it had more than doubled to over 30 million. Between 1890 and 1919, 2.6 million immigrants entered Brazil, mostly from Portugal, Italy, and Spain, but also from Asia and the Middle East.[14] Brazil today has both the largest population of Afro-descendant people outside of Africa and one of the largest populations of Japanese-descendant people outside of Japan. Much of this early wave of immigration concentrated in the state of São Paulo, a region that needed laborers for its vast coffee plantations. Both external and internal migrations shifted population growth from the north to the southeast of Brazil and changed Brazilian cities demographically and structurally. Brazil's urban centers grew in population and transformed in terms of industry and economy. Rio de Janeiro, the country's capital, expanded as a hub of the federal government and for the importation and consumption of manufactured goods. The city of São Paulo, the capital of São Paulo state, was the eventual destination for many migrants who found work in textile and food factories, among other sectors. A "sleepy town" of 35,000 people in 1880, the city swelled to 600,000 in 1920, and 2.2 million by 1950.[15] The growing urban centers reflected Brazil's racially and culturally diverse population with pockets of ethnic communities, including Jewish, Japanese, European, and Black communities, as well as neighborhoods and hubs where they mixed.[16]

These shifts in population growth and urbanization occurred during the Brazilian Old Republic (1889–1930), which sought to instill "order and progress"—a motto still emblazoned on the country's flag—in the nation's political, cultural, and racial order. Though implementing republican ideals of electoral democracy, like many young nations, popular democratic participation was an uneven process. Women, for example, were not accorded the right to vote until 1932, after the end of the Old Republic.[17] However, although only 1 to 3 percent of the population voted in federal elections that were more perfunctory than democratic, there was popular participation in "layers of republicanism," especially among the growing urban milieu.[18] Politicians and intellectuals expressed affinity with Western European and North American models of "progress" that influenced policies toward urban reform, education, and public health, which met with degrees of resistance and negotiation.[19]

Amid these transformations in demography and politics, gender norms also underwent change. In the early twentieth century, in Brazil and across the world, women became increasingly visible in mass media and urban spaces of leisure. From shopping to driving automobiles and acting on movie screens, women gained greater prominence in sites of consumption and sociability.[20] Of course, women had previously inhabited the streets to work and shop,[21] but new forms of femininity appeared on the pages of glossy magazines, newspapers, and advertisements. The "melindrosa" in Brazil, like other global manifestations of the "modern girl," presented a gendered quandary to notions of progress and social change.[22] These women frequented public spaces like department stores, amusement parks, and cafés, as well as movie theaters. The new media of the time period, including cinema, radio, and the attending "paratexts" such as print advertisements, reviews, and commentaries, amplified these visions and sounds of modern femininity.[23]

In Brazil, women also entered the workforce in greater numbers. For centuries, free and enslaved women labored inside and outside the home as domestic servants, market sellers, seamstresses, and more.[24] However, the twentieth century introduced a greater array of occupations tied to the commercial economy, including those in industry and retail shops. New sectors of the female population entered the workforce in "white-collar" professions, performing salaried, nonmanual work, such as secretaries and teachers. While still a minority, the number of women in white-collar professions rose rapidly; between 1920 and 1940, male participation in public administration doubled while women's participation increased by over 600 percent.[25] As Susan Besse has shown, however, even as some advocates encouraged women to work and contribute to household incomes and to broader society, critics still worried about the effect of women's work on Brazilian children and families.[26]

Figure I.1. "Afternoon on the Avenida on a Sunny Day," photographs of women walking on Avenida Rio Branco, a central avenue in the center of Rio de Janeiro and location of the city's elite cinemas. "A avenida á tarde em dia de sol," *Para Todos*, no. 122, April 16, 1921, RC Para Todos, Cinemateca Brasileira São Paulo.

The relative respectability of these "public" women was a point of great debate, especially considering the importance of gendered honor in Latin America. In Brazil, honor was both a social and legal concept that regulated individuals' adherence to codes of sexual and gendered behavior. The degree of one's honor was a factor in determining one's social and even racial status. In contrast to North America, Brazilians have traditionally based racial identity on skin color and phenotype, as well as factors like class and moral status, and they have also recognized mixed-race categories of identity like *pardo*, or being "brown."[27] For women, honor meant the preservation of virginity and the display of chastity, among other expectations for gendered propriety.[28] For men, honor might mean their ability to command public respect equal to their status and self-worth, or their participation in rituals to prove masculinity, social rank, and even ethnic superiority, for example by publicly dueling with those who offended them.[29] Sueann Caulfield has demonstrated how intellectual, political, and popular understandings of gendered honor persisted well into the twentieth century in Brazil, and how it was not a concept limited to or imposed by elites.[30] Caulfield and Martha de Abreu Esteves have examined court cases of "deflowering" to show how Brazilian women and their families, some of whom were poor women of color, asserted their possession of honor through the legal system by bringing sexual assailants and other offenders to court. While some intellectuals reduced women's sexual honor to the definitive possession or lack of a hymen, others took a more nuanced approach that bent with the changing social context. For men and women in the early twentieth century, honor could also mean belonging to a good family, not displaying sexual desire, or avoiding heterosocial spaces like cinemas and dance halls.[31]

Even seemingly mundane perambulations—moving between public and private spaces, from home to work, or from café to movie theater—had implications for women's honor. Women who circulated in public walked a fine line as they walked the city, and their spatial practices informed their moral status. According to Brazilian sociologist Roberto da Matta's framework of "house and street," home is the arena of family, safety, and morality, while the street represents danger, conflict, and anonymity. As in other languages and countries, the Brazilian Portuguese term for a "woman of the street" (*mulher da rua*) is euphemistic for a female sex worker. In contrast, a woman of the house enjoys the safety and status accorded to her place within a family unit.[32] Historians of Brazil have pointed out that the house was only a safe space for elite women. For servants and enslaved people, the house was a space of danger and repression while the street offered comparative liberty.[33]

Moviegoing adds to this discussion by demonstrating how these debates about honor, respectability, and social status extended well beyond the courtroom and permeated the realm of leisure and popular media. In the private/public space of the cinema, sexual respectability was both nuanced and nebulous. Outside the medical definition of virginal chastity and the legal language of honor, sexual respectability was a standard that moviegoers determined in fleeting social and physical interactions. As historians have previously shown, women's social status was heavily dependent on their sexual honor. Moviegoing, however, reveals how valuations of sexual morality and social status were often fluid rather than fixed, determined in the moment and shifting with context, precariously balanced within the social etiquette measured by the flirtations and desires within the movie theater. Moviegoers determined their own and others' social and moral status based on their quotidian interactions and spatial practices. The same woman who might be perceived as a "lady" when she sat in the private box of a morning matinee might be perceived as sexual prey or predator if sitting alone during a nighttime show. Social mobility was not without limits, and women continued to encounter barriers to their spatial movements. The movie theater was not a utopia in which people otherwise marginalized by race, class, and wealth became suddenly liberated from social expectations. Quite the opposite, the movie theater could function as a microcosm that reflected Brazilian society's social differences, where women who had fewer liberties outside the movie theater might have fewer inside as well. However, in the eyes of the multiple people who depicted moviegoing in the early twentieth century, moviegoers' identities were both intersectional and multifaceted, with aspects dependent on transient social practices: how they went to the movies, where they sat, and what they did in the darkness.

Examining these quotidian interactions reveals a diversity of emerging gendered identities and enriches our knowledge of femininity in this era. An evolving lexicon labeled women as *melindrosas* (modern girls), *mademoiselles*, *senhoras* (ladies), and *moças* (girls), among other terms, to describe them in varying shades of respectable behavior and sometimes racially tinged sexual allure. These feminine identities existed on a continuum and were differentiated by imprecise mixtures of fashion, consumption, and leisure habits. They were discrete yet mutable entities, and one could be mistaken for or become another by changing minute details: style of hat, length of skirt, choice of movie theater. The greatest disruption that these women posed, however, was not only that the boundary between a "mademoiselle" and a "senhora" could be so easily transgressed, but that it was not clear where the boundary lay.

Moviegoing highlights the complex sociability of urban Brazil, showcasing the various shades between black and white, the spectrum of femininity that existed between the binary of women either with or without honor.

Gender and Urban Space

In Brazil and in other national contexts, women's increasing liberation from domestic space was intertwined with questions about urbanization and what it meant for structures of family, health, and gender. Some of this discourse was aimed at women's "place" in the city—where they belonged, or conversely, how much of the city might belong to them. This question had both literal and symbolic meanings, as people debated where women should physically circulate and, more broadly, how increased spatial mobility might result in greater freedom from other strictures of confinement. This discussion was fundamentally gendered in the premise that women should be confined to any space at all. In contrast, the concept of the *flaneur* emerged around the same time, a de facto male observer of city spaces who walked anonymously in the crowds. In Brazil, *crônistas*, short-form writers who wrote journalistic and sometimes whimsical accounts of city life, provided this urbane perspective.[34] In an analysis of turn-of-the-century public amusements in Chicago, historian Lauren Rabinovitz asks whether there was a female counterpart to the flaneur, a "flaneuse," a rambling, urban woman who observed and consumed urban pleasures, or if her gender would instead cast her as a "streetwalker," a sexual commodity rather than a consumer herself.[35] The question extends to turn-of-the-century Brazil, where a woman's relationship to a moviegoing male flaneur might be as the object of desire, whether on the streets or on screen in erotic or even pornographic films.[36]

Historians of the Americas have explored urban spaces of leisure and consumption, such as movie theaters, amusement parks, and restaurants, tackling the question of what women's presence within them meant for a more traditionally defined public sphere. To clarify, I differentiate between public space and public sphere, as I do domestic space and domestic sphere, as activities in the public sphere did not always occur in public spaces.[37] Separating the terms recognizes how marginalized groups like women might participate in one but be excluded from the other.[38] While Jürgen Habermas's definition of the public sphere emphasized the process by which public social activity might generate public opinions and politics, scholars have taken an expanded view of the public sphere to examine how mass media, popular culture, and broad engagement with public life were involved in the creation of communities, subjects, and one's sense of place in the city. At the turn of the twentieth century, the image of women as active participants in urban life, whether in seeking pleasure or politics, contradicted stereotypes of women's passive domesticity. Kathy Peiss's landmark discussion of "cheap amusements" shows how the congregation of working women in dance halls and movie theaters ultimately overlapped with their presence in New York's union halls and ballot boxes.[39] Historians of Brazil have examined workers' congregation in sites of urban leisure culture, and how bars, restaurants, and cabarets might be sites of identity formation or loci of state surveillance.[40] Across the Americas, working men and women formed connections between politicization and consumption, finding intersections in sites of sociability like restaurants, shops, and cinemas.

Aside from these direct links between labor, consumption, and politics, cultural historians have analyzed art, architecture, literature, and theater to assess women's visual or cultural impact on urban landscapes.[41] By "landscape," I refer to the interaction between people and space, or the spaces that hold meaning for individuals and communities.[42] Women were sometimes the architects directly responsible for forging the modern cityscapes, and other times they were the muse-like visual inspirations for the male architects and artists who designed or depicted the city.[43] For example, Ageeth Sluis's work has analyzed how Mexican architects and artists used the spectacle of the art deco female body to inform the aesthetics of the modern Mexican landscape.[44] I also point out Maite Conde's work in *Consuming Visions*, which examines the image of the female consumer in literature as a spectacle that was both a product of and an active contributor to the modern landscape of Rio de Janeiro.[45] In São Paulo, Margareth Rago has deftly discussed female prostitution as a type of spectacle, an expression of commodified desire, symbolically key to the construction of the modern city.[46] In a related vein, historians of sex work and prostitution in Latin America have demonstrated how the state enforced ideologies of gender and public health to implicate female sex work as a key marker of the health, hygiene, and morality of early twentieth-century Latin American cities.[47]

Specific to cinema, historians have looked to movie theaters and audiences to elucidate the perspectives of people who were often shut out of film production, including populations marginalized by gender, race, class, or location. For example, significant work on female spectatorship has explored the potential of cinema to expand women's participation in an "alternative" public sphere in a time when they were excluded from mainstream politics.[48] In reception studies and audience studies, scholars have emphasized that in their love for specific films and movie stars, spectators of films were developing their own identities and defining their place in society.[49] Audiences could create new communities, and individuals could explore their own tastes and interpretations. In Mexico, for example, Mary Kay Vaughan relates how the young painter Pepe Zuñiga remembered moviegoing as integral to his circulations of a vibrant Mexico City. For Zuñiga, movies were an experience that he and his father shared, but Hollywood movies and Mexican movie stars were also vehicles for them to differentiate their tastes, to contrast their reactions and preferences.[50] Aside from the reception of films, spectators as audience members created new rituals and social practices that informed their performances of gender and belonging. Anne Rubenstein has examined how Mexican men might go to the movies with their families as a way to publicly demonstrate their role as the paternal head of the household.[51]

In the Darkness of the Cinema is indebted to these works but also contributes in many ways. While exploring the themes of modernity and changing gender roles that were key to the formation of Brazilian national identity, this book focuses on cinema and movie theaters as an exploration of gender and urban space, and how the rituals of dating, love, and romance were part of the social codes that built a modern city. It thus explores an arena of sexual morality that was linked to and informed by the discussions on gendered honor, public health, sexuality, and women's bodies, but that occupied the overlapping and ambiguous space of flirtation and romance. In so doing, the book examines a sector of urban life that was both frivolous and ephemeral—not as concrete or regulated as female prostitution, nor as "productive" as various types of women's labor, and outside of the formal, judicial judgments of female honor—and yet as I argue, still essential to the construction of urban space in a crucial time period. In addition, unlike histories that have linked consumption habits to political activity, this book locates the ways in which women were part of the modernization of Brazilian cities even when not explicitly involved in organized labor or politics, elucidating how frivolity and desire engendered their own effects on the shape of Brazilian cities. Similar to Sluis and Conde, this book accepts the premise that women's participation in urban spaces of consumption and leisure was key to emerging urban visual and literary cultures. However, it combines the analytic framework of gender as spectacle with a focus on gendered social interactions—the physical rituals of dating, romance, and flirtations, in sum, the everyday social practices of women—and how these too were part of the landscape of urban Brazil. This book, therefore, is not a history of the making of urban Brazil so much as a recognition of the central role that gender and sexual morality played in constructing it.

While focusing primarily on women's participation in film culture in the 1920s, the book follows how the intertwining of gender, sexuality, and urbanization persisted into later time periods. The final chapter thus extends these questions into the late twentieth and early twenty-first century, asking how moviegoers in these time periods reflected on the last century of moviegoing. Memoirs and oral histories from this later era reveal that the combination of fear, anxiety, and excitement from the 1920s about the future of Brazil had metamorphosed into nostalgia and longing about Brazil's past. Yet this societal transformation was still assessed by similar metrics—shifting gender roles, sexual practices, and their perceived deviation from accepted norms.

Cinema, Modernity, and the Rise of Brazilian Film Culture

Entrepreneurial Brazilian filmmakers and exhibitors were eager to experiment with the new technology of film almost as soon as it was available in the waning years of the 1800s.[52] Vicente de Paula Araújo has referred to the era between 1908 and 1911 as the "golden age" of Brazilian cinema because domestic film companies held a substantial share of the exhibition market.[53] In this time period of "early cinema," filmmakers around the world produced short narrative films and documentaries, and experimented with the potential of the medium. By the 1920s, however, the nature of filmmaking changed from a technological novelty to a full-fledged global industry. Hollywood studios began to produce narrative, feature-length films that were exported to movie theaters around the world.[54] While Brazilian filmmakers produced an average of 16.7 feature-length films a year, Hollywood films dominated over 80 percent of the Brazilian market.[55] Hollywood's ascendance may have overshadowed Brazilian film production in this respect, but Brazilian film historians have emphasized how domestic production persisted in the form of documentary and short-form films.

Movie theaters and exhibition circuits in Brazil reflected global changes in filmmaking. In the early 1900s, movie theaters proliferated across the country and acted as nodes within national and international networks of film exhibition. Ambitious entrepreneurs, many of them European immigrants like Jacomo Staffa, an Italian Brazilian, and Francisco Serrador, a Spanish Brazilian, established early conglomerates that supported networks of distribution and exhibition in multiple cities and regions. By 1911, for example, Serrador had consolidated a network ranging from Porto Alegre and Curitiba to Salvador and Recife, serving one thousand cinemas around the country.

Moviegoers in Manaus, on the edge of the Amazon, were outside of Serrador's network, but they accessed films directly through European distributors.[56] As such, a movie theater could be an entryway to a larger and more cosmopolitan world. Across multiple scales, the distribution of films and film culture might connect audiences across neighborhoods, regions, and nations. For example, a moviegoer from a peripheral neighborhood might journey to the city center to see a particular film, or moviegoers in Porto Alegre, in the far south of Brazil, might watch films from Rio de Janeiro or Hollywood.[57] In one curious example from 1932, one avid cinephile in a remote "little nook" of the Azores islands in Portugal wrote a fan letter to the Brazilian actress Eva Nil declaring his admiration and requesting her to send an autograph.[58]

Beginning in the 1910s, movie theaters became grander, more technologically advanced, and more elaborately furnished. Elite *cariocas* (residents of Rio de Janeiro) and *paulistanos* (residents of São Paulo city) increasingly attended these upscale cinemas in downtown centers.[59] While this trend continued, pushing out the itinerant film exhibitors and smaller theaters, cinemas ranged from giant movie palaces to small shacks with occasional screenings into the 1920s.[60] A billiards manager or restaurant owner might rent or buy a projector and some old reels and liven up their establishment with a weekly film screening. Before and in between films, some exhibitors had musical performances and circus acts, creating a dynamic, multimedia social space. In this sense, movie theaters overlapped with theaters, in that both might display films and theatrical performances (though they diverged in purpose and use in the 1920s), and both spaces were important avenues for sociability in São Paulo.[61] The moviegoing public was likewise diverse—young and old, rich and poor—though sometimes separated in different theaters, spaces, or days of the week. As an imperfect snapshot, in 1927, a male factory worker in São Paulo making 16$000 (16 *mil-réis*, which was the Brazilian currency in use at the time until 1942) a day, or a female factory worker making 8$500 a day, might purchase a "half-price" ticket for 1$000 to 1$500, prices offered to children and sometimes to women on special "girls' nights." Cheaper seats could be found in balcony sections for as low as $600, though as will be discussed in chapter 4, these were mostly for men. Keeping in mind that cinema was more accessible at the beginning of the decade and that the prices of goods overall increased rapidly in the 1920s, tickets were still less than the cost of a daily lunch at a restaurant in the same year.[62] The cost of a ticket was not insignificant and could be out of reach to many working women, especially those in low-paying sectors like domestic servitude, which paid little for egregiously long hours. However, women might use their wider social network and relations with higher-earning men, who might make twice as much per hour, to pay for leisure.[63] At the same time, well-off paulistanos who could afford a seat in a private box would pay anywhere between 7$500 and 25$000.[64] In this way, and as evidenced by anecdotes, memories, and stories from the time period, cinema was a leisure activity that was both elite and popular, where people of varying racial and social statuses congregated. Moviegoing, as a paid leisure activity, was not as integrated into street culture as music, dance, or drinking and likely excluded impoverished paulistanos who were similarly peripheral to other forms of entertainment. However, the movie theater was a microcosm of the broader population of Brazilians who participated in urban commercial culture.

As film exhibition and moviegoing grew, so did film criticism and intellectual production related to cinema. There was a vibrant and variegated intellectual scene in early twentieth-century Brazil and a flourishing domestic print culture that, though male in majority, included prominent female writers. In the city of São Paulo, the number of newspapers and periodicals increased from thirty-eight in 1910 to seventy-nine by 1927.[65] Writers, artists, and intellectuals from a variety of regions and ideological perspectives wrote about the impact of cinema in Brazilian society. For example, moralizers associated with the Catholic Church, republican politicians, elite intellectuals, and radical artists all addressed what the growth of cinema meant for gender norms, children's education, and Brazilian society. "Cine-clubs" dedicated to appreciating cinema as art arose in various cities around Brazil, and this nascent group of film critics published specialized film magazines dedicated to the discussion of films and moviegoing, resulting in weekly and monthly publications like *Cinearte*, *Scena Muda*, *Selecta*, *Palcos e Telas*, and *Foto-Film*.[66] And though I refer to these *críticos* as film critics and film intellectuals somewhat interchangeably, both terms are apt to describe the writers who mixed their reviews of specific films with their pontification on the meanings of cinema, exhibition, and their role in Brazilian society.[67]

This book focuses primarily on the cities of São Paulo and Rio de Janeiro, though mostly São Paulo, with some exploration of films and literature from Recife and the interior of Minas Gerais. Choosing the oft-studied cities of São Paulo and Rio de Janeiro risks recentering the largest and most prosperous cities of Brazil as being representative of the nation. However, each city provides a particular and exclusive portrait of Brazilian society in this time period, and neither city can stand in for the whole. Whereas Rio de Janeiro was the long-standing political and cultural capital, São Paulo was booming with new industrialization and population growth. The participation of European immigrants in the early Brazilian film industry, and the concentrations of European immigrants in both Rio de Janeiro and especially São Paulo, fed the advancement of movie theaters in these cities. In São Paulo, moviegoing culture expanded concurrently with the city, providing a unique window into the city during an era of accelerated growth. In addition, factors such as the rise of the famed São Paulo modernist art movement, the growth of an industrial working class, and the state's attempts to regulate the unwieldy explosion of movie theaters contributed to a swirling, vibrant moviegoing scene that was reflected in a flourishing urban print culture. As the final chapter of this book winds into the mid- and late twentieth century, it also follows the story of movie theaters in the city center and how these mammoth institutions played a central role in memories of urban life, emphasizing how, over decades, the city's moral fiber might be represented in the actions that took place in or around cinemas. In the case of Rio de Janeiro, the then-capital was home to an outpouring of cultural production, including major film-related publications like *Cinearte*, which gathered film intellectuals and producers who influenced production and criticism for decades. In addition, scholars have pushed back against São Paulo's claim as the bastion of modernism, reclaiming space for the rich modernist scene in Rio de Janeiro, including the Afro-Brazilian artists and the popular cultural production that emerged from it.[68] Between the two cities, there was a public rivalry that played out on the pages of magazines and newspapers, each vying to be recognized as the epicenter of cultural production and moviegoing in Brazil, such as when Rio de Janeiro–based critics envied the fact that São Paulo would be the first city in Brazil to exhibit a sound film or "talking picture."[69] While other urban centers of Brazil also participated in these conversations, both Rio de Janeiro and São Paulo provide a panoply of sources to examine the ways in which moviegoing habits engendered discussions regarding the interplay of gender and urbanization in Brazil.

Brazilians' participation in this explosion of film culture was tied to intellectual and popular understandings of the relationship between film culture and modernity. In Latin America, scholars of early twentieth-century film culture have focused on how filmmakers, exhibitors, and moviegoers used cinema to participate in, circulate, and produce their own meanings of modernity.[70] Ana M. López has revealed how Latin American elites from many different national contexts used cinema as a tool to represent and construct their nations as modern.[71] Laura Isabel Serna has stressed that even when in dialog with a domineering US film culture, Mexicans participated in national, modern film culture in a transnational context.[72] Rielle Navitski has shown how, from intellectuals in urban centers to adventurous filmmakers in rural areas, Latin Americans recentered the production of modernities through their production of films and participation in film culture. Flora Süssekind and Sarah Wells have discussed cinema as being integrated into a larger aesthetic of modern art and literature in Brazil.[73] The trend in literature has bent toward contextualizing cinema and film practices in terms of specific varieties of modernity that are not merely "hybrid" blends of modernity and tradition, but nationally and locally specific versions of modernity that existed in parallel across Latin America.[74] Scholars of the moviegoing experience in Latin America, such as Camila Gatica Mizala, have linked moviegoers' social practices to locally specific ideas of progress and modernity.[75] *In the Darkness of the Cinema* also frames modernity as variable and distinct in Brazil, but it focuses less on defining modernity than on what—during the time period of study—this sometimes nebulous and contested concept meant for gender roles.

As a place of the "light," cinema was an art form, mass medium, and social space that some Brazilian elites imagined as a tool of progress, one that could "uplift" the racial, moral, and intellectual profile of the populace. Throughout the early twentieth century, filmmakers, educators, and politicians hoped that "educational" or "good" cinema could be a powerful tool of moral guidance and propaganda, countering the effects of the "bad" cinema that was mostly from Hollywood.[76] The republican statesman Rui Barbosa made a speech as early as 1918 praising the use of "educational cinema" in the Rio de Janeiro school system.[77] Jonathas Serrano, a Catholic intellectual who focused on the effects of cinema on children, wrote several treatises in the early twentieth century that later influenced federal educational policy.[78] Collaborating with other intellectuals, Serrano proposed the production of Brazilian educational films that, in contrast to Hollywood films, would demonstrate "healthy emotions, without cheesiness, without ridiculousness, more humane, patriotic, socially superior."[79] Filmmakers and film intellectuals espoused similar ideas about cinema, maintaining that the domestic production of high-quality films would demonstrate Brazilian mastery of modern technology and taste. By excluding actors of color, films could also be a means of exhibiting Brazilians as white rather than a mixed-race population to domestic and international audiences.[80]

On the other hand, a slew of thinkers and policymakers across multiple sectors of Brazil, from writers and religious authorities to civil engineers and medical professionals, associated cinema with "the darkness" of modernity. Artists and intellectuals depicted cinema as a powerful force that would poison and destroy Brazilian womanhood and family life. As shown by Shelley Stamp and Hilary Hallett, intellectuals and writers in the US worried particularly about the effect that Hollywood films, with their sensational pleasures, would have on female fans in the United States.[81] Brazilian moralizers echoed similar concerns, but worried that in addition to spurring improper sexual desires, Hollywood films would colonize Brazilian minds and mannerisms. Similar to what Laura Isabel Serna has shown regarding the "yanqui invasion" of Hollywood films in Mexico, or what Fernando Purcell has shown in Chile, some Brazilian intellectuals and artists saw Hollywood as a potential threat to Brazilian cultural autonomy.[82] Across various ideological perspectives, Brazilian intellectuals worried that moviegoers would be overcome by the powerful verisimilitude of cinema and its all-too-real scenes of sex, violence, and undignified buffoonery of Hollywood films. The weak minds of moviegoers would then imitate these scenes in their real lives, with deleterious effects on norms of gender and sexuality in Brazil.

Hollywood films presented a double-edged sword in terms of racial ideologies in Brazil. Despite the fluidity of racial categorization and interracial social relationships that led to the myth of Brazil as a "racial democracy" in the 1950s, scholars in multiple disciplines have cataloged the systematic and personal racial prejudices against Black Brazilians.[83] Brazilian intellectuals also espoused an ideology of "whitening" or *branqueamento*, a concept rooted in eugenics promoting that, through European immigration and racial mixing, Brazil's Black[84] and mixed-race population would effectively be "whitened" over generations.[85] Whitening also manifested in engineering of the environment, with policy-makers hoping to endow the Brazilian populace with the characteristics they associated with whiteness, such as cleanliness, morality, and respectability through education and social reform.[86] While some salient voices, particularly in the Black intellectual community, presented alternative visions for the future of Brazil's multiracial society, it was whitening that informed federal policy on issues like immigration and education.

Where did Hollywood cinema and other contemporary media fit within these racial hierarchies? This was a time period in which artists and intellectuals across the globe experimented with primitivism and orientalism, from Brazilian modernist painters and poets to cultural imports like jazz and the Charleston dance, with their roots in African American culture.[87] As Ismail Xavier points out, Hollywood films presented sanitized visions of whiteness and affluence that satisfied Brazilian film intellectuals invested in eugenic ideology.[88] On the other hand, Hollywood studios participated in the vogue of orientalist and primitivist modern art, simultaneously embracing and exploiting African American cultural products like jazz and presenting images of exotic, foreign sexuality. Stars like Rudolph Valentino, Dolores del Río, and Pola Negri performed the role of the sexually aggressive ethnic "other," portraying Middle Eastern sheiks, Mexican "spitfires," and Egyptian cabaret dancers in films that sought to both shock and titillate.[89] Given US morals and even legislation, these films provided narrative arcs that both upheld the virtues of sexual chastity and condemned mixed-race coupling, punishing women who exhibited sexual vice and rewarding those who were pure.[90] However, these narrative frameworks merely condemned, not erased, the visual, visceral images of sexuality and ethnic otherness that made their way around the world. In this sense, Hollywood and North America remained an aspirational model for Brazilian film culture, but Hollywood films were not so unequivocally white, and certainly not always chaste.

In terms of urban space, the movie theater itself invited both adulation and anxiety. Apart from stories of the "dark and light" and the ambivalence regarding sex and romance inside the movie theater, issues like public health, class, and immigration also came to the fore. On the one hand, newspapers and magazines reported on the inauguration of opulent new movie theaters, praising the new technologies, services, and glamour associated with the social activity, not to mention the elite society that peppered the audience. The same film intellectuals who advocated for the growth of Brazilian film production touted the value of movie theaters, proclaiming, "A country's progress should be measured by its number of movie theaters."[91] Yet lurid stories of sexual assault, robberies, and violence appeared in Brazilian newspapers when describing the inner workings of the cinema. Urban reformers targeted ramshackle movie theaters that, due to the flammability of celluloid, were prone to fire and disaster. Public health officials also found fault with the moviegoing populace, worrying that overcrowded movie theaters would be breeding grounds for dangerous contagious diseases. The same film critics also maintained an ambivalent attitude toward the class of film entrepreneurs, mostly European immigrants, who established movie theaters in Rio de Janeiro and São Paulo. Film critics characterized these entrepreneurs as ranging from purveyors of progress and cosmopolitanism to greedy merchants without an understanding of the seventh art.

Cinema was key to the formation of urbanization, nationhood, and modernity, according to intellectuals of the time period. And within this triangulation, norms of gender and sexuality were also thrown into flux. Film culture expanded rapidly in Brazil, and intellectuals across the political spectrum were enthused and concerned about the new medium. Just as they were ambivalent about the influence that cinema might have on Brazilian society—was it a tool of uplift or a distraction from progress?—they were concerned about modernity at large. An examination of moviegoing amplifies and refracts the dynamics of modernization and gender, race, and urbanization.

Sources, Methodology, and Book Structure

This book takes a decentralized approach to the study of gender, moviegoing, and film, recognizing that the individuals who sat in the audience were as much participants in this phenomenon as the filmmakers who pioneered Brazil's film industry. Thus, the book weaves together sources from multiple sectors of Brazilian society, some more "traditionally" located within film culture and others more peripheral. Within film culture, I espouse an expansive view that examines Brazilian films of the early twentieth century as well as the corpus of material related to film spectatorship, such as film reviews and fan magazines. While some histories of film delineate between the sectors of film production (making movies), exhibition (showing movies), and reception (watching and reacting to movies), this book reflects historiography that shows how these sectors were strongly interrelated.[92] Early Brazilian filmmakers were the country's earliest film critics and intellectuals, such as Adhemar Gonzaga, who founded the patriotic film magazine *Cinearte* in the 1920s and then went on to become one of the most successful film producers and directors of the 1930s. Moviegoers, both men and women, assumed the role of amateur film critics when they wrote their thoughts on film in anonymous "letters to the editors" of domestic film magazines. Film exhibitors and businessmen became celebrities in their own right and made appearances in magazines and newspapers that critiqued their perceived contributions to the film industry. Across the variegated film community, the boundaries between cultural producer/consumer, artist/entrepreneur, or film intellectual/film fan were blurred, and each of these roles is valuable to the study of film culture in this time period.

Additionally, this book recognizes the wide effects of cinema by looking at sources from commentators who were not actively included in such film circles, but who still thought, wrote about, and published their musings. They thus contributed to public discourse on the social effects of cinema, including how it related to gender and sexuality. I look at "leisure magazines" and art magazines, in which writers and commentators reported on film and moviegoing with humor, alarm, and admiration. These might be called "mainstream" sources in that they generally aligned with and spoke to regional elite tastes. However, I also look to more marginalized sectors of the moviegoing population and intellectuals from disparate communities. For example, in the local Afro-Brazilian newspapers of São Paulo, intellectuals both commented directly on the effects of cinema in the Black community and also mentioned film more casually in humorous gossip and society columns. Patrícia Galvão, also known as Pagú, one of Brazil's most famed female writers of the early twentieth century, is another example of an intellectual who was not embedded within the circles of Brazilian film production and criticism, but whose distinctly Marxist ideals on film and mass media were in conversation with discussions of gender and marriage and notions of progress. Even technocratic building inspectors and municipal legislators can be included as agents in the shaping of film culture, as they and other local officials tried to regulate and contain the construction of movie theaters in Brazil's growing cities. They, too, touched on the intersections of gender and urbanization through the lens of hygiene and urban reform. Casting a wide net to look beyond traditionally defined film culture reveals the broad influence of cinema across multiple sectors of Brazilian society, revealing how individuals from different political spectrums, racial identities, and class statuses perceived the effects of moviegoing and modernity on gender roles in their communities.

Given these disparate sources, I read film sources for clues about gender and sources related to gender and urbanization for clues about cinema. It is less a process of "reading against the grain" and more about pulling specific threads out of the available material, triangulating them to fill in the gaps of what we know about the gendered experience of urbanization in early and mid-twentieth-century Brazil. The end effect enriches our knowledge of the lives of young women in the time period, as well as the complicated expectations for how they should behave and where they should circulate, how they might be "modern" while still contributing to patriarchal definitions of womanhood and family, and how they might occupy and be seen in urban spaces of public leisure while maintaining their duties to the domestic home.

Chapter 1 explores the burgeoning print culture of the early twentieth century in Brazil, and how writers, intellectuals, and artists saw the fate of the city as intertwined with the fate of the melindrosa, the Brazilian "modern girl." They viewed Hollywood films and movie theaters as alluring but potentially threatening additions to Brazilian society, especially in how moviegoing women challenged the division between private and public spaces. These depictions demonstrate fears of women's greater mobility in time and space, traipsing to previously taboo spaces during day and night. Their fears underlined the precarity of women's social status, how one wrong move might transform a respectable woman into a disreputable one, a mother into a sexual victim, a sister into a prostitute.

Chapter 2 turns to the work of Brazilian filmmakers in the era of silent cinema. Examining three films from three different cities, the chapter explores how prominent filmmakers expressed their anxiety regarding the effects of urbanization on Brazilian families and gender norms. By incorporating film reviews from the film magazine *Cinearte*, chapter 2 also reveals how film critics organized national filmmaking into racialized regional hierarchies. From the perspective of Rio de Janeiro–based cinephiles, Brazilian narrative films were a means to define Brazilian national identity and a platform to exhibit a racially and morally idealized society. While these film critics developed their own aesthetic economy that accorded value to films according to their definition of "good cinema," the three films analyzed in this chapter all exhibit similar themes. Primary among the filmmakers' concerns was whether they could imagine a modern city, with somewhat modern gender roles, that could still accommodate traditional standards about sexual morality.

Chapter 3 pivots to a very different sector of film culture through the concepts of "hygiene" and "safety," and how these terms took on gendered meaning in the construction of movie theaters. Municipal officials and medical professionals in the growing field of public health adopted medical discourse from the sanitation movement as they sought to contain the growth of and regulate the construction of movie theaters. Through medical publications, municipal legislation, blueprints, building inspections, and newspaper articles, this chapter elucidates the real and perceived hazards of movie theaters, including fires, overcrowding, and "stale air." Yet through close reading, this chapter also reveals how these perceptions of health and safety (or lack thereof) of movie theaters were imbued with notions of their appropriateness for women.

Chapter 4 examines hierarchies of class, race, and gender in the city of São Paulo. In accounts of moviegoing in literature, film criticism, personal letters, and oral history, Brazilians evaluated their own and others' social statuses based on choices about where to go to the movies. Moviegoers developed new hierarchies of morality and taste, evaluating neighborhoods and areas of the city based on the quality of their movie theaters. However, while exploring the ways in which diverse moviegoing audiences came together or apart based on factors like class and race, this chapter also argues that romance and desire were formative in how paulistanos chose to move about the city.

The fifth and final chapter of this book visits moviegoing and film culture into the mid- and late twentieth century in the city of São Paulo. Rather than provide an exhaustive or chronological survey of moviegoing across the era, this chapter contrasts memories of moviegoing in the mid-century versus perspectives of moviegoing in the late twentieth century. Drawing primarily from oral histories but also memoirs, literature, and popular songs, this chapter demonstrates how moviegoers continued to link the fate of the city through the acts that occurred within and around its movie theaters, viewing illicit sexual activity as symbolic of the city's perceived deterioration. Whereas in the early twentieth century, intellectuals and artists wondered what movie theaters meant for the future of Brazilian cities, the late twentieth century offered a chance for moviegoers and film critics to take a nostalgic view of the past. Movie theaters built in the mid-century functioned like a repository of memories, refracted through decades, holding visions not necessarily of what the city of São Paulo was, but what it could have been.

The five chapters track the ebb and flow of moviegoers who were attempting to forge their place in a dynamic social scene. Through their actions and condemnations, they both pushed and challenged the boundaries of what was acceptable and unacceptable for men and women in these exciting new city spaces. This multifaceted perspective on moviegoing and film culture confirms, as previous histories have shown, the important role of sexual morality in ascertaining social status in twentieth-century Brazil. However, it also highlights the ways in which the very meanings of sexual morality were being negotiated through the realm of film culture. As much as women in public discomfited commentators of the time period, women were also key to the imaginings of a modern, urban Brazil. In a somewhat paradoxical process, even as commentators expressed their anxiety about changing gender norms, they made these norms ever more present in the expanding avenues of popular expression, including in print culture and cinema. In effect, commentators both reflected and contributed to imaginings of the modern city and women's role within it. And in their perceptions of whether moviegoing activities were acceptable or illicit, whether they were of the "dark" or the "light" or in between, these commentators also read the destiny of Brazil's cities—their past, their future, their promise, and their threat.

1

MELINDROSAS AND MOVIE-STRUCK GIRLS IN BRAZILIAN PRINT CULTURE

In 1913 a Rio de Janeiro newspaper reported on a shocking story of seduction and robbery, but with a twist on gender roles. "A certain Charlotte Bessiere, a beautiful, intelligent lady," was always present during the most stylish sessions at the Cinema Parisiense.[1] She possessed "the skill of enchantment," and the many men who competed for her attentions would "throw themselves at her without scruple."[2] Appearing to be offended by their pleas, Charlotte would move her chair away or even leave the cinema altogether after they approached her. In her hands, however, were the "bills, watches, chains, and tie pins" of the men who had fallen for her charms.[3] Unfortunately, although Charlotte disappeared with the jewels she had stolen, "vestiges" of her personality remained in the "innumerable" Charlottes, "hundreds" of whom plagued Rio de Janeiro's cinemas.[4] According to the author, Charlotte Bessiere was not a singular case but symptomatic of a larger problem that would lead to the moral decay of the city.

This chapter examines domestic print culture in early twentieth-century Brazil, and how artists and intellectuals perceived women's susceptibility to cinema and other temptations of the era, whether as victims or, like Charlotte, as the aggressors. A key point of their concerns was how women's presence in cinemas and outside of the home would change the calculus of urban life, particularly by destabilizing "traditional" markers of identity and status. That

Charlotte Bessiere had a French name and went to the Cinema Parisiense was no coincidence, but was indicative of how these modern habits were interwoven with notions of the foreign and ethnic other. Modern, moviegoing women not only participated in new attractions but presented challenges to the dichotomy of house and street. These anxieties were channeled into the figure of the melindrosa, or Brazilian "modern girl," whose appearance and proclivities bore similarities to other global iterations like the US "flapper." Across spectrums of politics, class, race, and culture, Brazilian artists and writers maintained a highly ambivalent attitude toward the moviegoing woman. Even as cartoonists drew the modern girl breaking up marriages, getting carried away by the movies, succumbing to prostitution, and endangering the future of the Brazilian nation, they were fascinated by this figure of cosmopolitan culture. Although she was condemned, she became a new icon of femininity in Brazil. And like Charlotte, other versions of the modern girl were "always present," fixtures of urban leisure—spectacular visions that represented the fate of the city, whether for progress or for ruin.

Modern Girls and Racial Anxiety in Brazilian Print Culture

Moviegoing modern girls were a recurring figure in early twentieth-century print culture, which flourished on a national scale, especially from the cities of Rio de Janeiro and São Paulo.[5] The number of daily newspapers increased, as did "illustrated magazines," weekly publications with text and artwork that focused on current trends in fashion, films, leisure, and the arts. In addition to these mainstream publications, print culture expanded in racially, ethnically, politically, and artistically based communities. A growing Black press in São Paulo, mostly based around local social clubs, produced several newspapers aimed at the local Black community, including *O Progresso*, *A Liberdade*, and *O Clarim da Alvorada*.[6] The diverse immigrant populations of Brazil published newspapers in a mixture of Brazilian Portuguese and their home languages of Italian, Portuguese, Spanish, Japanese, and Arabic. Leftist political organizations and working-class communities contributed to this diverse print culture through newspapers such as anarchist Edgard Leuonroth's publication of *A Plebe*, which explicitly called for working-class activism and touched on issues of gender and feminism.[7]

Most of the writers and artists across these publications were male, with notable exceptions. Women writers did appear as regular columnists in the press in the more mainstream illustrated magazines, as well as in niche artistic and political newspapers like *A Plebe*.[8] Some writers, their real identities unknown, used feminine monikers like "Mademoiselle X" and took on the vantage point of female archetypes who were themselves the muses of Brazilian print culture—chic modern girls or the socialites ever-present at concerts, shows, and films.[9] The famed Marxist writer Patrícia Galvão, or Pagú, was a frequent contributor to discussions on gender and moviegoing, and her thoughts on cinema are discussed in this chapter and in chapter 4.

Weighing in on the vagaries of modern life included commentary on cinema and its effect on gender norms. The priorities and objectives of these writers varied extensively, and no community was monolithic. Many of these publications, even if not explicitly invested in upholding traditional gender norms, nevertheless acted as literary arbiters of proper social norms and gendered behavior. For example, the anarchist press in São Paulo, while exalting the role of working women, was still wary that women would be compromised by the temptations of urban leisure and capitalist consumption.[10] The glitzy illustrated magazines of Rio de Janeiro and the São Paulo Black press, while in some ways mutually exclusive, shared similar vantage points in their extensive discussion of respectability and leisure practices. These various publications reflected on the place that their diverse readerships held in the shifting hierarchies of urban Brazil.

The growing coterie of journalists, writers, and artists in Brazilian print culture are today perhaps less internationally famous than the artists associated with the São Paulo Modern Art Movement. This group of vanguard artists ignited a "Week of Modern Art" held in the city's municipal theater in 1922. Experimenting with primitivist aesthetics, painters and writers like Tarsila do Amaral and Oswald de Andrade gained international attention for their innovative artistic styles. Reinterpreting European accounts of Indigenous cannibalism, one of the modernists' key philosophies was "anthropophagy," or the concept of cannibalizing another culture and then regurgitating it to produce something new. Although the São Paulo–based artists later became synonymous with Brazilian modernism, they were one among many communities of artists grappling with the meanings and aesthetics of modern life.[11] In addition, though their innovation propelled them to great prestige, their work was still comparatively limited to artistic and intellectual circles. *Klaxon*, their short-lived weekly publication, was not popular beyond its immediate contributors. And for all the bombast of the São Paulo Week of Modern Art, it appeared as barely a blip even in Rio de Janeiro's newspapers.[12]

In contrast, outlets like illustrated magazines and newspapers were reaching wider audiences in 1920s Brazil. The national literacy rate in Brazil remained low in this time period; in 1920, it was under 30 percent for men and women. However, it was higher, between 52 and 66.5 percent respectively for women and men, in the urban centers of Rio de Janeiro and São Paulo.[13] The publishers of illustrated magazines attempted to attract readers with both text and design by featuring graphic art and photography. Although illustrated magazines and newspapers were far from ubiquitous among poor and rural populations, these texts nevertheless represented a shift from the elite literary production of the nineteenth century to a more accessible—albeit not quite "mass"—product. In particular, the growing population of white-collar urban professionals, which rose to about 20 percent of the population in Rio de Janeiro and São Paulo by 1920, turned to newspapers and illustrated magazines to view an aspirational "cultivated" lifestyle.[14] In the pages of magazines like *A Cigarra*, personal ads and letters to the editor reveal a socioeconomically diverse reading audience, with submissions from seamstresses and telephone operators.[15] The concept of a "middle class" was not a rigidly defined, stable category in 1920s Brazil, nor were magazines necessarily a reliable indicator of "middle-class" sentiment. However, we can examine these magazines as a barometer for the habits and fashions of those who both practiced and aspired to the habits and fashions of a bourgeois lifestyle.

On the pages of such publications, the melindrosa appeared as an iconic female figure, a variation on the modern girl that developed around the world in the 1920s—for example, as the "flapper" in the US, "mago" in Japan, "neue Frau" in Germany, or "kallege ladki" (college girl) in India. As described by the Modern Girl Working Group, each iteration sported a similar image of "bobbed hair, painted lips, provocative clothing, elongated body, and open, easy smile."[16] In magazines, films, and popular culture, these modern girls were associated with "'frivolous' pursuits of consumption, romance, and fashion."[17] The modern girl also represented societal anxieties regarding modernization, globalization, consumer culture, and the liberation of women from the domestic sphere, "a harbinger of both the possibilities and dangers of modern life."[18] Whereas the "new woman" was a potential suffragette, law student, and "cerebral bourgeois woman," the modern girl was the threatening figure of consumption and leisure.

The melindrosa channeled Brazilian writers' deep ambivalence regarding changing gender roles. At her best, the melindrosa represented the rise of a new, exciting consumer culture, the glamour of a cosmopolitan, urban Brazil. Maite Conde links melindrosas directly to the rise of the Brazilian film industry, as Brazilian films and film magazines targeted female audiences and capitalized on the melindrosa's habits of consumption and leisure.[19] At her worst, the melindrosa was a harbinger for the destruction of the Brazilian family and, by extension, the nation itself. Margareth Rago has found that while the melindrosa became a fashionable icon of consumer culture, the "specter of prostitution" constantly haunted her. She was simultaneously oversexed but not fit for motherhood.[20] The São Paulo women's magazine *Revista Feminina*, a nationally circulating magazine, producing over twenty thousand print copies of each issue,[21] frequently published articles that cautioned women to wear skirts of reasonable length, or to wear less makeup, lest they be perceived as prostitutes.[22] Other commentators interpreted the melindrosa's androgyny as the inversion of proper femininity, and read in her style the destruction of gender roles and the end of matrimony.[23] Advertisements, medical advice, and essays in women's magazines promoted the image of the domestic "queen of the household" as an antidote to the melindrosa's abandonment of the domestic sphere.[24]

While the modern girl's appearance and habits were broadly uniform across the world, this figure generated culturally specific images and anxieties. In Latin America, the modern girl encapsulated deeply complex notions of modernity, as well as its relationship to race, progress, and gender. Swathed in imported French clothing and watching the latest Hollywood films, the modern girl represented a type of urbane cosmopolitanism, proof that Latin American nations kept abreast of European fashions. Yet she also threatened cultural loss—the idea that an imagined traditional national culture would be subsumed by foreign fads. The Modern Girl Working Group argues that in Europe, the modern girl sported orientalist and primitivist styles in both phenotype and clothing.[25] Across Latin America, the modern girl's dalliance with both foreign and primitivist styles caused unease as to her racial identity.[26] In Mexico, Joanne Hershfield has analyzed versions of the "chica moderna" that combined visions of European fads and Mexican indigeneity, sometimes wearing the latest French styles, and other times traditional Indigenous rebozos.[27] Ageeth Sluis has found evidence of dark-skinned, Indigenous versions of the *bataclana*, a scantily clad, hypersexualized variation of the modern girl.[28] In Argentina, the press similarly lauded the *joven moderna* or "modern youth" as a symbol of Argentine progress, but also feared her explorations of transatlantic Black culture.[29] Brazilian renditions of the modern girl echoed the qualms in Mexico and Argentina. In appearance, the melindrosa faithfully mirrored the global type, with, as described by literary scholar Beatriz Resende, "short hair, in the garçon style, lips in the shape of a heart, a curled bang falling on her forehead, thin and transparent clothes, short skirts and long necklines, sometimes with a small hat or cloche, sometimes without, always seductive."[30] Similar to the Modern Girl Working Group's "global" definition of the modern girl, Resende emphasizes a combination of bodily form, sexual desirability, and specific commodities (lipstick, hat, skirts).

While modernist artists might have flirted with indigeneity, the habits of the global modern girl fell into conflict with the prominent ideology of branqueamento, or racial "whitening" of the Brazilian population. Based on eugenics, or the ideology of racial engineering, proponents of whitening espoused education and public health, along with "positive" racial mixing with white and European people, to "uplift" the Brazilian nation.[31] For the politicians, medical professionals, and intellectuals invested in eugenics, women played a central role. Through "scientific motherhood," women were responsible for both reproducing and raising the next (whiter) generation. Within this context, public health initiatives across different regions of Brazil sought to improve maternal and infant health.[32] Intellectuals and artists vested in puericulture, or the scientific raising of children, viewed women as mothers whose bodies and caretaking labor were charged with the racial uplift of the populace. Even women who were not yet mothers were "protomothers," whose ultimate destiny was to bear and rear children. As such, intellectuals and eugenicists scrutinized women's bodies and habits, holding them to the ideals of sanctified motherhood. As Sueann Caulfield points out, police chiefs and public health officials worried that modern girls, with their habits of smoking, drinking, and enjoyment of public leisure, were ruining themselves for future maternal duties.[33] The modern *girl*, by definition, was not a mother or protomother and thus was a threat to proper gender roles and their larger role in the national whitening project.

The male counterpart to the melindrosa was the *almofadinha*, a dandyish young man who eschewed family responsibility in favor of urban pleasures. The almofadinha was depicted wearing a flat straw hat pushed high on the head, often with a cigarette, baggy suit, and pointed shoes. Like the melindrosa, the almofadinha was seen in spaces of leisure like the cinema, the cabaret, and restaurants and bars. According to cartoonists, humorists, and writers, the almofadinha's primary offense was his divergence from traditional codes of masculinity. Although regional ideals varied, if masculinity was industrious, serious, and solitary, then the almofadinha was the inversion: lazy, decadent, overly social, and frivolous.[34] Literally meaning "little pillow," the almofadinha was soft and feminine. The use of the diminutive "inha" also hints at the almofadinha's arrested development, stuck in a state of perpetual youth, eschewing the responsibilities of maturity and fatherhood. Like the melindrosa, the almofadinha was caught up in the new culture of consumption. His habits of grooming, fashion, and leisure were both feminine and foreign, imported from North America and Europe via retail and the movies. In one cartoon, the young "Juventino," whose name gestures to his youthfulness or *juventude*, wears glasses like Harold Lloyd, a comic actor who wore signature thick-framed glasses and a straw hat, and floppy shoes like Charlie Chaplin. The overall effect, as his father insinuates, is that in mimicking these famous comic actors, the young man looks like a clown. While illustrated magazines sometimes depicted the almofadinha alongside the melindrosa, the former did not attract the same volume of attention or consternation.[35]

A single page of cartoons from the magazine *Para Todos* provides a snapshot that distills the many criticisms that surrounded both the melindrosa and the almofadinha. The graphic artist J. Carlos (pseudonym of José Carlos de Brito e Cunha), sometimes credited with first designing the Brazilian melindrosa, was the magazine's artistic editor and was particularly prolific in producing images of the melindrosa in the magazine's pages.[36] *Para Todos* stands out among similar publications because it was the original platform for a one-page section that eventually became the film magazine *Cinearte*, a source of Brazilian film intellectual production analyzed in subsequent chapters.

In one set of caricatures, J. Carlos depicted a "Masieur" and "Mondemoiselle"—each title mixing the French words for "Mister" (Monsieur) and "Miss" (Mademoiselle). One is named "Maria José" and the other "Zé Maria," combining common masculine and feminine names (Zé being short for José). Their appearance and their names mirror each other, both blurring binary gender roles. Short riddles poke fun at the idea of their gender-bending habits, implying that it is hard to distinguish one from the other. The melindrosa is "crazy about boys / already smokes, takes snuff / all the same, not a man / She's Maria José." For the almofadinha: "Looking like a girl / radiating beauty / With lips painted red / It's the little Zé Maria."

Just below these androgynous figures, J. Carlos drew another cartoon lobbying yet another criticism of modern gender roles, depicting a husband whose wandering eye is caught by the sight of a melindrosa walking by. The wife, called "the old woman," cries out, "Florentino, contain yourself!" The husband, or "old man," responds, "Wait, Eulalia, we need to have vacation days from marriage too!" In the bottom cartoon, the melindrosa is depicted as a solitary woman strolling in public. She is an object of desire, and her very

Figure 1.1. J. Carlos, "Untitled," *Para Todos*, no. 277, April 5, 1924, RC Para Todos, Cinemateca Brasileira São Paulo.

"What's this, Juventino? Do you have something in your eyes? What's with the bicycle?"

"Hey Dad, this is the style. Glasses like Harold Lloyd."

"And your shoes, my son, they are like Charlie Chaplin?"

presence in public presents a threat to the married couple's respectability. At the same time, the most foolish character is not the melindrosa, but the cartoonish "old man" who cannot "contain himself" as the melindrosa calmly walks by. In fact, the melindrosa is not out of place in the cartoon so much as Florentino, who cannot seem to function in an urban landscape where young women freely circulate. The melindrosa appears to fit in naturally with the

Figure 1.2. J. Carlos, "Ai, ai, meu Deus!" *Para Todos*, November 29, 1924, RC Para Todos, Cinemateca Brasileira São Paulo.

background of other passersby, with her spotted cloche hat appearing almost like a little flower or ladybug blending in with the leaves. On the other hand, the married couple, Eulalia and Florentino, are oversized and cartoonish, clashing harshly with their surroundings. Eulalia has a round red nose, and Florentino has lips in the shape of a duck's beak, both reminiscent of clowns. J. Carlos's point here is not so much that the melindrosa is a disrupting force, but that the urban landscape has already evolved. An old-fashioned couple like Eulalia and Florentino, outlandishly oversized, quite literally do not fit in anymore in this new urban scene.

These cartoons represent the ambivalence about what the modern girl and boy signified for Brazilian society. Social commentators like J. Carlos expressed anxiety about these youthful, gender-bending, and frivolous figures. At the same time, this unease was expressed not with panic but with humor and fascination. While the "specter of prostitution" hung around the solitary, street-strolling melindrosa, and while she might have threatened what appears to be a less-than-perfect marriage, she was incontrovertibly a part of public society. Commentators analyzed both how the modern girl would change Brazilian society, as well as how Brazilian society would need to adapt to a world that contained the modern girl.

The melindrosa's adoption of French monikers and foreign styles was also a source of debate. Margareth Rago points out that while Afro-Brazilian women had traditionally been the symbols (and had borne the burden of exploitation) of sexual promiscuity in Brazilian history, at the turn of the twentieth century, the foreign prostitute was "the principal signifier of sexual immorality."[37] In particular, French prostitutes, or women who presented themselves as "French" prostitutes, were sought after as exotic and even "prestigious" symbols of sexuality,[38] and commanded the upper tier in the social and ethnic hierarchy of sex workers in Rio de Janeiro.[39] Rago writes that "the charm of the *francesa* [the Frenchwoman] . . . was her greater capacity of seduction and her dominance of the rules of civilized behavior."[40] The theme of the melindrosa's moral decay as originating in Europe, and particularly France, reverberated across other illustrated magazines and popular literature of the time period.

For example, a writer using the pseudonym "Mademoiselle X" wrote a fantastical piece in *Para Todos* on the "origins of the melindrosa," in which God summons women from "all the nations"—though in this Eurocentric story, "all" only included Europe, the USA, and Brazil—to hear out their pleas. The women meet St. Michael in heaven and perform variations of the modern girl mixed with stereotypes of their nationalities. The Frenchwoman is charming, seductive, and loved by all, but complains that there are not more films, cigarettes, jewels, or cabarets on earth. The Englishwoman is athletic and plays sports; the German loves to work, drink beer, and eat; and the Spaniard likes to tango. The North American shimmies to a ragtime rhythm, declaring her love for dancing and movies, only lamenting that there are not more men to marry and then divorce. St. Michael rewards the wholesome Brazilian woman by commanding her to "take a bit" of culture from all the nations in Europe in order to become "perfect." The Brazilian woman, however, ends up "acquiring an excess dose of foreign products that were recommended in small portions, which in large quantity destroy the greatest treasure that a woman's heart can possess—goodness and love. And so arose the 'Melindrosa.'"[41] In an uncanny reversal of the concept of anthropophagy, the "problem" with the melindrosa was her excessive consumption of goods, literally overdosing on foreign products like cinema, cabarets, and alcohol, until she was no longer "good and loving," but an amalgamation of fashionable habits. Mademoiselle X warned that consumption would destroy the "good and loving" woman and result in the morally devoid melindrosa. And yet even as she made these ominous claims, "Mademoiselle X" herself adopted a French moniker for "young woman," hinting at her own possible proximity to the modern girl. The story itself is humorous, and with this tongue-in-cheek approach, the writer implies that the fun and glamour of the dancing, smoking, movie-watching modern girl might outweigh the moral apprehension.

Another example of a moviegoing "mademoiselle" appeared in Benjamim Costallat's 1922 novel *Mademoiselle Cinema*, which details the sexual and shopping/leisure exploits of an ill-fated melindrosa. In the novel, Rosalina is a decadent, upper-class carioca who partakes in all of the sins of the decade—overshopping, using cocaine, and taking lovers. *Mademoiselle Cinema* was the bestselling novel in Brazil that year and an example of the modern literature that arose from Rio de Janeiro. Maite Conde describes how the main character of the novel, Rosalina, is at home on the streets of Paris, a setting that functions as a symbol of moral degeneracy; she is enviably fashionable and compelling, but also morally and sexually decadent.[42] Religious organizations condemned the enticing and scandalous novel. However, an essayist using the pseudonym João Escreve (literally, "John writes") claimed that the dangers of the novel itself were trivial compared to the real threats presented by the young women who were "real-life Mademoiselle Cinemas." According to Escreve, real women in Rio de Janeiro were "prostitutes of pain and shame, dragging the misery of their momentary weakness, crumbling, lifeless, without will, defeated, contemplating death, without the courage to kill herself."[43] For Escreve, the melindrosa's habits were representative of moral and physical decay, with the dramatic outcome of a good woman's literal death.

Writers in the São Paulo Black press also deplored the influence of French fashions on gender norms in the Black community. In the November 15, 1925, edition of the Afro-Paulista newspaper *O Clarim da Alvorada*, Horacio da Cunha criticized the men and women who frequented the "bars and confeitarias of Paris," who cut their hair in the same bobbed style of the "garçonne." In sporting the same hairstyle, men and women affronted "centuries of tradition and God's own creation of women with long hair and men with mustaches." *O Clarim da Alvorada* was highly invested in the politics of respectability, in the uplift and "aggrandizement" of the local Black community, and it is not unexpected that Horacio da Cunha maintained the same worries about youthful fashions that white elites did. For da Cunha, the "garçonne" challenged proper gender norms, though it is indeterminate whether he also meant that the fads were a specific betrayal of how Black people should wear their hair. Regardless, da Cunha transposed the concerns of the negative influence of Parisian fashions not just to the Brazilian national body, but more specifically to the respectability and cultural autonomy of the Afro-Paulista community.[44]

Despite these criticisms, advertisements in the Afro-Brazilian press, even in publications that similarly emphasized the respectability of the local Black community, betrayed how European fashions and transnational hairstyles were desirable and not quite such dangerous fads. The "Salão Brasil," which specialized in "haircuts for Black people," published weekly advertisements in the newspaper *O Progresso* with the slogan, "We cut ladies' hair a la garçonne, bebe, semi-garçonne, etc.," variations of the iconic short bob associated with the modern girl.[45] Another advertisement called "The Beauty of a Woman" appeared in the Afro-Paulista newspaper *A Rua* and promised women, "In order to shine like a star, become a bride or dear wife, or belong to the highest, most luxurious social circles, it is necessary to dress with purity and elegance. . . . Visit the tailor Mademoiselle Mathilde Dias da Cunha, who works with the most modern figures coming directly from Paris and Italy." The tailor also advertised "prices within reach of all, from the luxurious and lofty aristocrat to the most impoverished workers, specialties in veils, jackets, and wedding dresses."[46] The promises of the advertisement reveal the many layered complexities of what it meant to be "modern" and what it meant to be respectable. The ultimate goal for women was marriage, "to become a bride or dear wife," and to sport the vestments of purity, "veils, jackets, wedding dresses." However, in order to achieve this, the advertisement promised that "Mademoiselle Mathilde"—again the use of the alluring French moniker—would summon the melindrosa's style, particularly in the form of "the most modern figures coming directly from Paris and Italy." The advertisement presented the melindrosa as an attractive but transitory identity that naturally preceded the role of "dear wife."

Black women in the role of "modern girls" gained some fame via the theatrical stage. The Parisian theatrical revue *Bataclan* toured and found great success in Brazil, Argentina, Uruguay, and Mexico, appearing in Rio de Janeiro multiple times from 1922 to 1924.[47] Although the mainstream press in both Rio de Janeiro and Mexico City responded to the scantily clad dancers with disapproval and even outrage, the revue was wildly successful, and carioca retailers capitalized on its popularity with shoes, fashions, hotels, and music groups named after the *Bataclan*.[48] Black musicians and actors also adopted their own version of the *Bataclan*. Headed by João Candido de Ferreira, who used the stage name "Chocolat," the Companhia Negra de Revistas performed their own version of the *Bataclan* with Afro-Brazilian performers.[49] Historian Micol Siegel refers to the show as "cementing its position in the

Figure 1.3. "O Bataclan preto: As Blacks girls [sic] genuinamente brasileiras," *A Careta*, no. 947, August 14, 1926, p. 36, Acervo da Fundação Biblioteca Nacional–Brasil.

chain of cultural exchange powered by Afro-Brazilians' embrace of Parisian cultural conditions."[50] In the show, Afro-Brazilian women were prominently on display as Black modern girls, with both their racial identity and "modern" status as selling points in theater advertisements. They used the intriguing title, written in English, of "Blacks [sic] girls," yet described themselves as "truly Brazilian," accentuating the transnational dimensions of the gendered, raced, and generational identity. The affirmation of Brazilianness, comingled with English, reflects the specific ways in which the modern-girl identity combined both globally and locally specific influences.

For elites and intellectuals, the racial ambiguity of the modern girl was representative of the larger allure and peril of modernity. In a magazine cover for *Para Todos*, J. Carlos contrasts the melindrosa with the apelike figure that he sometimes used to derogatorily depict Black individuals. The contrast between the melindrosa and the apelike figure serves to highlight the melindrosa as having white skin and elongated features. However, the contrast also serves to underscore the melindrosa's flirtations with racial nonwhiteness.

Another prolific graphic artist of the time, the São Paulo–based Belmonte (pseudonym of Benedito Bastos Barreto), also produced images of the melindrosa. Belmonte is best known for inventing the cartoon character "Juca Pato," a self-proclaimed champion of the "middle class" who was consistently confounded by modern life. Highly influenced by J. Carlos, Belmonte touched on similar themes in the 1920s.[51] He titled one of his paintings *Civilization and Barbarism*. The title recalls former Argentine president and writer Domingo Faustino Sarmiento's novel *Facundo: Civilización y Barbarie*. In *Facundo*, Sarmiento contrasted the "barbarism" of rural *gaucho* culture in Argentina

Figure 1.4. J. Carlos, untitled cover of *Para Todos*, no. 441, May 28, 1927, Acervo da Fundação Biblioteca Nacional–Brasil.

with the enlightened "civilization" of Europe. Belmonte instead poked fun at the primitivist aesthetic of the cosmopolitan modern girl, comparing it to a stereotype of an Indigenous woman. The two variations of femininity share the same blunt bob, hoop earrings, necklaces and bracelets, and an immodest display of skin. However, what separates them is their racialized phenotypes. The melindrosa is pale skinned with large blue eyes, a small nose, and small, clearly lip-sticked lips. The Indigenous woman is brown skinned with closed eyes and a larger nose and mouth. The insinuation is that the melindrosa is phenotypically "white" but that she risks being interpreted as racially nonwhite, or via Indigenous styling, "barbaric" because of how she dresses. The irony is that in becoming too modern, the melindrosa is actually antithetical to elite notions of progress and has become primitive. Which one is civilization and which one is barbarism? Belmonte's joke is that we should ask that question at all. According to these illustrations, although the melindrosa appeared white, her habits of consumption and leisure were contrary to both progress and white womanhood.

Figure 1.5. Benedito Carneiro Bastos Barreto (pseudonym Belmonte), Civilização e Barbárie. Enciclopédia Itaú Cultural de Arte e Cultura Brasileira, "Civilização e barbárie," last modified December 4, 2024, http://enciclopedia.itaucultural.org.br/obras/103711-civilizacao-e-barbarie.

For these writers and journalists, the fashions and habits of the melindrosa were a destabilizing force on gender roles and the ideologies of whitening and whiteness. And for writers in the São Paulo Black press, the melindrosa with her European and Hollywood habits similarly challenged Black respectability. Melindrosas risked harming their bodies for future motherhood, symbolized by their flirtations with foreign products and "primitive" fashions. Cronistas depicted the symbolic "death" of "honorable" women when they became infatuated with the commodities and leisure activities of modern urban life. In writers' exaggerated imaginings, as men and women went to cabarets and movies, they jeopardized their health and that of the nation and were scourge to the future of the Brazilian race. Yet the *Bataclan* revue was a huge success across Latin America, including in Brazil, and the melindrosa continued to allure consumers and admirers, even if only as a transitional stage before respectable marriage, demonstrating widespread fascination with this figure.

Movie-Struck Girls

Another figure related to the melindrosa was the "movie-struck girl," a term that I borrow from Shelley Stamp's work on female moviegoers in the US.[52] Although Brazilian writers did not use this exact term, they voiced similar concerns about women's susceptibility to Hollywood's seductive images on screen, the abandonment of the private, domestic sphere, and ultimately, victimhood to the predation of sexual aggressors. So prevalent was the fear that men would sexually assault women in movie theaters that a specific colloquialism—bolina—was developed to refer to men who groped women, implicitly nonconsensually, in cinemas.[53] Brazilian writers sometimes grouped Hollywood films with commodities like lipstick and short skirts or social activities like dancing as one entry in the era's many temptations. However, they also voiced specific concerns surrounding cinema and its verisimilitude. Religious authorities, politicians, writers, and artists from across different ideological spectrums were both hopeful and wary of cinema's power to entrance and influence viewers, particularly the "weak minds" of women and children. As one editorial in *Revista Feminina*, a magazine advocated by a prominent Catholic bishop and aimed at women, claimed, cinema "sows in the innocent hearts of loyal wives the poison of discontent, seducing their weak spirits with the false beauty of unrealistic heroes."[54] While critics sometimes singled out the melindrosa as a "movie-struck" fan, they also worried about cinema's influence on other types of feminine identities, including wives, mothers, and working women. These broad concerns, though not always implicating the modern girl, echoed the same concerns—that the consumption and viewing of Hollywood films were tied to cultural loss and breakdown of the Brazilian family.

Critics of melindrosas and "movie-struck" women focused not just on the dangerous content of Hollywood films, but on how moviegoing lured women away from the home, changing the dynamics of the urban street. Crônicas and cartoons featured these moviegoing women as fascinating new fixtures of the urban landscape who attracted attention both inside and around the movie theater. The cinema and other interior public spaces did not fit neatly into the traditional house/street dichotomy. Both within the darkness of the cinema and in the street outside of it, women vacillated between sexual prey and sexual predator. Their visibility in the street generated both fascination and anxiety about changing social relations between men and women and between women and their families, and about changes within the urban landscape of Brazil. In da Matta's framework, the street was the site of danger, particularly for women who ventured away from the confines of home and family. However, in these new calculations of urban life, the street was doubly perilous because women, influenced by Hollywood films and European fashions, could become seductresses who victimized the men who were susceptible to their charms.

One writer in the São Paulo newspaper *O Correio Paulistano* went into great detail as to how children faithfully mimicked love scenes they saw on Hollywood films, and how these actions were visible in everyday street encounters. The author of the story, Lellis Vieira, was a prolific journalist and member of the "Colmeia Group," an informal nucleus of intellectuals, writers, and artists in São Paulo.[55] He described his shock at seeing two children around "eight years old" (the boy not even old enough to wear long pants) seated together on a bench outside. The boy "wildly caressed the little brown-haired girl, with sighs, little hands over his heart. She, full of caprice and 'don't touch me's,' responded to the baby Lovelace, throwing him kisses and twisting her innocent, angelic, little body."[56] Yet like "Floriano" in J. Carlos's cartoon, who was unable to "contain himself" in the presence of the alluring melindrosa, Vieira's character is also out of place in this new environment. When he expresses his shock at seeing their actions, the children respond, "Mister, are you a country bumpkin? You don't go the movies? The movie that we saw yesterday was just like this. It was so beautiful that we dreamed about it."[57] Poking fun at him, the children point out that it is not their habits, but his own shock, that is inconsistent with the modern city. Similar to Floriano, who cannot contain himself at the sight of the melindrosa, it is the narrator who is out of touch. In his story, Vieira praised the efforts of an elite local women's group who organized wholesome film screenings for children and disparaged the symbols of modern youthfulness, including "the smelly almofadinha, the frivolous melindrosa . . . [who] affirm that the movie theater is a delight."[58]

Reflecting the same concerns that cinema tempted girls away from home and respectability, one advertisement presented the ideal way that a woman might enjoy the movies—with her family at home. The Pathé-Baby was a home video recorder and projector launched by the French Pathé film company, which was represented by the Ferraz brothers in Brazil. The home video

Figure 1.6. Advertisement, "O cinema no lar (Pathe-Baby)," *Para Todos*, April 26, 1924, RC Para Todos, Cinemateca Brasileira São Paulo.

recorder engendered a small circuit of amateur "home movies" in Brazil, and the advertisement for the project proclaimed the tantalizing idea of "cinema in your own home, feasible within your family circle."[59] The illustration would have appealed to a very elite family, marked by home ownership, the purchasing power to afford an appliance costing 425$000, and lavish clothing and furniture. As context, a price of 3$000 for Rio de Janeiro's "select" cinemas was considered nearly prohibitively expensive in the same year.[60] The advertisement pushed the ideal that, through the Pathé-Baby, elite women could participate in modern consumption and leisure (the movies, automobiles) and access the excitement of the outside world, but still enjoy it from within the safety and intimacy of the domestic/family sphere. Women should remain in their "family circle," and even as they might enjoy the new technology of cinema, they could maintain the gendered and class divisions between "house" and "street." Interestingly, however, advertisements for the Pathé-Baby camera presented a different scenario, depicting a female camera operator in a swimsuit at the beach, filming family members with children and capturing their "happy memories and laughter."[61] A woman behind the camera already contradicted stereotypes, but swimming, along with other sports, generated a multitude of questions about women's health, athleticism, and modesty in public.[62] Surrounded by family, with the privilege of either being ensconced in the home with a Pathé-Baby projector or enjoying public leisure at the beach with the Pathé-Baby camera—this was both the contradiction and the ideal of modern womanhood.

Even from different sides of the class and political spectrum, writers and popular songs echoed concerns about women abandoning their family home, lured by the movie theater. São Paulo writer Antônio de Alcântara do Machado collected and compiled popular neighborhood songs, one of which condemned a working mother who is by turns threatening and coaxing her child to sleep because "Mommy is going to the movies / To see the craziness of love. . . . Mama works too much / And she needs escape."[63] The "escape" in this scenario is liberation from the responsibilities of family and industrial work, but also from the domestic space of the home.

The leftist writer Patrícia Galvão differed radically from those writing in mainstream newspapers and illustrated magazines. Even as she saw the power of cinema as a tool of workers' consciousness, she echoed worries that Hollywood was a threatening force of cultural imperialism, especially for women.[64] In the experimental newspaper *O Homem do Povo* (Man of the people) that she self-published with her husband, modernist writer Oswald de Andrade, she wrote a film review of the Hollywood film *Our Modern Maidens* (MGM, 1929), starring Joan Crawford. Galvão lamented, "Anyone in South America who saw *Garotas Modernas* and knows of the decisive influence that cinema has on the mentality of our young girls—will be alarmed."[65] She accused Crawford of "filling the empty heads of Brazilian girls with fairy tales."[66] Crawford represented a "rags to riches myth" both in her public persona and in the films she made. In *Our Modern Maidens* and similar films like *Our Dancing Daughters* (MGM, 1928), Crawford starred as a spirited, impoverished heroine who eventually marries a rich hero.[67] As a Marxist communist, Galvão believed that worker consciousness and collective class struggle were the keys to ending poverty and exploitation, so she criticized the materialistic Cinderella fantasy of Crawford's films.

Galvão expressed how this cultural imperialism played out in her imagined streets of São Paulo. In a comic that she drew for *O Homem do Povo*, Galvão depicted the image of a "movie-struck girl" attempting to escape the confines of home, with the added element of Hollywood's cultural imperialism. A mother holds back her daughter, who responds, "If I don't go to the Paramount Cinema, I'll run away from home." The large letters "Paramount" loom in the background like the Hollywood letters of Los Angeles, and a car waits to take her away. Although for Galvão the threat of Hollywood was primarily as a capitalist opiate, it also represented young girls' liberation from the domestic sphere. The role of the mother was not at the movies, but as a moral safeguard against Hollywood's deleterious temptations. Wearing her hair in curls and sporting a beret, the daughter in the depiction might be read as a stand-in for Galvão herself, who sported a similar appearance. At the age of sixteen, Galvão also attempted to leave home for Hollywood dreams and entered an international beauty contest to become the next "Latin" star of the Hollywood studio Fox Films.[68]

Victims and Vamps on the Way to the Movies

Alarmist stories that predicted the downfall of the Brazilian family because of the movies were printed alongside many other stories that were more equivocal. In these literary and graphic depictions, the moviegoing *melindrosa* was an alluring object of sexual desire, but one that was fascinating rather than dangerous or distraught. In short stories and poems, writers described the visibility and desirability of melindrosas as an extension of the allure of cinema itself. In a recurring column called "Bataclan," João da Avenida wrote humorous poems about moviegoing women like "Mademoiselle of Futility," who has forty "flirts" per month. She goes to the beach, the *confeitaria*, and at 4:30 in the afternoon she drives to the Cinema Pathé, where the author responds, "What a delicious fate, to see you every day. And what beautiful clothing, so transparent, and such elegance so unique. You don't know how I suffer when I am near your gaze." These writers depicted melindrosas as highly visible objects of desire who both commanded and courted attention as they wandered the streets and entered the movie theater.

In several cartoons J. Carlos represented the division between house and street—between private and public—as a deciding factor in the moral status of both the melindrosa and the space of the cinema. Throughout these cartoons the commodities associated with the melindrosa (cloche hat, lipstick, short skirt, cinema) remain the same. However, her moral status changes depending on her physical location in the house or on the street. In these images, the cinema ranges from an innocent, female-centric diversion to one of danger and sexual predation.

One comic presents a relatively benign portrait of the melindrosa's moviegoing habits. The cartoon, entitled "Out on the Town," satirizes the centrality of moviegoing as an urban experience. "Going to the city" or "out on the

Figure 1.7. J. Carlos, "Out on the Town," *Para Todos*, no. 373, February 6, 1926, p. 18, RC Para Todos, Cinemateca Brasileira São Paulo.

"We'll go to the movies first or after?"

"After what? There is no after."

town" was synonymous with moviegoing, as one figure asks, "We'll go to the movies before or after?" and the response is "There is no after"—no other activity worth their time. The women in this cartoon feature the elongated figures, painted lips, and bobbed hair characteristic of the modern girl. However, they differ in one aspect, in that they are depicted within the morally safe space of the home. The three women are in a homosocial environment without much suggestion of sex. There are other interpretations of the cartoon; what might be the activity that happens either before or after the cinema? Why is one figure's face hidden in a red shadow? Although these might be hints at a more subversive or sexual meaning, the overall visual depiction is of a domesticated, nonthreatening melindrosa.

In contrast, another J. Carlos comic portrays the melindrosa in the street, presenting another perspective on her moviegoing habits. In the cartoon, a man approaches a woman who is standing alone outside and asks, "Are you waiting for someone?" She responds, "Yes, someone to pay for the movies, tea, a car."[69] She has a stylized appearance similar to the domesticated melindrosa in the J. Carlos cartoon but clearly has a different agenda. In addition to being outside of the home, this modern girl is not within a homosocial, feminine environment as the previous melindrosas were. She is by herself but waiting for a man. Although the man who approaches her declines her open invitation for a

Figure 1.8. J. Carlos, "Alguem que pague o cinema, o chá, o automovel . . . ," *Para Todos*, no. 315, December 27, 1924, RC Para Todos, Cinemateca Brasileira São Paulo.

He: Are you waiting for someone?
She: Yes, someone to pay for the movies, tea, a car.
He: Keep waiting. He won't be long.

Elle — Espera alguem ?
Ella.— Sim. Alguem que pague o cinema, o chá, o automovel...
Elle — Continue a esperar. Elle não deve tardar.

date, he remarks that she would probably not have to wait long for someone else to come along. Among multiple interpretations of this cartoon, the melindrosa is conscious of her appearance and sexual desirability, and she strategically uses men to pay for her leisure habits. Yet while waiting in the street for a man to approach her with money, the melindrosa in this comic closely mirrors the soliciting sex worker, or "woman of the street."

While the "waiting" melindrosa consciously attempts to attract male attention, another moviegoing woman is represented as sexual prey rather than predator. In this cartoon, a man again approaches a woman on her way to the cinema. He asks her if the young boy by her side is her little brother. When she replies yes, the little boy says, "Alright, man! I'm there, I'm at the movies!"

Characteristics of the melindrosa, like bobbed hair, painted lips, and *cloche* hat, appear again in this J. Carlos cartoon. However, the elongated figure and short skirts characteristic of the melindrosa's sexuality are not shown in this comic. Instead, her figure is obscured by her little brother, which foregrounds that this woman has a place within a family. Rather than the solitary woman in the "Waiting for someone" comic, this woman has a chaperone, which affirms her moral status. The comic, however, pokes fun at the idea that her chaperone is so young. Alternatively, one might interpret the man to be confirming whether the woman is with her own child (and therefore married and symbolically protected by her marital status) or her little brother (and therefore single and, in his eyes, sexually available). While the presence of the little brother signifies that this woman is not the street-strolling, single

Figure 1.9. J. Carlos. "Guaranteed Business," *Para Todos*, no. 352, September 12, 1925, RC Para Todos, Cinemateca Brasileira São Paulo. He: Is this your little brother?
She: Yes, sir.
The boy: Alright, man! I'm there, I'm at the movies!

melindrosa, the "specter of prostitution" is present and sinister. The title of the comic is "Guaranteed Business," insinuating that the men leering in the background are "guaranteed" to find women, in whatever capacity, at the popular movie theaters. The word for business, *negócio*, also means "transaction," and "guaranteed business" could be read as a financial/sexual transaction. In this final cartoon, taking place on the street on the way to the cinema, the melindrosa unknowingly risks becoming a sexual commodity.

J. Carlos's perspective as a satirical observer of modern life exhibits the great variance of women's social and moral status as they went to the movies. Like the cartoon at the beginning of the chapter, J. Carlos presents each of these scenarios with whimsical humor. At times it is the melindrosa, frivolous and movie-crazed, who is the butt of the joke; other times it is the old-fashioned men who cannot "keep up" with the new social codes by which she lives. The significance of the house and the street informs their status as either innocent, fun-seeking women, morally ambiguous prostitutes, or sexual prey. In these comics, the space outside the cinema, "on the way to the movies," is represented as a transient space where melindrosas' moral status was in flux. They could be on their way merely to enjoy a film, or on their way to the sexual/moral downfall associated with the darkness of the cinema. Moreover, J. Carlos's cartoons exemplify print culture's simultaneous fetishization and condemnation of the melindrosa's visibility in public space.

In the early twentieth century, a diverse and variegated set of publications were expanding in number and audience in Brazil. The writers and artists across these publications were intrigued by the figure of the melindrosa, the Brazilian "modern girl," but worried that her habits of consumption and leisure threatened her racial and moral status. Intellectuals from an array of political and ideological positions feared the cultural imperialism of Hollywood and how it might lure women from home and family. Amid this dual threat, the moviegoing melindrosa walked a fine line between sexual victim and predator in satirical cartoons and *crônicas*. Across these representations in the flourishing print culture of the time, writers and artists publicly assessed the effects of moviegoing women on the moral division between private and public, house and street—a division that they feared was blurred by the darkness of the cinema. What was at stake was not just the moral or social status of these "movie-struck" women, but also the urban landscape, where women's sexual allure might be on full display. Melindrosas and moviegoing girls changed the calculus of urban life so that the street was a place of temptations for men and for women. The thrill of this developing landscape was the subject and vision of filmmakers and film critics as well. The following chapter examines how filmmakers asked similar questions, exploring how changing gender norms and urbanization affected the visions of Brazil that they crafted on the silver screen.

REGION AND RACE, GENDER AND URBANIZATION IN BRAZILIAN SILENT CINEMA

> When I saw the announcement for *Unknown Brazil* . . . I was afraid of those animals and naked Indians, let loose among the finest and most aristocratic audience. . . . The film was a disaster. It nearly closed the cinema. The "chic" public left complaining and the film was only shown until Sunday. . . . Will we continue to produce films that exhibit wilderness, naked Indians, monkeys, and etc.? Isn't it apparent that this puts us back, and does not even educate us, Brazilians? And don't we also risk showing trash like this to foreign audiences (For none of these producers of "exploration films" have scruples about this)?
>
> —**Adhemar Gonzaga,** *Para Todos***, 1925**

Writing for *Para Todos* in 1925, film critic Adhemar Gonzaga's quote demonstrates his concerns surrounding Brazilian film production and reception. Gonzaga was a leading film intellectual and film critic in the 1920s and later a successful filmmaker himself. He was part of a coterie of like-minded film intellectuals who believed cinema could be a platform of nationalist rhetoric, a medium that advanced a modern, urban, and morally upright image of Brazil for both domestic and international audiences.[1] *Unknown Brazil*, a documentary about the Brazilian Amazon, did not conform to this ideal. Gonzaga was appalled not just by technical and artistic failings, but by what he considered to be racially backward and sexually explicit images. Contrary to the title *Unknown Brazil*, Gonzaga complained that the Amazon was a region already well known through other Brazilian documentaries.[2] For Gonzaga, "animals and naked Indians" were a stereotypical vision of Brazil completely contrary to the sophisticated, urbane image that he and his fellow critics supported. These images were also sexually inappropriate for the "chic" audience in Rio de Janeiro. In contrast to his reaction to *Unknown Brazil*, Gonzaga wrote an article in 1932 explicitly stating that Brazilian filmmakers should produce high-quality, fictional films that presented Brazil "as beautiful, well-dressed, modern, with its skyscrapers and its factories, many factories."[3] Consistent with Gonzaga's campaign of promoting narrative films over documentaries, his comment also betrayed a preference for featuring Brazil's burgeoning cities as an urban counterpoint to visions of rainforests and remote areas.

Despite Gonzaga's adulation of urban wonders, Brazilian filmmakers of the 1920s displayed an ambivalent attitude, portraying cities as double-edged. In several films, cities were spaces of cosmopolitan fashions, impressive engineering, and social progress. They were also places where women drank, danced, and worked in public, and where men lost themselves in decadent leisure and evaded their familial responsibilities. As presented in Brazilian silent films, when women and cities became too modern, they represented a challenge to traditional gender norms and social hierarchies. Images of women who deviated from norms of sexual chastity and men who abandoned codes of male paternalism and chivalry were simultaneously thrilling and moralistic visual attractions. In contrast to the idealization of urban progress, filmmakers and film critics were wary of how urbanization affected gender roles in Brazil.

This chapter closely analyzes three films from the era of silent film: *The Lawyer's Daughter* (Aurora-Film, 1926), *Lips Without Kisses* (Cinédia, 1930), and *Fragments of Life* (Rossi Film, 1929). All three films center on overlapping themes of family, sexual morality, and gendered respectability, and how these values might be reconfigured in 1920s Brazil. The filmmakers centered sexual morality and gendered propriety in their visions of whether the traditional Brazilian family would survive the social disruptions wrought by modernization and urban growth. Brazilian filmmakers were as anxious about masculinity and family structure as they were about femininity, and how these might change amid urbanization, the expansion of consumer culture, and a widening professional workforce.

By the 1910s the "traditional" Brazilian family, defined as rural and multigenerational, disintegrated as an ideal, giving way to images of an urban, nuclear family.[4] This was an era of shifting social hierarchies, in which one's social position was increasingly determined by a multitude of "modern" signs such as profession, consumption, taste, and social habits, rather than the "traditional" hierarchies of family and legal status. How would one determine the moral certitude of "good" people if men and women alike adopted androgynous styles and mingled together in public? Like the artists and intellectuals discussed in the previous chapter, filmmakers attempted to define codes for men's and women's proper behavior in this new environment. In these films, characters weave between dichotomous representations of the urban and the rural, the public and the private. As the symbolic meanings of these spaces shifted and changed, filmmakers offered models for how men and women should navigate them. In their films, these pioneering Brazilian filmmakers put forth varying visions of the modern city as a site of hope, progress, and disillusionment, and envisioned how men and women might reconcile traditional gender norms with the modern attractions of the city.

At the same time, the writers at *Cinearte* organized Brazilian films and filmmakers into their own hierarchies of race, region, and sexual morality. In film reviews published in the magazine, this newly formed group of film intellectuals and film critics assessed whether Brazilian film productions conformed to or deviated from their conservative vision of Brazilian modernity and national identity.[5] Based primarily in Rio de Janeiro, still the largest city and political capital of Brazil in the 1920s, these critics participated in wider intellectual conversations regarding Brazilian regionalisms and the relative status each held within a national body politic. In this way, the *Cinearte* film critics placed themselves as the arbiters of the images and identities that would represent Brazil on the silver screen.

Cinearte and Regional Film Production in Brazil

The nucleus of intellectuals at *Cinearte* came together in 1917 as the Paredão Club, one of the multiple "cine-clubs" or film appreciation societies that arose in this time period. The members of the Paredão Club, mostly young and male, met weekly to watch and discuss films at the Cine Iris in Rio de Janeiro, and they eventually formed foundational outlets for film criticism in Brazil.[6] While part of the cine-club, Adhemar Gonzaga began to write a "Cinema Section" in *Para Todos*, the illustrated magazine whose artistic director, J. Carlos, popularized the image of the melindrosa, discussed in the previous chapter. Due to the success of the cinema section, Gonzaga and Mario Behring, a Rio de Janeiro intellectual who was the editor of *Para Todos*, established the film magazine *Cinearte*. As film intellectuals and critics, the writers of *Cinearte* produced both intellectual treatises on the potential of cinema and weekly reviews of the latest films. Other film critics from the Paredão Club, including Pedro Lima, Álvaro Rocha, Paulo Vanderley, and L. S. Marinho, contributed articles to *Cinearte* over the years.

Cinearte was a relatively popular magazine with a circulation of 60,000 weekly subscriptions by the end of the 1920s.[7] By contrast, *Revista Feminina*, which was the most successful women's magazine, sold 20,000 copies a month in 1922.[8] Although other film magazines like *Palcos e Telas* (1918), *Cine Revista* (1919), and *Scena Muda* (1921) existed before, *Cinearte* stands out for its longevity (published until 1942), for its wide circulation, and for being a nucleus for some of the most prominent film intellectuals and producers of twentieth-century Brazil. Founder Adhemar Gonzaga not only produced the film *Lábios sem Beijos*, discussed in this chapter, but also eventually became a successful Brazilian filmmaker in the 1930s. He founded the Cinédia film company that produced popular musical films called *chanchadas*, through which stars like Carmen Miranda and Grande Otelo became internationally famous. Pedro Lima, who wrote for *Cinearte* from 1926 to 1930 and later for the illustrated magazine *Selecta*, continued to be a prolific film critic for multiple decades.

In this time period, filmmakers and film critics, rather than representing opposing sectors of film production and reception, were part of overlapping circles of cinephiles. Filmmakers like Humberto Mauro, Mario Peixote, and Canuto Mendes appeared frequently on the pages of *Cinearte*, where they offered their own thoughts on the meanings and purpose of Brazilian cinema. These early filmmakers were all moviegoers and cinephiles, blurring the distinctions between producers, critics, and consumers of film. *Cinearte* enthusiastically publicized domestic film production and each success of the fledgling national industry.[9] Pedro Lima developed one of the magazine's slogans: "Every Brazilian film should be watched with great attention."

As part of their nationalist vision of Brazilian cinema, *Cinearte* emphasized an image of progress, highly inflected with the ideology of eugenics and largely in keeping with the policy of branqueamento, or whitening, in Brazil.[10] Filmmakers whose vision of Brazilian society conformed to *Cinearte*'s vision had their voices amplified in the pages of the magazine through publicity stills, in-depth interviews, and news coverage. On the other hand, the critics filtered out productions that did not conform to their idea of Brazil's proper image on screen, a process that Paulo Emílio Salles Gomes calls the "policing" of Brazilian cinema.[11] Gonzaga's review of *Unknown Brazil* implicitly criticized the "producers of 'exploration films' who had no scruples" about showing "trash" to Brazilian and foreign audiences. The critics at *Cinearte* decried these films as unwatchable, not worthy of being labeled Brazilian cinema. Paulo Emílio Salles Gomes and Ismail Xavier have discussed the film intellectuals' nationalist discourse as inseparable from their adulation of prevailing notions of North American modernity.[12] Scholars like Taís Campelo Lucas have systematically surveyed the nationalist perspectives in *Cinearte* in the 1940s.[13] Maite Conde points out that by addressing a presumptively female reading audience, *Cinearte* explicitly cultivated women's fandom practices and consumption of Brazilian films. For the film critics of *Cinearte*, eugenic concerns about modernity, hygiene, and whiteness, as well as gendered moviegoing practices, were not distinct from, but rather implicit in, the formation of Brazilian national identity.

While *Cinearte* emerged from Rio de Janeiro, film production in 1920s Brazil had great regional range. Centers of production cropped up in the cities of Rio de Janeiro and São Paulo, but also in Recife and in the countryside of Minas Gerais. Historians of Brazilian cinema have thus traditionally organized production in various "regional cycles," such as the cycle of Pernambuco or the cycle of Cataguases.[14] However, film scholars have recently challenged the boundaries of regional cycles. Arthur Autran, for example, has called for scholars to think of Brazilian cinema less as a collection of spatially and temporally interrupted series of fits and starts, and more as a continuum of film production across various regions.[15] In his study of the cycle of Pernambuco, Paulo Carneiro da Cunha Filho examines film production as a regional project, but one that was in constant dialog with, and constitutive of, national ideas of Brazilian cinema and modernity.[16] Also in the context of Pernambucan films, Luciana Correa de Araújo reminds us that interpreting Brazilian film production as "cycles" is a perspective that privileges the ebb and flow of narrative film production rather than the more constant and prolific output of documentary films.[17]

Gonzaga's comments reflected the efforts among politicians, filmmakers, and artists to harness the potential of cinema for fashioning modern nationhood across Latin America. Cinema, like concurrent technologies such as the radio or the telegraph, was a way to connect the nation, from coast to interior, and center to periphery, or even across national boundaries to construct transnational and regional identities.[18] Maite Conde has referred to early Brazilian films as "foundational" texts enmeshed with the political and cultural project of nation-building and modernity.[19] While film scholars have debated the extent that Brazilian cinema in different time periods or genres was "colonized" by the dominance of Hollywood, these debates still emphasized the importance of cinema as part of national history and identity.[20] Yet it was precisely this capacity that made cinema a great arena of debate across Latin America. While some sectors of Brazilian intellectual production had long looked to the rural "backlands" and regional hinterlands as the "core" of Brazilian national identity, others, like Gonzaga, looked to the growing urban cities as the locus of a modernizing Brazilian nation.[21] What was at stake was not just how Brazil might be represented to itself and to the rest of the world through film, but also how these images would educate Brazilian audiences.

Brazilians produced films that were uniquely relevant to their local urban context, yet also part of a wider, global conversation about the disruptive influences of city life on traditional gender norms. Images of "fallen women" and sinful cities were a trope in various national cinemas around the world. German director F. W. Murnau's *Sunrise* explicitly presents the "woman of the city" as a flapper who seduces a man from his innocent country wife. The first Mexican sound film, *Santa* (1932), based on the 1903 novel by Frederico Gamboa, told the classic story of a woman who, seduced and abandoned by her lover, leaves her small town and becomes a prostitute in Mexico City. In Mexican cinema, the dichotomy between the "virgin" and the "whore" appeared during the silent era and continued into the high-quality "golden age" productions of the 1930s and 1940s.[22] Similarly, Brazilian silent cinema presented feminine archetypes of the "innocent" and the "vampire." As Maria Fernanda Baptista Bicalho has demonstrated, the politics of casting these archetypes was set within nationalist projects to represent a white, eugenic nation. Brazilian silent films presented dualistic narratives that were both seductive and moralistic, but in which female figures functioned primarily as passive objects of desire.[23]

Through the lens of gender, sexuality, and race, films from various regional cycles are bound together by overlapping ideologies and modes of representation. The renowned films *The Lawyer's Daughter* (Aurora-Film, 1926), *Fragments of Life* (Rossi Film, 1929), and *Lips Without Kisses* (Cinédia, 1930), like pieces of a jigsaw puzzle, each relay particularities tied to their region and unique circumstances of production, but together create a larger picture of the role of urbanization and shifting gender roles across Brazil. Film criticism at *Cinearte* was both a unifying and divisive force. The magazine's writers integrated these films into a national corpus of "Brazilian cinema," but also measured each film against their ideal of what this cinema should be. At the same time, they pointed out regional distinctions and hierarchies, deeming some visions of Brazil as more valid than others.

Restoring Fatherhood and Patriarchy in *The Lawyer's Daughter*

The Lawyer's Daughter is one of the most famous films from the "cycle of Recife," a burst of roughly fifty films, both fictional and documentary, produced from 1924 to 1930 in the largest city of the northeastern state of Pernambuco.[24] The film was produced by the Aurora-Film Production company, which also produced documentaries and the feature films *Retribuição* (1924; Retribution) and *Aitaré da Praia* (1925; Aitaré of the beach), among others. From the perspective of regional identity, the analysis of any of the films from the cycle of Recife must account for the relative position of the northeast in relation to the south, and to Brazilian national identity. The "northeast" comprises nine states of Brazil including Pernambuco, Ceará, and Bahia. It is the traditional sugar-producing region of Brazil, but in addition to physical geography, it also represented distinct economic, cultural, and racialized spaces in Brazilian intellectuals' imaginations. In the 1920s a few northeastern intellectuals represented the interior areas of the region, or sertão, as a kind of "heartland" of traditional Brazil.[25] From a different perspective, the famous intellectual Gilberto Freyre, born in Recife, focused on the coastal northeast in his depiction of Brazil as a mixed-race society with foundational African roots, predicated on the culture of Afro-descendant enslaved people but also on their subservience and exploitation.[26] These assertions of the northeast's foundational roles in national identity were not uniformly accepted across Brazil. From the vantage point of intellectuals in São Paulo, who promoted their region as the engine of Brazil's progress and future, the "northeast" became an imagined place of backwardness, poverty, and racial degeneracy.[27]

In contrast to the paulista perspective, the producers of Aurora-Film represented the region's traditions and progress as coterminous with the nation's. Paulo Carneiro da Cunha Filho has argued that Pernambucan filmmakers adopted the modern technology of cinema in order to showcase their modernity to the rest of the nation, but thereby adopted the aesthetic standards of the center while remaining on the periphery.[28] This regionalism is evident in the production and reception of Aurora-Film's second film, *Aitaré da Praia*. The opening intertitle declares the film to be the "first super-production, created in truly national circumstances," but at the same time, it pays homage to regional traditions: "In the customs of our heroic jangadeiros [fishermen], the true sons of the forgotten northeast. Let the spontaneous pride of these brothers, of these pioneers, vibrate in your souls." Beautiful poems from regional poets like Adelmar Tavares pepper the film, praising the simple life of poor fishermen.[29] The critics at *Cinearte* took the perspective of southern intellectuals who saw the northeast as impoverished and inferior. They criticized these regional particularities in *Aitaré da Praia* as a showcase of poverty and backwardness.[30] Yet even in *Aitaré da Praia*, the filmmakers erased the presence of the region's Black and Indigenous populations, casting white or white-presenting actors in the film.

In contrast to *Aitaré da Praia*'s poor fishermen, *The Lawyer's Daughter* presented a more sanitized version of both urban and rural spaces. In the film, a well-respected lawyer travels abroad, leaving his illegitimate daughter Heloísa and legitimate but wayward son Helvécio in Recife. Heloísa, who has until then lived in the countryside with her mother, keeps her parentage a secret when she moves to the city. Her half brother, not realizing Heloísa is his sister, falls in love with her, and when she resists, he attempts to rape her. In the rather graphic struggle that ensues, Heloísa kills Helvécio with a gun that her father had given her to "protect her honor." She is put on trial for murder, but her lawyer-father returns home in disguise to defend his daughter. In a dramatic flourish at the end, he takes off his glasses and mustache to reveal his identity and formally recognize Heloísa as his daughter. In the end, Heloísa marries Lúcio, her father's trusty assistant (and cousin), and the multigenerational family lives happily ever after in Recife.

The film presents the clash of modernity and tradition through the portrayal of gendered archetypes, often putting these archetypes in direct visual contrast and narrative conflict. First of all, the film provides commentary on a variety of contemporary, gendered "types" from the era. An intertitle describes Helvécio (played by the director J. Soares) as "the only legitimate son of Aragão, orphan of his mother, libertine and wastrel, victim of the world's mad crazes." He is dressed exactly as an almofadinha, to borrow a phrase from Beatriz Resende, "as if he came from the pen of J. Carlos." J. Soares's physical form conforms exactly to the "skyscraper" aesthetic of the time: tall, thin, with a long face and angular nose. He wears his hair slicked back, and the film features an extended scene in which he carefully combs it. He also wears a suit with pants that reveal his socks and pointed shoes, a large pocket square, and to cap it off, a straw hat pushed back to reveal his groomed hairline.

Like the cartoons of J. Carlos discussed in chapter 1, the film mocks the almofadinha's fashions and grooming procedures as both effeminate and juvenile. Lúcio, in contrast, represents the masculine, virtuous, and hardworking counterpart to Helvécio. Lúcio sleeps in a spare, modest apartment

Figure 2.1. Traditional Masculinity vs. the Almofadinha. Lúcio (Euclides Jardim) threatens the preening Helvécio (J. Soares). *A Filha do Advogado*, directed by J. Soares (Aurora-Film, Recife, 1926), restored by the Cinemateca Brasileira, Cinemateca Pernambucana, Jota Soares.

at night, while Helvécio carouses during the night and sleeps all day. Indeed, most of Helvécio's moral failings are presented as perversions of traditional binaries of gender or standards of sexual morality. A scene at a lively cabaret features Helvécio dancing and drinking, holding various women close and kissing them. The music appears to be that of a "jazz band," complete with a trombone. When Lúcio reads the newspaper in the morning, he discovers that a rowdy Helvécio not only broke furniture but also hit women, symbolizing his lack of masculine chivalry. Helvécio's perversion of sexual mores culminates in him falling in love (albeit unknowingly) with his own half sister and attempting to rape her.

The film establishes a marked contrast between Lúcio and Helvécio when they nearly come to blows. Upon reading about Helvécio's scandal at the cabaret, Lúcio goes to Helvécio's apartment, where the latter is half dressed and grooming himself, demonstrating his effeminate habits. When they meet, Helvécio's actions are exaggeratedly cowardly, hiding his face from a fight as he sprays perfume in his hair. Lúcio, by contrast, appears larger and asserts his traditional masculinity by intimidating but not beating him.

Figure 2.2. Antonieta (Olyria Salgado), the law student and bookish "new woman." *A Filha do Advogado*, directed by J. Soares (1926, Aurora-Film, Recife).

As yet another symbol of his perverse sexual/romantic relations, Helvécio is engaged to Antonieta, a materialistic, androgynous woman, and he is not even faithful to her. Antonieta is represented as a mixture of the "modern girl" and the "new woman." According to the Modern Girl Working Group, while the "modern girl" was associated with improper consumption, the "new woman" was overly educated or politicized. Whereas the modern girl was identified by her cloche hat and lipstick, the new woman was identified by glasses and other "fads" deemed unconventional for women, such as bicycles and trousers. If the modern girl went to the cabaret or the cinema, the new woman went to university or even more radically, a meeting in support of suffragism or feminism.[31]

In *The Lawyer's Daughter*, Antonieta is a law student, and she sports the characteristic round eyeglasses of the new woman and bobbed hair of the modern girl. She first appears in the film wearing an androgynous suit and, as a student, is poring over a large book. Later, she teases and flirts with Helvécio while ignoring his obvious drunkenness when he stops by her house. Antonieta's glasses, bobbed hair, and her demonstration of both unwomanly bookishness and libertinism might as well be scarlet letters; here is a bad woman, a villainess without traditional morals. Like Helvécio, her image as a modern "type" is indicative of her aberration from traditional gender roles and perversion of romantic and marital relationships. Both she and her parents ignore Helvécio's own personal faults because they plan to have Antonieta marry Helvécio for his money. Thus, the film presents Antonieta as the female counterpart to Helvécio, both of them androgynous perversions of proper gender norms who sully the institution of marriage.

Antonieta's version of too-modern, aberrant femininity is in direct contrast to Heloísa, the illegitimate daughter. When the film first introduces her, Heloísa wears her hair long, symbolic of her feminine virtue. The first time that Lúcio sees her (voyeuristically through a window no less), Heloísa is in her home, cleaning. She is a picture of female domesticity, hard at work within the private space of the home. Conforming to the conventional Hollywood visual narrative style that portrays women as passive objects of the active "male gaze," she remains unconscious of his objectifying admiration.[32] Heloísa presents the archetype of a woman who knows her "proper place" and conforms to appropriate gender roles.

The Lawyer's Daughter establishes these archetypes through both narrative and visual images. The primary narrative arc is the restoration of a respectable and nuclear Brazilian family. Instead of blaming women and their loose ways for the breakdown of family and society, the film explicitly blames men for abdicating their proper responsibilities. The main narrative conflict is Helvécio's incestuous attraction to his half sister. However, this attraction is facilitated by his father's "youthful extravagances" and subsequent failure to publicly recognize his illegitimate daughter. By abdicating his fatherly role, Aragão facilitates his son's misrecognition of his sister, resulting in the incestuous sexual attraction. The end of the film, in which Aragão stands on his balcony, looking over his daughter, Lúcio, and their child, creates a tableau in which proper familial relations and hierarchy (with the paternal head visually at the top of the balcony) are restored. Heloísa, with her bobbed hair and fashionable dress but bouncing a baby on her lap, represents a vision of femininity that is simultaneously modern but respectable. The prodigal son Helvécio also returns to the roost, albeit in tragic circumstances. After being shot by his sister, he is rushed to the hospital. On the hospital bed, he has a dream of his father begging him to be a better person. He shouts, "My father, my father!" affirming his role as faithful son before he dies.

Heloísa's narrative arc is perhaps the most revelatory in the symbolic meanings of urban and rural spaces. Heloísa is less a fully fleshed character

Figures 2.3 and 2.4. Restoration of the patriarch looking over the urban, nuclear family, including the Afro-Brazilian nanny. *A Filha do Advogado*, directed by J. Soares (1926, Aurora-Film, Recife).

than an object of male admiration and desire, a symbolic placeholder for the film's meditations on urbanization and social change. The film establishes a firm geographic distance between Recife and the countryside where Heloísa has grown up. In an extended scene, Lúcio takes the train to Heloísa's house, passing through urban and then rural environments, which establishes visual and symbolic contrasts between the two. Where the city is bustling, the country is peaceful. Where the city holds danger, the countryside is pure. Heloísa, in her country home, has long hair and has been isolated from society. When her father tells her that she must move to the city, he tells her that she must also cut her hair. At first, her shorn hair symbolizes her loss of innocence, and after she moves to the city with her short bob, Heloísa is exposed to sexual violence and predation.

Significantly, the city is such a threat that it breaks down the division between public and private, so that even in her home, Heloísa is not safe. Indeed, she encounters the greatest danger within her domestic and family circle. Helvécio first notices her at a public outing, but he continues to pursue her and follow her home. At her house, he bribes a servant into delivering love letters, spying through the gate and garden into the house. He sneaks into her room to attack and rape her, threatening to "demoralize" her. As he grabs her, their physical struggle is tense and disorienting. Heloísa's subsequent shooting of Helvécio is graphic, and a close-up of Helvécio shows blood trickling down his face.

Helvécio's incremental invasion of Heloísa's space, first circulating around her in public, then around her garden, then inside her home, her room, and finally her body, creates a claustrophobic narrative of enclosure and entrapment. In the moment in which they struggle, Heloísa has a flashback to her father giving her the gun, instructing her, "Use this to defend your honor." The flashback takes place in their countryside home, and it provides a brief, visual respite outside the predatory clutches of Helvécio and the city. The fatherly advice and mention of honor provide a temporal and ideological escape to traditional moral hierarchies, a reminder of the values that are supposed to dictate proper gendered behavior. At the same time, Aragão's words of warning are unintentionally ironic, given that both he and Helvécio have abdicated their expected roles of guarding Heloísa's honor and the privileges accorded to her place in the family. From a contemporary perspective, the situation is also a reminder that for marginalized women such as domestic servants, or in this case illegitimate family members, the "home" presented more danger than the street, and that the structures of patriarchal power were sometimes the greatest threat.

The film's narrative depicts an idealized dichotomy between the dangerous city and bucolic country, yet it concurrently showcases the progress and potential that the city affords.[33] Shots of elite men and women at the jockey club and panoramas of urban avenues in Recife are nonnarrative spectacles that celebrate feats of modern engineering. These recall a genre of documentary-like films, called "natural films," produced in Latin America and Brazil in the same time period. These natural films exhibited the modern "wonders" of Brazil—sometimes urban and other times natural—for domestic and international audiences. Such scenes demonstrate aesthetic continuity between narrative "feature films" and documentary "natural" films, as well as their shared ideological motivations, to celebrate the image of a bounteous and wonderful Brazil, which in this case was modern, urban, and advanced.[34] A scene showing Aragão boarding a large ship at the port features people waving at the boat, with pedestrians and streetcars crisscrossing among buildings. Lúcio's long train ride to the country also exhibits carefully orchestrated shots of the oncoming train, which Paulo Carneiro da Cunha Filho points out as echoing early nineteenth-century films that fetishized trains and railroads as modern marvels.[35]

Lúcio in particular navigates multiple arenas of the city, weaving between streetcars in a busy street, passing a movie theater advertising the Hollywood film *Wages of Wives*, coming out of a posh bakery, and receiving and sending telegrams. His long train ride to the countryside represents his ability to navigate both urban and rural environments, and by extension, urban modernity and rural tradition. A symbol of a growing class of urban professionals, Lúcio's romance with Heloísa represents a perfect marriage of urban and rural, modern and traditional. With the support of a proper paternal figure, the newly redeemed Aragão, their union fortifies the nuclear family and literally gives birth to a new generation of respectable urban society.

The critics at *Cinearte* enthusiastically reviewed the film. In contrast to the depiction of makeshift straw huts and rafts in *Aitaré of the Beach*, *The Lawyer's Daughter* presented a more urban and advanced image of Brazil.[36] In terms of racial politics, the sole Black figure, played by Ferreira Costa, is Gerôncio, the servant whom Helvécio bribes in order to attack Heloísa. Mario Mendonça praised the acting of Costa, but his character otherwise embodied negative stereotypes of Afro-Brazilians, and he is portrayed as a villain. In the film, Gerôncio is disloyal, deceptive, and easily bribed into betraying Heloísa. When he finally confesses at the end of the film that he was the one to help Helvécio sneak into Heloísa's room, he does so not out of moral

Figure 2.5. Lúcio at home in the urban environment. *A Filha do Advogado*, directed by J. Soares (1926, Aurora-Film, Recife).

certitude or integrity, but because he is superstitiously haunted by his guilt, dreaming of blood at night.[37] Furthermore, he is a minor character in an otherwise all-white-presenting cast, conforming to the "structuring absence" of Afro-Brazilian actors and characters in Brazilian cinema.[38]

Mario Mendonça reviewed the film in *Cinearte*, enthusiastically relaying that the film was "considered unanimously by the Recifense press and all that have seen it to be not just the best Pernambucan film, but also the best national film that has been shown on the screens of Maricéa."[39] However, revealing the regional prejudice against the northeast, Mendonça added a backhanded compliment: "*The Lawyer's Daughter* perhaps does not have the perfection of *The Bachelor's Wife* or of *Flash in the Pan* [films produced respectively in the southeastern states of Rio de Janeiro and Minas Gerais], but I judge—perhaps it is outrageous on my part to say this—that the Pernambucan film will stand alongside the great triumphs of the southern studios, without at all tarnishing these forceful achievements."[40] The not-so-hidden insult, embedded in the compliment, is that it would typically be "outrageous" to suggest that a Pernambucan film could be as good as a film from the more "advanced" states of Rio de Janeiro or Minas Gerais. Mendonça ended his review with a nationalist call to arms typical of *Cinearte*: "To the men of Aurora-Film, as advised by Lord Douglas, 'Never retreat'—let this also be our war cry! Onwards, always onwards, it is necessary to show to the world that we also have cinema!"[41]

Mendonça's enthusiasm for *The Lawyer's Daughter* must be tempered by *Cinearte*'s mantra that "every Brazilian film should be watched with great attention" and thus every Brazilian should be predisposed to celebrate domestically produced films. Yet the touch of condescension that he displayed in his description of northeastern productions lends some credibility to his positive review. The fact that Mendonça declared *The Lawyer's Daughter* to be a prime example of Brazil's forward progress, worthy of an international audience, demonstrates how the film's representations of sexual morality, gender, and race were largely compatible with *Cinearte*'s vision of forward progress. The film's presentation of modernity embraced traditional hierarchies such as women's sexual chastity and the stability of a family headed by a paternal father. In the eyes of filmmakers and critics, while the Brazilian family might have been shifting from multigenerational to nuclear, and from rural to urban, it still upheld patriarchy. While Brazil might have been adopting the accoutrements of urban life (streetcars, movie theaters, railroads), and women might have been sporting markers of feminine consumption (bobbed hair, hats, dresses), these changes were morally acceptable so long as they remained skin deep.

In contrast to Mendonça's praise, Pedro Lima wrote a more critical review of the film for the film magazine *Selecta*: "The film is bad, it does not attract, in fact it's detestable." Lima compared J. Soares unfavorably to other Brazilian actor-directors whom Lima found more talented and advised him to focus on directing rather than acting. If Soares were to continue acting, Lima suggested, "only act in the role of the '*bad man*' and never the hero; your ears ruin everything."[42]

Lips Without Kisses: Undressing the Melindrosa

Lips Without Kisses is a film written by Adhemar Gonzaga and directed by Humberto Mauro. Gonzaga was the aforementioned film critic at *Para Todos* and founder of *Cinearte*, and Humberto Mauro is sometimes called the "father of Brazilian cinema" for his illustrious decades-long career. An early film for both producers, *Lips Without Kisses* features experiments in their directorial styles.[43] In the film, the protagonist Lelita is a melindrosa who falls in love with a man named Paulo Morano. Her cousin Didi is also in love with a man who, unbeknownst to Lelita, happens to have the same name. When Didi cries that "Paulo" seduced and abandoned her, Lelita assumes they have been duped by the same man. When the characters come to Lelita's aid after she is in an automobile accident, the mix-up is revealed, and Lelita's Paulo Morano becomes a hero. Lelita realizes that she loves Paulo, and both couples reconcile in the end.

In contrast to the Recife-based *The Lawyer's Daughter*, or *Aitaré of the Beach*, which proclaimed its regional specificity in its opening intertitle, *Lips Without Kisses* emphasizes its cosmopolitanism rather than its regional roots. Across shots of urban Rio de Janeiro, an opening intertitle relays a tongue-in-cheek meta message from the filmmakers: "We could have filmed in London, but to avoid the snow, we filmed in Rio, in spite of the rains." The not-so-subtle claim is that this is a story so cosmopolitan and sophisticated that it might as well have been filmed in London as in Rio de Janeiro.

With depictions of women lounging in negligees and bathing suits, as well as the seductive elements of its storyline, the film was deemed "inappropriate for youth and young women" by the existing board of censorship, which provided more guidance than mandate.[44] Yet despite the risqué material and sexy glamour, the film's narrative arcs focus on the restoration of gender norms and family. In *Lips Without Kisses*, women might sport the trappings of modern life, but deep down, they adhered to traditional codes of sexual morality. In a reversal of Heloísa's move from country to city in *The Lawyer's Daughter*, the main protagonist Lelita begins the film as a bobbed-hair melindrosa in the city and ends the film as a long-haired woman in the countryside. Lelita's narrative arc loosely echoes similar Hollywood films about the US flapper, which show that the "modern girl" persona can be a misleading performance. Modern girls may dress as if they were sexually liberated, but underneath the costume, they can still be chaste and pure, and thus deserving of the male protagonist's love. Joan Crawford, for example, played this type of character in *Our Dancing Daughters* (MGM, 1928). In both US and Brazilian contexts, the titles of these films, *Lips Without Kisses* and *Our Dancing Daughters*, hint at the limits that filmmakers placed on women's sexual liberation in the 1920s. While filmmakers might accept women wearing short skirts or visiting a cabaret, these were only acceptable if they were superficial changes that did not threaten more rigorous expectations of virginity, chastity, and romantic love. This message is encapsulated in the scene in which Paulo says to Lelita accusingly, "You paint your lips, you paint the town red, you even paint your soul!" She asserts her sexual morality by responding, "These painted lips had never been kissed before I met you."

The first scenes portraying Lelita emphasize how her image as a melindrosa justifies criticism and aggressive sexualization. The film opens with Lelita dressed in a houndstooth suit with bobbed hair, a cloche hat, and of course, painted lips. In addition to this, she works outside the home in her uncle's office. The film directly satirizes the image of women holding a job, since she is shown to be not actually working, but reading frivolous magazines and stories with titles like "The Greatest Love Story" at her desk. She is a stereotype of a frivolous working woman who uses her wages for vanity and fun. An older male worker aggressively ogles her as close-ups focus on her ankles and high heels, fragmenting and objectifying her body in a common visual pattern that feminist film theorist Laura Mulvey has identified in Hollywood films.[45] The scene chauvinistically suggests that women's clothing choices willfully invite sexual predation. Her uncle chastises her, telling her that she has too much liberty but not enough sound judgment.

Throughout the film, Lelita's "romantic" encounters with Paulo are marked by coercion and objectification. At a party at her friend Gina's house, he pins her to a trellis and demands, "I'll only let you go if you kiss me," and he later makes a note about it in a journal, seemingly marking a conquest. They go for a hike on a cliff, and as he continues to pursue her attention, he mocks her intimidated reactions, telling her, "Don't pretend. You aren't afraid of me." While she declares, "I'm not afraid of anything," she also runs away. Although the film depicts the encounter to be a lighthearted frolic, she quite literally runs away from a man attempting to force physical contact. Lelita ends up falling out of a tree, and while she is stunned and physically vulnerable, Paulo embraces her and tries to kiss her again. Later, on an excursion to the beach, Paulo observes her body, recalling the opening scene in which the office worker aggressively ogled her legs. At the beach, Paulo films her as she models a swimsuit, and as in the earlier scene, extreme close-ups objectify her body. Paulo and Lelita do share one consensual kiss while sitting under a tree. However, after Lelita ignores his calls, thinking he is the same man who seduced her cousin, Paulo responds by sneaking into her apartment and grabbing her in bed. While arguing heatedly, he looms over her, appearing as if he might attack her physically and sexually. He stops when he sees the shadow of a cross above her head. The next shot reveals that the shadow is cast from the frame of a kite, a kind of fortuitous, divine intervention that dissuades him from his planned assault.

Within conventions of early twentieth-century cinema, sexual violence, attempted rape, even kidnappings, were normalized depictions of semilicit

Figures 2.6 and 2.7. A coworker ogles Lelita, dressed as a melindrosa. *Lips Without Kisses*, directed by Adhemar Gonzaga (1930, Rio de Janeiro, Cinédia).

"romance." These images were not just for male audiences; in the US, women-identified viewers expressed interest in fantastical depictions of "dangerous" sexual encounters.[46] In this context, Paulo's predatory sexual advances are not necessarily intended to depict him as villainous. However, even as these images of sexual assault might be normalized for the genre and time period, this does not erase their charged violence. In fact, feminist film theorists have demonstrated that cinematic representations of women as objects of sexual desire were embedded in the form and style of filmic language.[47] The extreme examples of the "male gaze" and the predatory relationship between Paulo and Lelita highlight how these conventions were also produced and circulated within Brazil.

Unlike *The Lawyer's Daughter* and its frequent, documentary-like panoramic shots of Recife's busy streets, *Lips Without Kisses* mixes a variety of styles to depict urban space. Much of the narrative occurs in spaces secluded from urban environments, inside luxurious bedrooms, on the grounds of large houses, at parks and beaches that appear quiet and secluded. In addition, there are unique tableaus of urban spaces presented through car windows and apartments. Film scholar Sheila Schvarzman points out that this mixture of visual styles reveals the contrast between the film's two authorial voices: producer Adhemar Gonzaga's preference for Hollywood-style luxury and glamour versus director Humberto Mauro's more realistic naturalism.[48]

In striking contrast to Lúcio in *The Lawyer's Daughter*, who easily weaves in and out of crowded streets, boards streetcars, and rides on trains, Lelita is constantly in conflict with public, urban spaces. Rather than an adept urban professional, Lelita is presented as an ineffective working woman whose perversion of gendered propriety leads to disruption and chaos. Lelita's first meeting with Paulo occurs when they both enter the same taxicab and argue over who should leave. Lelita angrily gestures and yells at Paulo, finally stopping the taxi on her own and instructing the cabdriver to let her off and "take this cad straight to hell." During the argument, there are close-up shots of the spinning steering wheel, and the taxicab visibly careens down the street. The camera shoots from within the car, facing the windshield and rocking dizzyingly back and forth. Through the windshield, the urban streets are further obscured by the rain that falls stochastically on the window. It is simultaneously a visually arresting and disorienting scene.

In another scene, Lelita, still thinking that Paulo has seduced her cousin, drives Didi through the streets of Rio to find Paulo and force him to marry her. "I know what I'm doing!" she declares as she careens wildly through the

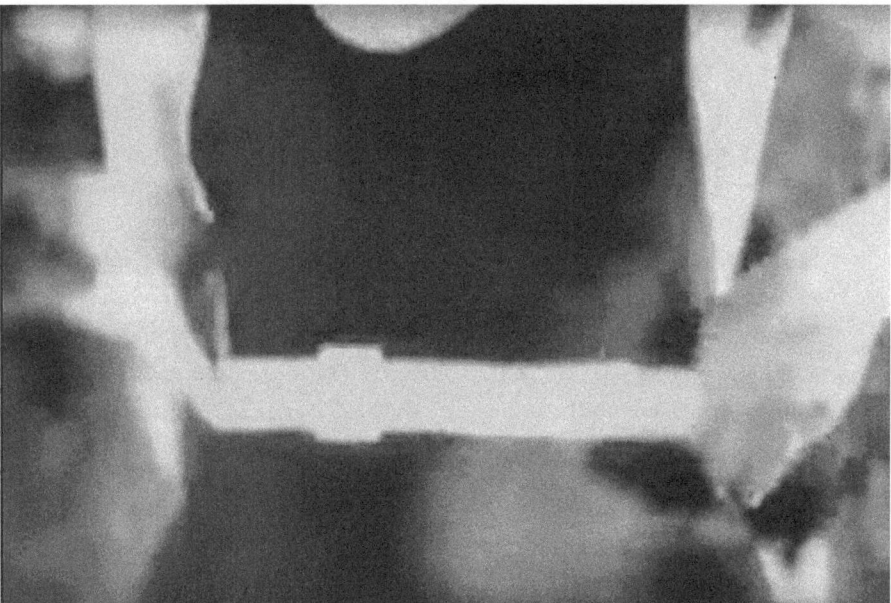

Figures 2.8 and 2.9. Paulo Morano "shoots" Lelita's body in extreme close-ups as she models a swimsuit. *Lips Without Kisses*, directed by Adhemar Gonzaga (1930, Rio de Janeiro, Cinédia).

Figure 2.10. A rain-soaked Rio de Janeiro through a taxicab windshield. *Lips Without Kisses*, directed by Adhemar Gonzaga (1930, Rio de Janeiro, Cinédia).

streets in her car. Shots from the dashboard again show the city through the windshield. Like the taxicab scene, the close-up shots of the windshield and the rocking back and forth of the car are visually disorienting. The scene partially pokes fun at the notion of women drivers, a phenomenon that writers and cartoonists lampooned at the time. Like concerns over women cyclists in the US or in Mexico, prejudice against women drivers originated in gendered notions of women's inability to master technology or have autonomy over their geographic movements.[49] Shots from outside Lelita's car show her careening out of control. At one point, Lelita almost runs over a man reading a newspaper in the middle of the street, and finally, the scene ends when she gets into an accident on the road.

In contrast to Lúcio's ability to navigate Recife's streets in *The Lawyer's Daughter*, Lelita is shown to be incompatible with the bustling urban environment of Rio de Janeiro, particularly in the contact with the men who are "naturally" present within public urban spaces. Ironically, she is not at fault in her road accidents. When she nearly hits a man in the road, it is because he is reading a paper in the middle of the street. When she has a car accident, it is because three men purposefully cause her to crash in a scheme to harass her. Nevertheless, the film establishes Lelita, as a woman, to be ill-equipped

Figure 2.11. Lelita, the woman motorist, in conflict with urban space. *Lips Without Kisses*, directed by Adhemar Gonzaga (1930, Rio de Janeiro, Cinédia).

to confront the dangers of navigating a city filled with men. In taxicabs and in her own car, she is out of control, constantly at odds with the men who command the spaces that she seeks to traverse.

After the confusion of Paulo's identity is resolved, the final scene of the film provides a happy-ending resolution. It is vastly different from the opening scene depicting the urban streets of Rio de Janeiro. Instead of Lelita at the wheel, Paulo drives her in his car in the countryside; a large dog in the backseat completes their protonuclear family. Lelita's appearance contrasts strongly with her image at the beginning of the film. Seated next to Paulo on a romantic outing, she is the placeholder for a wife/mother rather than a working woman in an office. Gone is the houndstooth suit with short skirt. Instead, she wears a long frilly dress, conspicuously white and bridal as a sign of her chastity. Her cloche hat is replaced by a large sun hat. Her hair, instead of slicked back or tucked under to appear like a bob, is loose and long past her shoulders. She looks more like a country maiden than an urban melindrosa. Lelita makes this redemption in the countryside explicit when she says, "Nature adorns itself to celebrate our love! Here everything is calm."

Fulfilled in love and romance, Lelita no longer needs to "adorn" herself with the outward appearance of the melindrosa, such as lips painted with

Figure 2.12. Melindrosa no more, Lelita in the countryside. *Lips Without Kisses*, directed by Adhemar Gonzaga (1930, Rio de Janeiro, Cinédia).

makeup. Instead, she finds nature to be its own adornment. Here everything is "calm," in contrast to the careening, disorienting car rides through the streets of Rio de Janeiro. In the countryside, gender roles, with women's proper place in a domestic family, are reaffirmed. Throughout the film, every romantic encounter is marked by nonconsensual contact, and Paulo's rakishness superficially masks his repeated threats of sexual violence. And yet at the very end, gender roles are restored when Lelita returns to the "nature" of a protowife/mother in harmonious deference to her husband. In this new dynamic, the two main characters finally share a consensual kiss. In an abrupt and comical interruption of the peaceful scene, a bull shows up out of nowhere and chases the couple across a field. Film scholar Sheila Schvarzman interprets this as Humberto Mauro's humorous undermining of Adhemar Gonzaga's Hollywood-style "happy ending."[50] However, in addition to this, the scene transfers the site of violence and aggression from Paulo to the charging bull. While in earlier scenes, Paulo is the aggressor, the animal forces Paulo and Lelita to run together, seek refuge in a tree against this shared comical threat, and romantically kiss. Now that Lelita is no longer "painted" by her urban lifestyle, the narrative depicts her as on a more equal footing with Paulo (quite literally, as they are both on the same level in a tree) and more deserving of romantic love.

Like *The Lawyer's Daughter*, the happy ending is a restoration of proper gender roles and the fortification of the nuclear family. The heroine transforms from a melindrosa and working woman to a future wife. Paulo also gains moral higher ground, his rakishness tempered into monogamy and more chivalrous physical contact with Lelita. Even Lelita's cousin Didi follows her own arc of redemption. After being jilted by her boyfriend, she too is redeemed when she announces that they will be married. In contrast to *The Lawyer's Daughter*, where Lúcio and Heloísa succeed in finding love and family in urban Recife, *Lips Without Kisses* cautions that consensual love can only be achieved by abandoning the city and its temptations. This return to nature is characteristic of Humberto Mauro's larger authorial work, in which nature is a consistent symbol of innocence and rejuvenation.[51] In terms of the film's message on gender, this innocence means that love, family, and romance will be purer in the countryside. The couple's rural redemption gives an ironic twist to the film's opening intertitle, which claimed that the story could have been filmed in any city around the world. However, *Lips Without Kisses* is not quite an ode to the potential of urbanization or the promises of the Brazilian city. In fact, in contrast to *The Lawyer's Daughter*, the film does not visualize a modern city that holds both the progress of urbanization and the traditions of love and family. The city remains chaotic and perilous, while innocence is ultimately found in nature.

Quite expectedly, given the connections between Adhemar Gonzaga and *Cinearte*, the magazine's film critics showered praise on the film. After weeks of publishing promotional stills, interviews, and news, the magazine reviewed the film when it premiered in Rio de Janeiro and São Paulo in late 1930. The critic of the week wrote admiringly of the film as "photographically perfect and technically irreproachable."[52] The critic also pointed to the film's outdoor scenes of Rio de Janeiro, especially the turbulent one in which Lelita drives Didi through the city, as "photographically the most artistic and beautiful thing that we have yet seen in Brazilian film."[53] The reviewer found minor flaws in the acting and direction, ultimately rating the film "7 points." However, the reviewer acknowledged that it was only the first production of Gonzaga's newly formed Cinédia studio, which was "now organized and ready to produce [films] in better conditions." The Rio de Janeiro newspaper *Jornal do Brasil* also declared the film "the best of the year."[54] Indeed, Gonzaga and Cinédia Studios went on to become the country's leading film production company in the 1930s, producing domestically popular musical comedies, or chanchadas, that turned Brazilian actors like Grande Otelo and Carmen Miranda into stars. From the perspective of *Cinearte*, Adhemar Gonzaga's Cinédia Studios represented both the present and future of Brazilian cinema.

The Other Side of the City: Work and Masculinity in *Fragments of Life*

In one scene of *Lips Without Kisses*, Lelita and her family are listening to music on a radio when her uncle suddenly shuts it off, declaring, "Leave that noise for São Paulo." The carioca reference to the "noise" of São Paulo references a degree of regional rivalry between the two cities and perhaps a general carioca disdain of its industrial neighbor. From the perspective of carioca intellectuals at *Cinearte*, São Paulo was a burgeoning center of film production and exhibition, but a city still comparatively smaller and more provincial than Rio de Janeiro. However, from the perspective of paulista artists, particularly the ones associated with the modernist art movement, São Paulo represented the vanguard of cultural production while Rio de Janeiro represented tradition. In actuality, intellectuals in both cities exchanged ideas, and modernism was never the sole purview of São Paulo.[55] More broadly, while the film's reference to the "noise" of São Paulo is a brief and ambiguous comment, historian Nicolau Sevcenko has characterized the "noise" of São Paulo to be dynamic and thrilling, depicting the city in this time period as an "ecstatic Orpheus," in which leisure-seeking paulistanos danced and walked to the beat of jazz bands and the hum of new machinery.[56] As seen in the introduction, they also moved to the rhythms of samba.

Fragments of Life (Rossi Film, 1929), like *The Lawyer's Daughter* and *Lips Without Kisses*, explores themes about urbanization and gender amid social change. However, the film presents a vastly different perspective on urban poverty, a topic elided in the other two films.[57] Directed by José Medina, *Fragments of Life* was shot by Gilberto Rossi, an Italian Brazilian film producer and camera operator. Produced and set in São Paulo, *Fragments of Life* was loosely adapted from the short story "The Cop and the Anthem" by North American author O. Henry. Like its original source material, the film blends a stark exploration of urban poverty with ironic outcomes, resulting in a dark comedy masquerading as a moralistic drama. In it, two men, the unnamed "Vagabond" and "Scoundrel," live homeless in the streets. With winter coming, they make a plan to commit crimes and be arrested so that they can seek shelter in jail. They each hatch a series of schemes that fail in comedic fashion. For example, the Vagabond eats robustly in a restaurant, but when he unabashedly reveals he cannot pay, a kind stranger buys his meal, sympathizing that he too has felt when "hunger was greater than shame." The Vagabond later throws a brick through a window, but the owner laughs him off when he confesses, claiming that it is impossible a criminal would be so honest. In a final plot, the two men attempt to scare a woman on the street by following her closely, thinking she would feel threatened. But she instead thanks them for protecting her as they unwittingly scare off two other men who had been following her.

The series of crimes fail because, within the harsh conditions of urban life, there is always someone who has done worse or been more desperate. Thus, when the Vagabond does not pay in a restaurant, he is absolved by someone who has also been poor and desperate for food. When he throws a brick, the owner does not believe him because in his experience, a thief should also be a liar. When they attempt to harass a woman, they end up protecting her because there are greater villains who are truly trying to assault her. The ultimate conceit of the film, borrowed from O. Henry's story, is that the two men find prison a comforting alternative to surviving the misery of the city.

Although *Fragments of Life* condemns the two main characters for not working, painting them as loafers and "scoundrels," it also demonstrates the desperation and futility of the working poor. This is distinct from J. Soares's depiction of the libertine Helvécio in *The Lawyer's Daughter* or Humberto Mauro's depiction of the indolent Luiz in his film *Brasa Dormida* (1928)—both characters are elite men who are wasteful and refuse to work. In contrast, *Fragments of Life* features poor men who are indolent because they find little difference between the desperate circumstances generated by either unemployment or labor. The film implicitly criticizes the main characters for being lazy when the "Scoundrel" suggests that jail is easier than living on the streets: "I prefer jail, where the government gives me room and board, rather than begging for public charity." Yet the opening scenes of the film speak to the dire fates of the urban workforce, suggesting that laboring in the modern city offers little compensation or uplift. The opening intertitle says as much directly in its description of São Paulo: "As if it awoke from a great sleep, the city of São Paulo, within moments, transformed radically . . . covering itself in skyscrapers, adorning itself in plazas, where the refinement and taste of its residents dominated, and where it affirmed its wealth . . . built on the sweat of poor workers." One of these "poor workers" is the Vagabond's father. A brief prologue features the Vagabond as a child, accompanying his father at work on a construction site, presumably to build a skyscraper or other "adornment" for the city's wealth. The Vagabond reacts in horror when his father falls from the building to his death. In his final moments, the father imparts

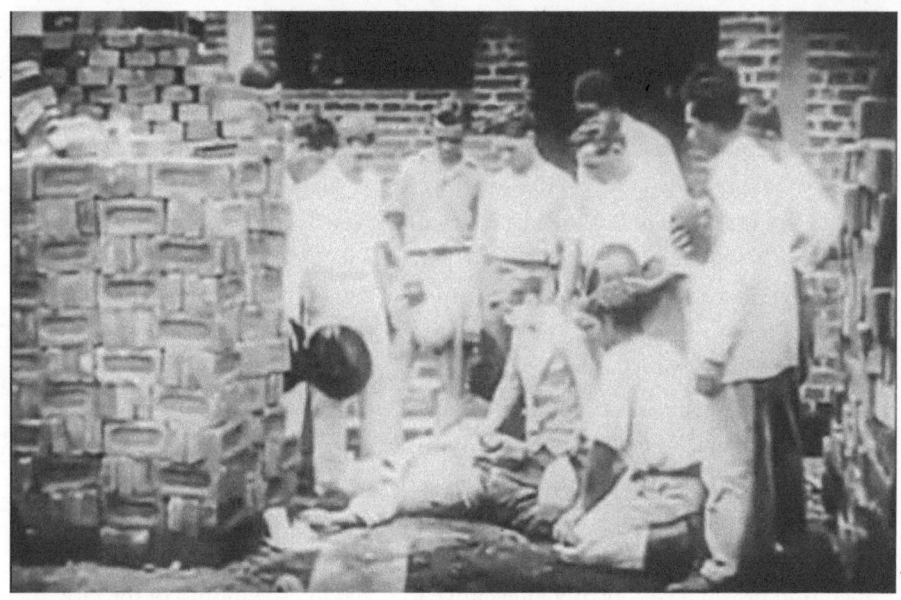

Figures 2.13 and 2.14. Visual contrast between progress and poverty. The vagabond's father falls to his death while building the modern city. *Fragments of Life*, directed by José Medina (1929, São Paulo, Rossi Film).

a final message: "Always be honest, always be a worker. Work will open the way to honor." Yet the opening intertitle, as well as the overall narrative of the film, affirms that the city and its wealth are built on the exploitation of the poor.

One of the metatextual ironies of the film is that Gilberto Rossi was the film's cinematographer. Rossi was an Italian immigrant who formed a prolific film production company in Brazil, producing mostly documentaries. Although the critics at *Cinearte*, with their preference for narrative films, rejected Rossi as an artistic upstart, Rossi held nationalist aspirations for Brazilian cinema that in some ways aligned with *Cinearte*'s views.[58] Rossi explicitly wanted to show the great bounty of Brazil, the impressiveness of its engineering, and the prosperity of its lands in his newsreels. In 1926 Rossi even shared his personal journey of immigrant success in a promotional pamphlet to attract cameramen to his production company—an earnest attempt at forming a national filmmaking corps that would "capture the marvels of Brazil."[59] Like similar scenes in *The Lawyer's Daughter*, Rossi filmed skyscrapers and squares to construct a visual narrative of the city's progress and urbanization.[60] Yet Rossi also poignantly juxtaposes images of wealth and poverty throughout *Fragments of Life*. Nearly every encounter that the two vagabonds have with other people establishes a visual contrast between rich and poor. The two men wander busy streets and restaurants, interacting with men wearing top hats and women wearing fur collars, yet they themselves are dressed shabbily in dirty clothes. The plot of the film also subverts the visual images of prosperity and modernity. The vagabond's father dies on a construction site, literally sacrificed to São Paulo's rapid urbanization. Patrons eat lavishly in a busy restaurant, yet more than one man inside has known "hunger greater than shame."

At the end of the film, the Vagabond remembers the words of his father and repents, vowing to find work and become worthy of "the air that I breathe." Yet his companion, the Scoundrel, frames him by placing a stolen watch in the Vagabond's pocket. In an ironic twist borrowed from O. Henry's original story, the Vagabond ends up in jail as he had wished at the beginning of the film, but only after he promised to redeem himself and seek work. The film diverges from the original short story by introducing another dark twist. In a final epilogue, a newspaper headline reveals that while in jail, the Vagabond dies by suicide. The city thus cannibalizes its citizens, expanding at the expense of the people who live within it, its growth built on the blood and sweat of the poor. It is a surprisingly raw story about the bourgeois exploitation of the worker (yet still extolling the necessity of working for "honor") for two producers, José Medina and Gilberto Rossi, who were not connected to radically leftist intellectual circles.

Figure 2.15. The "vagabond" stands alone in the middle of the city's prosperity. *Fragments of Life*, directed by José Medina (1929, São Paulo, Rossi Film).

Like Helvécio in *The Lawyer's Daughter*, the Vagabond and the Scoundrel are men who do not work. *Fragments of Life* portrays their indolence as a failure of masculinity and a rejection of patriarchal family values. Like Helvécio, the Vagabond and the Scoundrel leech on the excesses of the city rather than produce anything to contribute to its growth. For this, they are depicted as a destructive, aberrant, homosocial pair, two men who exist on the margins of society, more comfortable in jail than within a nuclear family/home. And while men in turn-of-the-century Brazil might prove their masculinity among other men in homosocial settings, whether in public squares, bars, or barracks, this might be through acts of violence and dueling rather than the purposeful evasion of paternal responsibilities.[61] As a "vagabond" and "scoundrel," these two characters resemble, in some respects, another variation of "aberrant" masculinity, the *vadio*, or "vagrant." During Rio de Janeiro's post-abolition antivagrancy campaign, legislation marked so-called vagrants as idle, weak, deficient in masculine honor, and incapable of supporting a family, specifically targeting this term toward Afro-Brazilian and poor men and women. And while their attempts at trickery and opportunism recall the Brazilian *malandro*, or the street-smart scoundrel, they significantly lack the actual ability to pull off their petty crimes, as well as the charisma or womanizing habits also associated with this figure.⁶² As a Brazilian adaptation of a US-based novel, *Fragments of Life* is reminiscent of these locally specific figures, but adapts cosmopolitan visions of failed masculinity to a paulistano context.

The women in the film appear as minor "extras," eating in restaurants, walking down streets, and owning shops. Like Heloísa in *A Filha do Advogado*, the women are less characters with their own motivations than archetypes of femininity that mark the male characters' emotional and moral growth. The first woman that the Vagabond and Scoundrel encounter in the city is a street-strolling melindrosa dressed in a fur-collared coat and cloche hat. When they concoct the scheme to follow and intimidate her, they see her merely as an object of desire and a means to an end. As evidence of their deviant masculinity, they intentionally prey on her, expecting to be arrested. However, the Vagabond ends up following the same woman not into a movie theater, but into a church. When he approaches her, he sees her in a nonsexual way, as a chaste and pious woman. In viewing the woman in this light, he becomes ashamed of his past behavior. Like Helvécio in *The Lawyer's Daughter*, his moral decadence is represented in his perverse sexual assault of women. When the Vagabond repents, his moral/spiritual growth is expressed through his respect for women's chastity. This also spurs his own recognition of proper familial hierarchies, symbolically returning home as a filial son, thinking respectfully of his departed father. Like Helvécio, he has a flashback before his death to remember his father's paternal advice about working hard and being a good man.

Fragments of Life takes a markedly different perspective on urban life in São Paulo than either *The Lawyer's Daughter* or *Lips Without Kisses*. It focuses on two "vagabonds" and the trials of poverty and crime rather than the romantic exploits of the elite. However, it similarly asks the question of whether proper gender roles and "family values" can survive in a modern city. The Vagabond's father's dying message of "work as the path to honor" gestures toward a certain type of idealized masculinity that is productive, diligent, and noble in toil. Yet other narrative elements of the film are more ambivalent. In *Fragments of Life*, the city exploits the "sweat of the working poor," which the film represents as the dark underbelly of glamorous urbanization. Ultimately, the film demonstrates that the perversion of masculinity and the breakdown of the nuclear family may be less an individual moral failing than an unfortunate byproduct of the city's too-rapid growth.

The film does not explicitly tell the story of working-class immigrants, but it was produced and set in São Paulo, a city that, during this time, swelled with expanding migrant populations from other parts of Brazil, Europe, and Asia.

The immigrant population of São Paulo is reflected in the film's production and exhibition. The film's cameraman, Gilberto Rossi, strongly identified himself as a hardworking Italian immigrant who "made it" in Brazil. The actor who played the "scoundrel" was Alfredo Roussy, but this was the Brazilianized stage name of Farid Riskallah, who may have been part of São Paulo's sizable Middle Eastern community. The film was shown in various cinemas in the city, including the Brás Políteama Cinema and the Mafalda Cinema, both located in the largely working-class neighborhood of Brás, which was home to a large immigrant and mixed-race population.[63] Shown in these São Paulo cinemas, the film would have been seen by working men, women, and children who recognized "the other side" of city life.

Cinearte ran a full-page spread of stills from the film to support its production, as well as a two-page interview with the director José Medina. Octavio Gabus Mendes, who was the magazine's resident film critic in São Paulo, wrote a half-page review of the film, conceding mixed results from the director, cameraman, and actors. He deemed the film to be, overall, "watchable." Noting that the film was completed in just under a month, the critic remarked, "Hurry is the enemy of perfection," but acknowledged José Medina was a "meticulous director." Mendes especially criticized Carlos Ferreira, the actor who played the Vagabond, denigrating his "horrendous makeup" and "excessively immobile" expressions. Describing a particularly dramatic scene in which the Vagabond is supposed to weep tragically, Mendes derided Ferreira for looking like "a little kid sent to sit in the corner by his teacher."[64] Gabus Mendes's other criticisms of the movie, however, were more pointedly directed against the camera operator, Gilberto Rossi. His critiques aligned with the magazine's overall disdain for Rossi and, more generally, the genre of documentary films that Rossi represented. Mendes wrote, as a backhanded compliment, "The [film's] photography is genuinely Rossi, but without doubt, it is much more careful than the horror that he is accustomed to putting in his documentaries."[65] Although Gabus Mendes was sparing in his compliments of *Fragments of Life*, he still considered it to be an achievement of Brazilian cinema. Film critic Pedro Lima also noted it briefly in his annual end-of-year review of Brazilian film production, counting it toward the magazine's final tally of the year's domestically produced films. Though Mendes, as a proxy for *Cinearte*, did not appreciate the film's focus on poverty and crime, as opposed to the elite adventures in *Lips Without Kisses*, he still found the film to have some merit as a Brazilian film.

Cinearte's tacit recognition of *Fragments of Life* was in distinct contrast to its reaction to another São Paulo film called *O Transito* (SPCF, Brasil Ideal

Filme, 1929). The film itself is lost, but descriptions of it still exist in *Cinearte*. *O Transito* had a plot similar to *Fragments of Life*. Two "vagabonds" come to São Paulo city for the first time and have a series of adventures until they have a run-in with the police. Mendes criticized *O Transito* as beyond redemption, a film that not only presented the city in an unflattering way but went so far as to sully the city's well-respected institutions. Mendes's criticisms pointed to both racial and sexual degeneracy in the film, with scenes featuring Black characters, drunkenness, and "unhygienic" and immoral behavior. "Is it right, decent, or beautiful to show such a depressing film? With such dirty people, with features so unhygienic?"[66] Describing what he considered to be a particularly notorious scene, Mendes said, "The Esplanada Hotel, for example. It's gained infamy with the scene filmed in its entrance. What would such a scene even suggest? With those two women, exiting together drunk from the inside [of the hotel]?" Mendes may have been appalled at the image of two drunk women in a centrally located, upscale hotel, one in fact that was associated with one of the city's premier movie theaters, the Cine República. Or, considering his outrage, he may have been accusing the film of insinuating a homosexual relationship between two female characters. Gabus Mendes was also explicit about the representation of race, criticizing the appearance of a paulistana actor in blackface: "And that Black woman was no other than Cohen, an individual that was always a 'fan' of Brazilian cinema and that played the role, in *Fragments of Life*, of the shop owner whose window was broken. What was that? What a scene, really!" Mendes's indignation was not a condemnation of blackface so much as the film's gesturing to Blackness. For Mendes, the film was so bad that it sullied even the movie theater in which it was shown. "Why have the audacity of premiering a film like this in a cinema as beautiful and nice as the [Cine] Dom Pedro II?" He continued, "José Pedro [the director] should . . . repay this chivalrous and noble gesture [of premiering at the Cine Dom Pedro] by never again even thinking of directing a film."[67] Mendes also claimed that in producing a film that was so morally corrupt, Pedro must have been influenced by only the worst of what he had seen "in North American films."

Although Mendes himself was a critic based in São Paulo, he lamented that *O Transito*, and by some extension *Fragments of Life*, reflected negatively on the city and its nascent film industry. "The paulista films, unfortunately, even today exhibit vagabonds, chicken-thieves, trolley ticket-takers, passengers of old trains, and suspicious launderers."[68] Pedro Lima, in his end-of-year review of all national film productions, even refrained from referring to *O Transito* as part of "Brazilian cinema." Lima pointedly excluded it, writing, "I am not including *O Transito*, made in 1928, the worst that has come out of our studios in the last few years."[69] Mendes had not found *Fragments of Life* to be so detestable, admitting, "Although [*Fragments of Life*] focuses on the less attractive aspects of our modern São Paulo, it is also a film full of agreeable adventures."[70] While the *Cinearte* critics distinguished between the two films, they nevertheless disapproved of both films' focus on the "less attractive aspects" of the modern city. If *Lips Without Kisses* represented the present and future of Brazilian cinema, shot and produced in Rio de Janeiro, featuring elite, white-presenting Brazilians who ultimately conformed to traditional family hierarchies, films like *O Transito* represented the dark side of cinema that showcased the moral, sexual, and social degeneracy that festered in the city.

This chapter has analyzed representations of gender and urbanization in several narrative films from Recife, Rio de Janeiro, and São Paulo. In each of these films, gender, family, and romance are key to the depiction of the ups and downs of city life. Where traditional gender norms were perverted, cities presented a dangerous threat. While Recife's *The Lawyer's Daughter* demonstrates how the modern city and traditional family might be united if given the guidance of a strong paternal figure, Rio de Janeiro's *Lips Without Kisses* finds the city to be both spatially and morally disorienting. The main characters never find their bearings until they abandon the city for the "natural adornments" of the countryside. Finally, *Fragments of Life* demonstrates the "other side" of urbanization, in which the city is not just chaotic but dysfunctional, where families are irreparably broken, men eschew family responsibilities, and lives are lost to urban growth—a city that cannibalizes its own citizens. In their nationalist interpretations, film intellectuals from Rio de Janeiro amplified the message that the true Brazilian cinematic vision was one in which cities were modern and glamorous, and where chivalrous romance between men and women blossomed into nuclear families. Similar to the cartoonists and writers in the previous chapter, filmmakers and intellectuals centered gender and sexual mores in their stories of urban Brazil, fashioning both idealized and threatening visions. The following chapter demonstrates how the implementation of such ideals was vastly different from the everyday reality of Brazil's growing cities. Turning to the movie theaters themselves, chapter 3 shifts from filmmakers and movie stars to municipal law, bureaucratic regulations, and the sometimes seedy realm of movie theater operations to demonstrate how gender figured into ideals of the safe and hygienic city.

3

MAKING CINEMAS SAFE FOR SENHORAS IN 1920s RIO DE JANEIRO AND SÃO PAULO

In the June 22, 1929, edition of the *Estado de S. Paulo* daily newspaper, illustrations of men and women embracing peppered several pages of movie advertisements. Tucked in between tantalizing titles like "The Fateful Woman," "The Heart of a Russian," and "Fast for Love" were advertisements for two films that, on first glance, were no more salacious than the others: *The Hygiene of Marriage* and *The Kiss That Kills*. With its illustration of a man and woman kissing, *The Kiss That Kills*, shown at the Cinema Paraíso, appeared similar to advertisements for other romantic films. But on closer inspection the description read, "Film about cerebral syphilis prophylaxis," preceded by the warning "Improper for minors and senhoritas." The advertisement for another film, *The Hygiene of Marriage* at the Cine Triángulo, was more direct, if not wholly transparent, about its main purpose: "*The Hygiene of Marriage* is a film that will impart the greatest, most useful teachings [on how to have a happy home]! Take note: This is a film awarded by the German government! A film made under the direction of doctors." Finally, the fine print read, just like in the advertisement for *The Kiss That Kills*, "Improper for minors and senhoritas."

Reading between the lines, both films were examples of semipornographic "exploitation films," or films that peddled images of nudity and sex under the guise of science and sexual education. In Brazil, such films were called

Figure 3.1. "The Kiss That Kills," advertisement, *Estado de S. Paulo*, June 22, 1929, Acervo Estadão, https://www.estadao.com.br/acervo/.

"scientific films," and as in the United States and other countries, they were part of the moviegoing scene throughout the first half of the twentieth century. In the case of *The Hygiene of Marriage*, the reference to approval by the "German government" was a gesture to the film's scientific legitimacy in a "developed" country, even if the actualities of Brazilian-German political relations were complicated in this time. *Cinearte* explicitly lamented the presence of such films in a lengthy editorial condemning these "spectacles only for men," and warning that they "incite the basest of human sentiments." *Cinearte* also hinted that such films did not necessarily exclude female moviegoers, as some films targeted their advertisements to "married people . . . , those that want to marry, and even those who want to know what married people do." The critic at *Cinearte* worried that through these films, cinema was "capable of further degrading . . . already relaxed social customs."[1]

Buried under the language of hygiene and purporting to demonstrate scenes of romance and marriage, films like *The Kiss That Kills* and *The Hygiene of Marriage* made clear that they were not intended for "*senhoritas*," a diminutive form of the word *senhora*, a term that typically signified women of somewhat elevated social or moral status, such as married or elite women. In the changing social scene of which moviegoing was a part, who was a "senhora," and which movie theaters did she go to, if any? The Cine Paraíso and the Cine Triángulo, despite their adoption of the concept of "hygiene," explicitly warned that they exhibited films that were inappropriate for senhoras or senhoritas. What, then, was a truly "hygienic" movie theater, and who were the senhoras who might be found within them? Often the films on screen, with their images of romance or violence, were cause for concern. However, another debate was brewing about the potential dangers of cinema, and it centered not on the films, but on the construction and use of movie theaters and their implications for public health.

This chapter contextualizes moviegoing and respectable womanhood within urban reform and the broader hygiene and sanitation movement of the early twentieth century. While "exploitation" or "scientific" films like *The*

Kiss That Kills or *The Hygiene of Marriage* hijacked the language of science to peddle baser pleasures, they were peripheral to the larger battle over hygiene in movie theaters. Individuals within the evolving public health sector, as well as those outside of it, such as film intellectuals and movie theater owners, fixated on movie theaters and their relationship to the hygiene and safety of the populace. These were the individuals who built, regulated, and assessed the quality of movie theaters, and in deeming some movie theaters appropriate for senhoras and others not, these intellectuals and public health officials utilized respectable womanhood as a symbol of the hygienic city. In this formulation, respectable women did not necessarily risk their health, safety, or status by going to the movies, but might instead sit in clean, comfortable spaces that protected their supposedly delicate sensibilities. In this symbiotic relationship between hygiene and respectable womanhood, "senhoras" even had a sanitizing influence, uplifting movie theaters and moviegoing as a social activity.

This vision of a city—safe and clean enough for "senhoras"—was in stark contrast to the reality of movie exhibition in Rio de Janeiro and São Paulo. While moviegoing in the 1910s "smartened up" and transformed into an elite leisure activity,[2] public health officials, film critics, and moviegoers found plenty of movie theaters that deviated from this standard. Similar to the scientific films that peddled a certain image (educational, for men only) that was far from its reality (pornographic, possibly appealing to "couples"), movie theaters themselves diverged from their advertised ideals. According to cinema's critics, ramshackle movie theaters prone to fire, disease, and overcrowding littered the city and threatened the broader health of the community. The movie theater industry in this time period was rife with extralegal maneuvering, safety irregularities, and evasions from the letter of the law. The men involved in founding and monitoring movie theaters, from immigrant cinema kings and small business owners to civil engineers and building inspectors, were part of bourgeoning entrepreneurial and professional sectors of the urban population. Though on opposite sides of urban regulation, they together hashed out the shape and status of movie theaters in Brazil, alternately implementing and twisting the language of hygiene to cast moviegoing as a social activity suitable for senhoras.

Movie Theaters, Urban Reform, and the Sanitation Movement

For public health officials, municipal officials, and state legislators, movie theaters were a key arena to test ideologies of hygiene—a concept intertwined with the history of race and eugenics in Latin America. Brazilian intellectuals participated in the contemporaneous global debates about eugenics and the engineering of fit and unfit populations. In contrast to the Mendelian eugenics of Germany and the United States, where eugenicists sought to engineer race through reproduction and mass sterilization, Latin American intellectuals selectively combined Mendelian and neo-Lamarckian eugenics, the latter of which maintained that environmental factors were the keys to racial uplift.[3] In this vein of thought, the improvement of the environment, whether through the education of the populace or the sanitation of a city, was a step to the racial improvement of Brazil. During the early twentieth century and beyond, Brazilian government officials embarked on campaigns to vaccinate, sanitize, educate, and otherwise elevate populations out of perceived poverty, racial degeneracy, and sexual deviance.[4] Urban planners in Rio de Janeiro and São Paulo razed, reformed, and pushed out neighborhoods that were home to poor, often Afro-descendant communities, and these populations resisted the state's incursions.[5] At the same time, urban reformers built up wide avenues, monumental architecture, ornate urban parks, and other symbols of the modern, hygienic city.[6]

In this context, movie theaters were again a discomfiting blend of both the "dark" and the "light." On the side of the "light," movie theaters could be akin to the bridges, train stations, and even the soccer stadiums that engineers erected across Brazilian cities to signify urban modernity and progress. Throughout the 1910s, movie theaters in Rio de Janeiro underwent a process of refinement, advertising new technologies and attractions like electric ventilation, the latest types of film projection, and Friday "matinees" dedicated to select audiences. According to film historian José Inácio de Melo Souza, these innovations in film exhibition strived to "demarcate [movie theaters as] territory destined for elegant people."[7] Movie theaters like the Cinema Odeon in Rio de Janeiro advertised themselves with words like "comfort" and "elegance." In one 1910 magazine advertisement, an illustration of women wearing ornate, fashionable clothing and holding a "Cinema Odeon" film program demonstrates the importance of elegant women in the branding of the movie theater.[8] Beginning in the 1910s in São Paulo, and continuing throughout the 1920s and later decades, movie theaters were also an opportunity to enforce new state and municipal regulations meant to ensure the city's sanitary rigor. State legislations, city ordinances, and municipal records demonstrate how state and local officials regulated the construction of movie theaters, often remarking on whether they satisfied sanitary regulations to ensure the "hygiene, safety, and comfort"—a phrase entrenched in municipal documentation—of the populace.

On the "dark side," film exhibitors used similar, aspirational descriptors precisely because cinemas could also be seen as a threat to an organized, sanitary city. For those who sought to regulate or comment on the state of movie theaters—public health officials, building inspectors, and even film intellectuals and moviegoers—movie theaters presented several affronts to an orderly city. First, the material of film itself conveyed real danger, as film contained elements of nitrate, making it highly flammable and even combustible.[9] Moviegoers were aware of and even exaggerated the dangers of nitrate film. The early twentieth-century writer and essayist Jacob Penteado recalled that in his working-class São Paulo neighborhood, moviegoers sat as far as possible from the film projectors because "they said the film could burn your eyes." In addition, before screenings, the movie screen would be doused in water with "the most primitive instrument possible: a cane of bamboo with a bulb at the tip."[10] This was supposed to make the cloth screen more transparent for the use of "rear projection," an older technology in which the film projector displayed the image through a translucent screen. However, some moviegoers were either mistaken or suspicious about the technology and "insisted that it was to prevent the screen from burning."[11]

In addition to the fire hazard, another disruption was the indeterminacy of what a movie theater really was in the early twentieth century. While by the 1920s, dozens of movie theaters dedicated to screening films existed just in the city of São Paulo, movies were also shown in hybrid spaces that combined cinema with other attractions like theater, dancing, and even dining. In some cases, a venue might bring in chairs and a projector to function temporarily as a cinema, and then clear these chairs to make way for a dance floor or even a boxing ring on another night.[12] With blurred boundaries surrounding the exact definition of a cinema, some establishments could evade building codes that sought to protect moviegoers against film-specific dangers such as fire or overcrowded exits.

The case of two competing businesses in São Paulo, the "Midnight Bar and Café" and "Kursaal Steaks," demonstrates how cinema weaved in and out of other types of leisure, and not always in a safe or orderly way. The Midnight Bar and Café, so named because one of its earlier owners had the unique surname "Meia Noite," which means "midnight," had peddled a number of popular leisure activities under one roof: ice cream, billiards, music, dancing, drinking, and elegant pastries. In 1926, in order to attract more clientele, the Bar and Café petitioned the São Paulo city government for a license to exhibit films, which they would screen for free as patrons enjoyed the bar's other pleasures. Though originally meeting some resistance, the Bar and Café was granted a license and began advertising itself as the "Midnight Cinema," with film screenings continuing from the late afternoon to midnight. In advertisements, the Midnight Cinema invited "distinguished families appreciative of the 'silent screen' to visit this establishment, the biggest and best adorned in South America."[13] In another advertisement that belied its somewhat salacious name, the Midnight Cinema purported to be "hygienic, comfortable, and elegant. In a league of its own in Brazil."[14] Despite that it most likely catered exclusively to men, the Midnight Cinema appealed to "distinguished families," alluding to a veneer of the respectability associated with "elite" clientele, and by extension the respectable women, mothers, and daughters of such families.[15]

Within months, a neighboring restaurant called "Kursaal Steaks" attempted to compete with the Midnight Cinema by offering free movie screenings to its patrons. The restaurant advertised itself as a hybrid "Brewery-Bar-Restaurant-Cinema" and also "the most modern and well-frequented movie theater" of the city.[16] This claim was certainly an overstatement when more than a dozen large cinemas sat between one and two thousand spectators each.[17] With the name "kursaal," which referred to the dining halls in German spa towns like Baden-Baden, the restaurant aspired to an image of elite, continental leisure.[18] Interestingly, the owner, a Mr. Galbasera, advertised his makeshift movie theater as "modern," in contrast to the Midnight Cinema and other large cinemas in the city that marketed themselves as "traditional" and "elite." However, in contrast to its cosmopolitan name, "Kursaal Steaks" was far from a marbled dining hall or a modern movie theater. Municipal officials in São Paulo, once they inspected the brewery-bar-restaurant-cinema combo, described it as a "wooden shack" and ordered Mr. Galbasera to shut his cinema down.[19] Given the flammability of nitrate film, housing both a cinema and a kitchen in a "wooden shack" may have warranted the business's closure. The incident certainly demonstrates the difficulty of regulating the sometimes spontaneous nature of film exhibition in this time period.

Yet another affront to urban reform was that movie theaters were necessarily dark, enclosed spaces. Although the prevalence of miasma theory, which blamed disease contagion on unhealthy "humors" was waning, the targeting of "bad air" and crowded social conditions remained influential in the growing arena of public health.[20] Medical professionals located risk in places where people might be crowded in close quarters, such as factories, tenement buildings, and schools, as well as movie theaters. The focus on factories and tenements demonstrates how fears of "toxic air" intersected with a more class-based wariness against poverty and urban density.[21] As moviegoing became a well-established leisure activity among the elite, this introduced the problem that people of different classes and racial statuses might mix and mingle together at the movie theater. This attracted the attention of public health officials who sought to contain the infectious diseases that they associated with racial degeneracy. Indeed, as historian Gilberto Hochman argues, the growing awareness among elites that they were as susceptible to germs as the poor was foundational in the formation of a national body politic and the concept of a shared "public," which fortified the advocacy of a national public health movement.[22] In Rio de Janeiro, medical professionals, public health officials, and film intellectuals participated in discussions and debates about the hygiene, or lack thereof, in the city's cinemas. Across mainstream newspapers, film magazines, and specialized medical publications, these intellectuals appealed to both specialists and the general public to remedy the "problem" of movie theaters. They disagreed on the root causes of unhygienic cinemas. The primary culprits could be the "unwashed bodies" of moviegoers themselves; the fact that cinemas were dark, enclosed spaces; or the neglect and misanthropy of cinema owners. However, they all wondered whether cinemas could be especially unhygienic structures that threatened the public.

In 1916, concurrent with an intensification of the movement for public health, Dr. Placido Barbosa gave an interview in the Rio de Janeiro daily newspaper *Jornal do Comércio* in which he criticized the city's cinemas as hotbeds of dangerous diseases. He faulted the "unwashed bodies" of the moviegoing masses as the primary cause of the lethal "carbonic gas" that pervaded cinemas. In response to Barbosa's interview, another group of medical professionals published an article in the well-established medical journal *Medico-cirurgica do Brasil*.[23] Taking particular aim at what they perceived to be bad science, they criticized Barbosa's logic but agreed that cinemas were indeed particularly dangerous structures that produced bad air. Comparing the "corrupted air" (*ar viciado*) of cinemas to that found in factories and prisons, the authors claimed that so many people crowded together produced a toxic, even lethal "carbonic gas."[24] The authors reported, "Even hours after being emptied, the smell characteristic of confined spaces persists. The reason for this is in the condensation of air, which comes into contact with walls, furniture, clothing, leaving tiny droplets of organic material that then permeate the atmosphere with this unmistakable odor." Reflecting the growing influence of germ theory, the public health officials and professors who wrote the article announced that even Rio de Janeiro's best cinemas had a shocking number of "germens" per cubic meter.[25]

Their language echoed the same rhetoric that medical professionals and public health officials used to condemn factories and slums. In the case of cinemas, however, the authors' main preoccupation was their heightened potential to spread disease beyond the working poor. The cinemas addressed in the article were all located on Avenida Rio Branco, a chic avenue in the center of Rio de Janeiro.[26] Thus, the discovery of the resistant, tuberculosis-causing "Koch bacteria" in a "well-frequented" (but unnamed) cinema was doubly dangerous, as the "corrupted air" could rise and infect nearby apartment buildings, spreading diseases to Rio de Janeiro's well-heeled elite.[27] Cinemas, therefore, were especially dangerous because they might affect all economic sectors of the population. The authors derided Barbosa's classist claim that it was the "unwashed bodies" that caused such dangerous "germens," instead faulting poor ventilation and lack of fresh air and light. Yet they, too, compared cinemas to factories and emphasized that cinemas were particularly unhygienic spaces that were contrary to the ideal of the sanitized city.

The ideas of the sanitation movement extended beyond medical literature, and journalists and film intellectuals incorporated medical discourse to organize the city's cinemas into hierarchies of race, class, and respectability.[28] While the 1916 study found fault with all cinemas in Rio de Janeiro, including and especially the "chic" ones of the Avenida, film intellectuals at the Rio de Janeiro–based film magazine *Para Todos* aggressively deemed some cinemas better than others. The same circle of critics who later wrote for *Cinearte* advocated for the construction and use of hygienic cinemas as a means of encouraging respectable moviegoing. They heaped praise on new cinemas that they considered to be clean and respectable but also frequently lobbed insults at cinemas they found to be dated, dirty, or structurally unsound. They especially criticized the *cinema do arrabalde*, or the cinema of the outskirts.

In 1925 a writer using the pseudonym "The [camera] Operator" reprinted the exclamations of a "Dr. Ciancio," who directly challenged Dr. Placido Barbosa to inspect the buildings and cinemas of the Avenida. Dr. Ciancio's primary concern was that although Rio de Janeiro health officials were targeting the spread of tuberculosis, they ignored the true place of its incubation, which was in the bustling "heart of the city." Dr. Ciancio especially condemned the "misery of air and light" typical of the "grand cinemas," referring to them as "gilded caves where the light has not penetrated since

1907." "The Operator" reiterated Dr. Ciancio's concerns and added that the public officials should also examine the cinemas of the "outskirts" and suburbs, which were "filled with ticks, if not worse, where people think they are enjoying themselves with an idiotic film but end up bringing home diseases that are sometimes even fatal."[29] Like the findings of the 1916 inspections, Dr. Ciancio and "The Operator" imagined cinemas as breeding grounds for germs and disease that could then spread from cinemas to the surrounding street and even to moviegoers' homes.

In sum, by the 1920s, movie theaters had undergone a process of legitimization in both cities. Film exhibitors and critics painted movie theaters as spaces that were destined for respectable types of people, sometimes depicted as "elite," "traditional," or "distinguished." Yet movie theaters still carried connotations of danger, disorder, and disease. Nitrate film presented a real threat of fire in all movie theaters, a threat that was exaggerated among audience members who went to older cinemas. Establishments like the Midnight Cinema and even a ramshackle restaurant like "Kursaal Steaks" adopted the language of hygiene and aspiration to paint their cinemas as respectable. Yet both were examples of how "cinemas" themselves were still evolving as distinct spaces, and this indeterminacy could mean skirting municipal regulations that were intended to keep cinemas safe and hygienic.

Sanitation and Respectable Womanhood

Although most of the medical discourse on the dangers of cinemas focused on the deleterious effects of infectious diseases on the general public, intellectuals implicitly associated hygiene with gendered respectability. The Rio de Janeiro–based intellectuals at *Para Todos* and *Cinearte* viewed gendered propriety and cinema as mutually constitutive; hygienic cinemas were appropriate for women, and respectable women only went to certain cinemas. One of the critics at *Para Todos* repeatedly took aim at the Cine Central in Rio de Janeiro as a ramshackle cinema, defective in both its physical construction and its audience. In one review, he described the Cine Central as such: "with chairs falling to pieces, between filth and bolinas [sexual predators who molested women in movie theaters] and people coming and leaving at all hours. 'You can't bring a senhora to the Central!' said my neighbor to the left. 'This is an outrage!' complained my neighbor to the front, as he and his chair fell into my lap."[30] In São Paulo too, Gabus Mendes complained of the Brás Polytheama, one of the largest cinemas in the city. His principal complaint was that smoking was allowed in the theater, which led to such a "large pillar of smoke" coming out of the cinema that firemen rushed to the area. Turns out there was no fire, but it was "just one of 'those' cinemas of the outskirts."[31] According to Mendes, the Polytheama had a horrible orchestra that played the wrong music and walls covered in advertisements, and on rainy days, "it leaked like cats and dogs." Yet on top of these defects, Mendes pointed out that moviegoers "filled the room with smoke, bothering the female audience," singling out women as the primary victims. Such comments about rundown cinemas in Rio de Janeiro and São Paulo assumed that women's delicate sensibilities made them the bellwether for determining improper standards of hygiene and behavior.

In 1926 *Para Todos* reprinted a letter they claimed to have received from a woman using the pseudonym "Mademoiselle Moreno." This "mademoiselle" reported that she never went to the cinemas of the Avenida in Rio de Janeiro because she "always felt bad in those tiny rooms of minuscule proportions, with little air, little hygiene, being forced into contact that was hardly ever agreeable, in an atmosphere corrupted by various perfumes (without mentioning other things), too hot, and with a deficient film projector."[32] Because of the poor quality of movie theaters, she knew nothing of actors and directors—topics in which her friends were "cap and gown scholars." Despite the claim that she avoided the movies, Mademoiselle Moreno wrote knowledgeably of film studios and the status of cinema as art rather than mere entertainment. For example, she complained that now she felt comfortable going to the "new cinemas, so good, so comfortable, so hygienic," but that the best films of "Metro-Goldwyn, Paramount, United" were still in the "cinemas of the outskirts."

Mademoiselle Moreno's specific complaints about the geographic distribution of films and the poor hygiene of the outskirts so closely mimic the criticisms made by writers at *Para Todos* that "she" may have been one of the *Para Todos* writers masquerading under a female pseudonym. The writers at *Cinearte* sometimes did this, planting letters to the editors by using anonymous pen names.[33] Whether Mademoiselle Moreno was actually a female moviegoer or a male film critic, she wrote as a moral authority, a voice of female respectability who condemned unhygienic cinemas as places where proper women did not belong. "Moreno" translates as "brown," and can refer either to hair and eye color or to someone of mixed African descent. The use of the French title of "mademoiselle" rather than the Portuguese and respectful "senhora" also hints at a foreign and sexually charged identity, as discussed in chapter 1. Although Mademoiselle Moreno's rhetoric and written assertion of respectability aligned her with ideals of white womanhood, her name also locates the feminine authority of moviegoing in a less determinate space, one that was cosmopolitan and at least gestured at racial variability, even as it claimed feminine virtue.

In at least two cinemas in Rio de Janeiro, women not only functioned as indicators of hygiene and cleanliness, but they also potentially elevated the cinematic experience. Mademoiselle Moreno's praise of the "new cinemas" of the Avenida was a reference to the Cine Capitólio, which had opened a few months before on April 31, 1925, to a "select audience" of elite cariocas. The Cine Capitólio was one of the many endeavors of the cinema king Francisco Serrador, a Spanish immigrant credited with the growth of high-end film exhibition in the 1920s.[34] *Para Todos* enthusiastically reported on the inauguration and all of its technical and aesthetic innovations. Each detail emphasized the cinema's hygienic structure and its difference from the dark, enclosed spaces and "corrupted air" of infamous movie theaters. Photos showed women and children prominently in the audience and in the lobby. While not necessarily a posed photograph, its publication was nevertheless a strategic example of the cinema's decency, a cinema that was appropriate for women and children. The Cine Capitólio had a mechanical ventilation system, which public health officials emphasized as necessary to produce fresh air. In addition, a special "automatic appliance" called the "Radio-San" (an amalgamation of "radio" and "sanitary") spread waves of perfume through the cinema's ventilators. Along with the Radio-San, the Cine Capitólio introduced another novelty: "female ushers located on the ground floor, the private boxes, and in the balconies."[35] Like the Radio-San, the women were accessories to a clean and safe environment.

In contrast to the "deficient" and unhygienic cinemas where one could not bring a "senhora," the female ushers were presented as a part of the overall appeal of the upscale Cine Capitólio. As women working in public, however, these usherettes did walk a fine line. What differentiated these female usherettes from other female domestic servants (who would not have posed for a publicity photo), or from women in "white-collar" positions who might also be criticized for working outside of the home? In her analysis of female volunteers for the collective regional war effort in 1930 São Paulo, Barbara Weinstein posits that the volunteers' use of uniforms was a way to convey gendered propriety while participating in public political activities that otherwise might be perceived as unconventional.[36] While in a different context and for different aims, the usherettes' use of uniforms served a similar legitimizing purpose, conveying a complex mixture of servile status but also gendered

Figure 3.2. "Girl Ushers" at the Cine Capitólio. *Para Todos*, "O Cinema Theatro Capitólio é o inicio de uma nova éra na cinematographia," May 2, 1925, RC Para Todos, Cinemateca Brasileira São Paulo.

respectability and sanitary hygiene. The usherettes represented a different type of femininity from the alluring melindrosa, or Brazilian modern girl, discussed in chapter 1. Whereas the melindrosa was depicted as a woman of consumption and leisure, the usherette was a working woman in a somewhat subservient position. The usherette similarly maintained an ambiguous social status as a woman whose femininity was on full display in public.[37] While the cinema strategically used the usherettes' appearance and uniforms to elevate the respectability of moviegoing, the usherettes themselves occupied a somewhat in-between status within the commercial economy.

Municipal Regulation of Cinemas: The São Paulo Department of Works and Film Exhibitors

Discussions of sanitation were not limited to medical or popular discourse, and both the state and city of São Paulo provide examples of how ideas of hygiene were incorporated into legislation. In 1917 São Paulo state passed sweeping legislation to revamp public health services that incorporated contemporary language about health and sanitation, as well as hints as to where "senhoras" fit into this vision of a hygienic city. Among the state's many targets of reform, such as schools, barber shops, hospitals, and butcheries, were movie theaters. On the municipal level, São Paulo city adopted the state legislation and developed its own ordinances and codes to ensure the "safety, hygiene, and comfort" of the city's cinemas. Cinemas, those crowded hotbeds of germs, toxic airs, and people, were an easy target for broader concerns regarding urbanization and women's place within it.

As Raquel Rolnik has demonstrated in her history of urbanization in São Paulo in the Old Republic, municipal authorities, influenced by the hygienist movement and accommodating the varying interests of the regional elite, attempted to regulate the city and reform its urban spaces through legislation, building codes, and zoning laws. This legislation helped codify the social and geographic boundaries demarcating the elite, residential neighborhoods of single-family homes, which were built on the city's dry hillsides and given names like "Higienópolis" for their supposed sanitary and hygienic environments. Yet at the same time, the development of self-constructed housing and tenements characterized the horizontal expansion of poorer neighborhoods, which were built in the city's swampy periphery. By 1931 this "clandestine city" of unregulated spaces was larger than the official one.[38] In addition, even areas that were part of the "formal," regulated city could be messy landscapes with auto-constructed "private roads" that deviated from the letter of the law.[39] Movie theaters were part of this symbiotic process, both the increasing regulation of city spaces and the extralegal or negotiated evasions of it. Lawmakers at both the state and municipal levels developed laws and ordinances to regulate the real and perceived dangers of cinemas, from fire and corrupted air to sex-segregated bathrooms.

In regulating the built spaces of movie theaters, municipal officials came into direct contact with the movie theater proprietors and film exhibitors who sought to construct these spaces. Civil engineers and film entrepreneurs were like two sides of the same coin. Although their differing goals pitted them against each other in municipal processes, they ultimately negotiated the construction of new cinemas and collaborated in the changing landscape of the city. In fact, cinema owners and municipal engineers were sometimes more similar than different. Cristina Peixoto-Mehrtens describes municipal organizations like the Department for Public Works as "cradle organizations for the new middle class," where the sons of immigrants and small business owners could become upwardly mobile professionals.[40] For example, Adriano Marchini, a Department of Works engineer, was the son of poor Italian immigrants.[41] Engineer J. Fraissat in fact navigated both sides as he worked for the municipal government but was occasionally also hired by cinema proprietors to design their movie theaters.

Municipal records show that 185 cinemas were built between 1916 and 1930, though not all functioned continuously through the 1920s.[42] The largest cinemas held thousands of moviegoers. For example, the Brás Políteama was a colossal theater constructed in 1922 that held 3,388 spectators, but there were at least a dozen more in the city with a capacity of around or above 1,000.[43] Small cinemas that held a few hundred seats or fewer were more common, and these were also scattered across various neighborhoods. Finally, there were ephemeral enterprises that were "cinemas" only in that they attempted to show films, either regularly or not. Like "Kursaal Bife," the bar-brew-house-steakhouse-cinema, many other "cinemas" were multifunctional spaces that combined film, theater, billiards, music, and dancing.

In contrast to republican ideals of ordered urban space, blueprints for cinemas often reflected months of conflict, and the end result did not always materialize the dream of order and safety. For example, cinema owners petitioned the municipal government to give them exemptions to these regulations, sometimes claiming their cinemas were too small, and other times too grandiose and modern, to be subject to such rules.[44] In this way, cinemas demonstrated that even buildings that were licensed, "official" enterprises did not conform to the letter of the law. José Inácio de Melo Souza has observed that if São Paulo's building codes had truly been enforced, then no cinemas would have been allowed to operate.⁴⁵ Film entrepreneurs and other businessmen associated with cinemas countered municipal laws by petitioning for exemptions, ignoring the government's demands for reforms, and sometimes simply buying time. In the most chaotic incidents, peddlers and theater owners resorted to convoluted subterfuge and even violence as they clashed with the law. In one bizarre case, two competing cinema/theater owners coerced neighborhood residents to sign petitions accusing each other's theaters of building code violations.⁴⁶ In another, an ice cream store owner threatened to kill a municipal official with a knife, blaming him for increased competition with ambulant ice cream peddlers who gathered around the nearby Marconi Cinema and therefore competed with his business.⁴⁷

Under the guise of not being a cinema, an establishment could beg exemption from adhering to the 1916 building codes, further flustering and evading municipal authorities. Building inspectors were repeatedly frustrated in their attempts to bring one such cinema, which functioned alternately as both the Cinema Apollo and the Imperial Dancing dance hall, to order, as a dance hall was not subject to the same set of laws as cinemas. The inspectors determined that as a cinema, the structure was deficient in hygiene, repeatedly pointing out that there were not enough bathrooms for either sex, that there was only "one vanity table for senhoras," and that the walls in the men's bathrooms were unhygienically painted with tar instead of tiled. All of this was "insufficient for a theater that seats 974 people."⁴⁸ In their reports, building inspectors parsed distinctions between how bathrooms were used in dance halls versus in cinemas. They emphasized that cinemas needed more bathrooms because moviegoers would crowd the bathroom at the same time, at the beginning or end of a film, whereas dancers might use the bathroom throughout the night.

Through thousands of municipal processes, a portrait emerges of a rapidly expanding urban environment dotted with cinemas and satellite spaces of leisure like bars, ice cream parlors, and music venues. There were a handful of very prominent cinemas like the aptly named "Cine República" or the grandiose Cine Central that municipal engineers found to be in "perfect" condition. But the government's overall judgment of São Paulo's hundreds of cinemas was that these spaces were neither particularly orderly nor hygienic. In fact, many were dated, and some were even dangerous. In contrast to the ambitious state law of 1917, cinemas were not places considered respectable for senhoras, nor were they in line with the republican state's ideal of sanitized hygiene.

The gap between municipal law and the built space of the city's cinemas prompted the newspaper *Jornal do Comércio* to print a sharp criticism of the government in 1928. The principal complaint of the article was that although cinemas were "spontaneously multiplying" in São Paulo, none of the cinemas were actually cinemas, but old theaters and buildings renovated to serve as cinemas. These renovated buildings were "full of defects," the main danger being the flammability of celluloid film and the possibility of electrical short circuits. With a lack of emergency exits, these old buildings were accidents waiting to happen. In addition, the writer advised that the engineers of cinemas should recognize the "excessive number of people who flock daily to shows" and adjust the maximum capacity of cinemas accordingly. The author of the article also ridiculed the claims that cinemas utilized "exhausts and ventilators with difficult names. If they exist, they are insufficient." Finally, he directly blamed the government: "The guilt against public hygiene lies with Sanitary Services, who easily close their eyes and ignore all of these details. The public (*público*) is the only one to lose. But what value do the people (*povo*) have?"[49] The article saw the growth of film exhibition as indicative of a badly governed and increasingly unruly city.

Senhoras and Sex-Segregated Bathrooms

In the 1917 law that overhauled sanitary services in São Paulo state, legislators sought to uphold certain markers of gendered propriety, namely through sex-segregated bathrooms, including in movie theaters. In reference to "places of amusement and commercial establishments of public character, such as theaters, cinemas, pastry shops, cafés, bars, breweries, diners, restaurants, and dairies etc.,"[50] the law demanded "a sufficient number of lavatories and urinals for patrons and for senhoras, a vanity (*toucador*) with the necessary hygienic appliances."[51] The mandate for a vanity, which really has nothing to do with going to the bathroom, was not an issue of hygiene but of gender. In contrast, the language for sex-segregated bathrooms in places of work was completely different. Article 120 specified that "factories and offices" should have "one latrine . . . separated by sex" for each group of thirty "workers" and one urinal for each group of fifty.[52] Though mentioning that bathrooms should be separated by sex, the law used the blanket term "workers," and made no mention of "senhoras" in the workplace.

The contrast between the state's language in reference to "places of amusement" and "factories and offices" points to subtle but embedded expectations about the gender, class, and respectability of the people present within each one. In this idealized dichotomy, "senhoras"—respectable women—might attend spaces of leisure. Yet while women might be present in "factories and offices," according to the state legislation, they were not necessarily "senhoras." Despite the state's neat division between leisure and work, historiography has shown how variegated distinctions of class and respectability cut through these broad categories. For example, there was a wide class division between the most elite cinemas on the "Avenida" in Rio de Janeiro, such as the Cine Odeon that featured elegantly dressed women in advertisements, versus the movie theaters that *Para Todos* critics deemed the "unhygienic" cinemas of the "outskirts." The gulf was even wider between elite cinemas and establishments like "bars and botequins," which were both typically masculine and working class.[53] These were spaces where women, but more particularly "senhoras," were not supposed to be present. For example, the growing popularity of nonalcoholic industrialized drinks like guaraná soda afforded women a more respectable alternative for public refreshment (as opposed to beer or cachaça). Women also had to follow unwritten rules of when and where they could drink in public, and when they should disappear.[54] Spaces of work, like the "offices and factories" mentioned in the legislation, were by no means monolithic either. The question of gender and respectability of working women was in fact a matter of debate, widely discussed in mainstream print media. Not only was there a perceived difference between women who entered "white-collar" versus "blue-collar" professions, but the respectability of these categories was also unfixed. For example, satirical writers and illustrators debated whether white-collar women threatened gender norms by entering the workforce (like Lelita in *Lips Without Kisses*, discussed in chapter 2), or if they were entitled to some respectability because of the nonmanual nature of their labor.[55]

Defining "Senhoras" in Public Bathrooms

In addition to the false division between women in places of amusement versus work, the legislation could not guarantee that standards of hygiene were uniformly applied across establishments, or even within them. Divisions of gender, class, and respectability existed even within the same movie theater. As Alice Gonzaga writes, movie theaters used a system of tiered ticket pricing and seating sections to actively differentiate members of a moviegoing audience. The largest cinemas in the 1920s were built in the style of nineteenth-century theaters and opera houses. In contrast to a large, flat audience, large movie theaters would commonly have private boxes (the most expensive seats, sometimes only available for rent on a monthly basis), ground-floor seats, and a balcony. Tickets were cheapest in the balcony, which was sometimes filled with rows of benches instead of individual seats. Whereas the state legislation had mandated a "sufficient" number of lavatories and "vanities" for "senhoras" within "places of amusement," film exhibitors implemented this mandate with great variety. The difference in how bathrooms were disbursed in the movie theater, especially among the different seating sections, reveals how laws of hygiene, meant to protect "senhoras," were unequally applied to women of different economic means.

The Cine Oberdan in the São Paulo neighborhood of Brás provides an example of such divisions. Reflecting the heavy concentration of Italian Brazilians in the neighborhood of Brás, the Oberdan was originally constructed as a mutual aid association for this community in 1889. It was named for Guglielmo Oberdan, an Italian nationalist during the Austro-Hungarian occupation of Trieste. Alongside other immigrant-based mutual aid associations in São Paulo, the Oberdan flourished in the early twentieth century. Francisco Matarazzo, among the most successful and richest Italian Brazilian industrialists of the time, was the society's honorary president. It first converted to a theater in April of 1929, and then held its inaugural session as a cinema in October of that year. Newspaper advertisements proclaimed that it would be the "premiere of the best regulated and in-tune sound film equipment in the most luxurious theater of Brás." According to newspaper advertisements from 1929, the year the theater was renovated and reopened as a cinema, seats on the ground floor and balcony area were 2$500, private boxes were 3$000, a half-price ticket was 1$000, and the gallery section, the cheapest seats, were 1$000. The half-price ticket was on par with cheaper theaters in 1927, when female and male factory workers made on average between 8$500 and 16$000 a day.[56] The theater seated nearly two thousand spectators across its different sections.[57]

What is striking is that only women's restrooms were available on the ground floor and second floor, where there were rows of seats and private boxes. In the blueprint, these restrooms were prominently marked for "senhoras." There were no men's bathrooms on either of these floors. Men's restrooms were located in a basement under the stage. In contrast, there were no designated spaces for "senhoras" in the top-floor gallery, the cheapest seats in the house. Instead, on either side of the stage, there were five urinals and a "W.C.," but no indication of a "toilette" or mention of "senhoras." Walls, flights of stairs, and separate entrances served to prevent moviegoers in the gallery from entering the other floors.

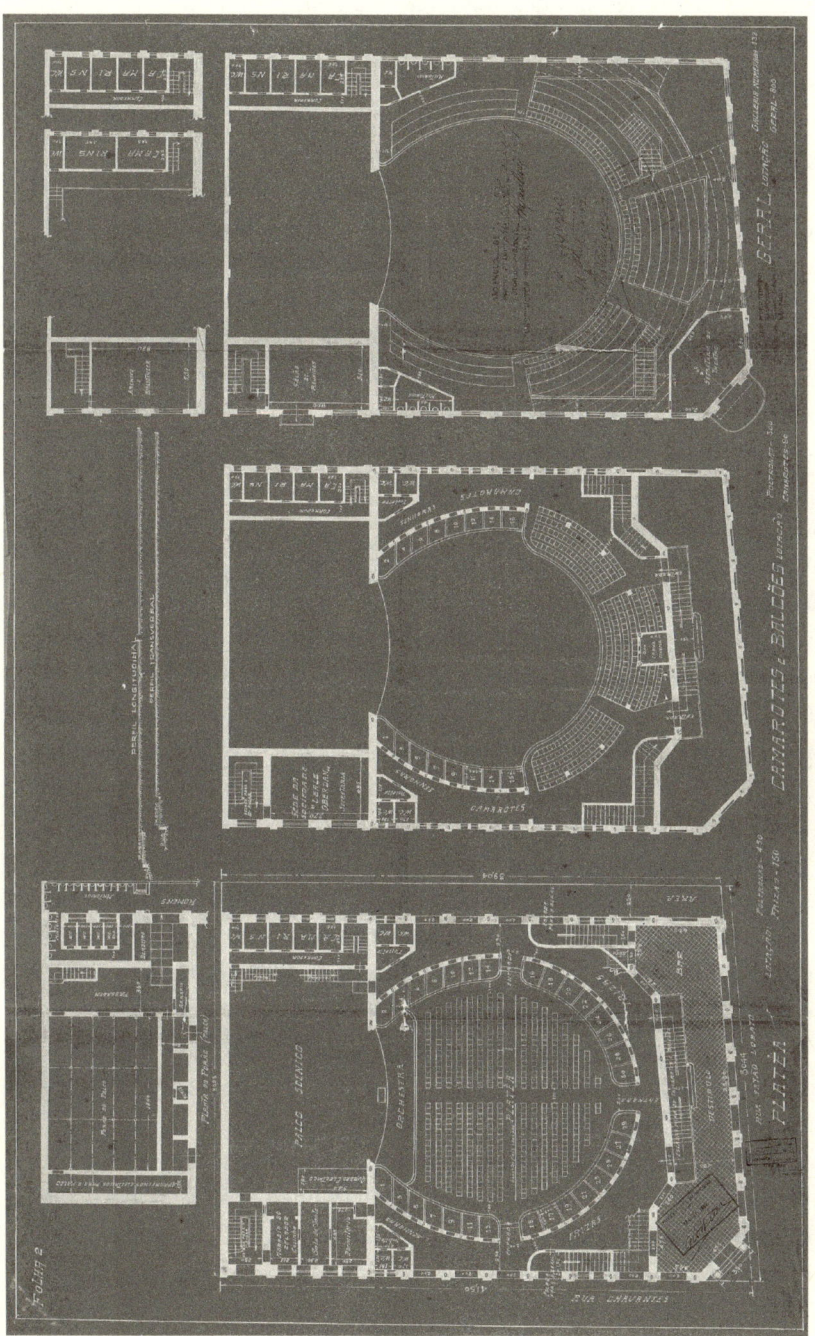

Figure 3.3. Cine Oberdan bathrooms on the second floor for private boxes and seats, with toilette and labeled "senhoras" on the left. Bathrooms in the gallery with only urinals and stalls on the right. "Cine Oberdan, junção das plantas 1929," 1929, Cinemas caixa 25, Cinemas 51, processo 1989-0.025.116-3, número da capa 0.024.117-29, Arquivo Histórico de São Paulo.

The "toilettes" were not designated for women, but for "ladies," which was as much a designation of class as it was of gender. By making such accommodations accessible only to some, cinemas like the Oberdan established physical boundaries around women who could be called "senhoras." And by altogether omitting women's bathrooms in the cheapest seats, such barriers clearly demarcated what class of women should be accommodated in this space. At the same time, these 1920s São Paulo cinemas did not have *cazuelas*, or explicitly female-only seating sections, found in Buenos Aires theaters at the turn of the twentieth century.[58] Anne Rubenstein has found that balconies were considered masculine spaces in Mexico City movie theaters throughout the mid-century, and that social mores created a stark gendered division between balconies and the ground floor.[59] While Rubenstein analyzes the social practices that constructed this gendered division, the case of São Paulo blueprints shows that such divisions were meticulously planned and physically constructed in dialog with municipal law.

While the architects of the Cine Oberdan may not have purposefully evoked this specific meaning of "senhora" when they drew up the blueprints, the labeling of the bathrooms reflects how the state government and the built space of cinema overlapped as voices that attempted to define the class and gender status of women in public space. The blueprints are also artifacts of the many layers of bureaucracy and ideology that attempted to enforce these divisions of class and gender, from the municipal legislators to the architects who drew up the designs, and the engineers and officials who examined, approved, and rubber-stamped each submitted blueprint (often multiple times, with each successive revision supposedly approximating the legal exigencies). The stark, thin lines of white on blue made visually clear how the movie theaters should be built, and how physical walls, stairs, and barriers should separate moviegoers on the basis of sex and class.

Yet while such physical divisions between the ground floor and the gallery were clear in blueprints, the price differences were not quite so vast. With discount movie nights that sold half-price tickets to women and other "matinee" promotions, it is possible that both sections were similarly priced on some nights. The same woman who sat in the gallery one night, or skipped the movies entirely, might become a "senhora" when she sat on the ground floor another night, shifting from "invisible" to "senhora" depending on whether she (or her date) had an extra 1$500 *milreis* that day. Could cinemas be an arena for women to perform as "senhoras," and when coming through the main entrance instead of the side, or when powdering their noses in the "toilette," might they temporarily enjoy the trappings of class and social status that this term included? On the other hand, the "senhoras" in the Cine Oberdan still had to share eight women's stalls. (If even a third of the six hundred or so seats on the ground floor and private boxes were occupied by women, that would be two hundred women for eight bathrooms.) Although the female moviegoers of Brás might be labeled "senhoras" in an idealized blueprint, this label might have been limited in reality by crowded bathrooms and long lines. In the work of Michel de Certeau, urban planners have strategies to construct the city from "above," but those who walk and use the city have tactics to challenge these plans and construct the city from "below."[60] In the case of São Paulo's movie theaters, movie theater owners and architects might have enforced seemingly rigid social divisions in blueprints, but moviegoers alternatively reinforced, contested, or created new divisions through their everyday use—a theme further explored in the next chapter.

The long history of the Cine Oberdan demonstrates the real effects of failed safety and hygiene standards. While the unequal distribution of bathrooms for "senhoras" caused inconvenience and perhaps uncomfortable distinctions of class, other physical aspects of the theater led to tragic results. In 1938 a stampede occurred at the movie theater, resulting in the deaths of thirty-one people, thirty of them children. On April 10, young moviegoers, mostly children from the surrounding neighborhood of Brás, had gathered to watch an early matinee. In the commonly known version of this event, a young child yelled "Fire!" while watching a scene of airplanes exploding on screen. Panic ensued, and moviegoers from all sections of the theater rushed to escape. The children in the crowded balcony, the cheapest seats, were in the greatest danger, having to descend narrow staircases and multiple floors to reach the exits. In contrast to this version, which places blame on the verisimilitude of cinema, police records show that a young boy had gone to the bathroom during the film, but found that the lights in the bathroom did not work. He lit a small fire to see, which caused another moviegoer to yell "Fire!"[61] The tragic results of this incident fulfilled the fears of the legislators, municipal officials, and moviegoers—that dark, crowded cinemas with outdated facilities posed a threat to the health and safety of the populace. And although in this case the threat was imaginary—the fire itself was not dangerous—the perceived perils of the cinema had real and terrible effects.

The Cine Oberdan temporarily shut its doors for a few months, but later reopened and remained active as a cinema until the late 1960s. In 1972 the building was purchased by Zelo, a linen store, which operated well into the twenty-first century. An advertisement flyer from the early 1960s shows that at least on one occasion, the Cine Oberdan exhibited "scientific films," similar to *The Kiss That Kills* shown at the Cine Odeon thirty years before. Sexually provocative films such as these never disappeared, and were screened in certain São Paulo movie theaters throughout the twentieth century. The 1960s Oberdan flyer featured "three grand, realistic films in just one program." One of the films was called "The Consequences of Sin," while the one most prominently featured was advertised as *Intimate Relations Between Man and Woman*, though it was actually a portion from a film called *Tomorrow I Will Be a Woman*. The illustrations of women and the provocative titles promised audiences scenes of nudity and sex. However, the advertisement continued the ruse that these were educational, scientific films that served public health, prominently placing the caduceus symbol for medicine opposite the figure of a nude woman. Unlike the scientific films shown in 1929 that warned of being "inappropriate for senhoritas," the advertisement at the Cine Oberdan specified that these films were "exclusively for adults of both sexes." The Oberdan's gesture to female moviegoers represents a cultural shift from the 1929 warning that excluded women, or at least any that might consider themselves "senhoras."

Within the context of eugenics, cinemas, with their dark, enclosed quarters and threat of fire, could be an environmental threat to the health of the people and the uplift of the race. Yet in São Paulo, cinemas were also an arena to implement new legislation and standards to protect public health. Urban reformers linked their idealized vision of a safe, sanitary city to one in which respectable women, senhoras, were welcome and protected. Movie theaters demonstrate the importance of including popular culture and gender in the growing debates about public health. Ideas about health and safety extended beyond medical and state circles, and involved film entrepreneurs, film intellectuals, and moviegoers. Whereas this chapter on hygiene has delved into the lofty intentions of the constructors of moviegoers, the next chapter focuses on the ways in which moviegoers also constructed social spaces. Paulistanos both created and challenged hierarchies and divisions of race, ethnicity, and class through their moviegoing habits. Together, the planning and the everyday use of movie theaters reveal the central role of gender and sexual practices in creating new rituals of romance, as well as defining the social contours of a vibrant São Paulo city.

4

CLASS, RACE, AND DESIRE AT THE MOVIES

Moviegoing in São Paulo

On a Saturday in 1929, movie theater advertisements in the state newspaper *O Estado de S. Paulo* presented an overview of moviegoing options in the capital city. The Cinema Odeon advertised a triple-feature with the novelty of two sound films: *O Noi de la Mare*, based on the Catalan folk song, which would be sung in "Hespanhol," a Brazilianized version of "Spanish," and a risqué Hollywood comedy called *The Belle of Samoa* (Fox, 1929) with scantily clad dancers in grass skirts. The Cinema Odeon also promised a 3 p.m. "Girls' Hour" or "Sessão das Moças" with reduced ticket prices for women. It was an attractive option for one of the most expensive movie theaters in the city, with tickets usually sold at 3$000 for a seat at the afternoon matinee and 4$000 at night. On the east side of town, the Teatro Colombo promised to show *The Bride of the Sea*, with tickets priced at 2$000. Several cinemas in different neighborhoods planned to screen the same films, including *The Dominions of Satan* and *Waterfront* (First National Pictures, 1928). Nestled in between these semisalacious advertisements were the seemingly inconspicuous advertisements for "scientific" films with their medical-sounding warnings about sexually explicit content. Theaters and circuses also promoted their shows and performances, with plays and actors that circulated from Europe and other parts of Latin America.

Figure 4.1. Cinema advertisements in *Estado de S. Paulo*, Saturday, June 29, 1929, p. 24.

Unlike the contemporary multiplex experience, movie theaters in the first half of the twentieth century typically had a single screen. Each night would be dedicated to a unique program of films centered around a main attraction, often a Hollywood film, but also European and Latin American features. Each movie theater, in its way, had its own personality and reputation. Nearly ever-present, however, were themes and images of romance, love, and modern womanhood. How and why did moviegoers choose to go to the Odeon to see *The Beauty of Samoa* versus going to the Cine Royal to see *Mocidade Leviana*, and why would they see *Plantation and Air* at the Capitólio or the Mafalda? While convenience of location from home or work, or the difference in movie ticket prices, were determining factors in moviegoers' decisions, they were not the only ones. Rather, moviegoers' quotidian actions in their circulations across the city's vibrant film scene were complex and layered negotiations involving identity, social status, fandom, and interpersonal relationships. Moviegoing begs additional questions: Who did moviegoers meet at the cinema, and where did they sit? What did their choices and reactions to the transnational media of cinema, circulating through Europe and the Americas, say about their identities, tastes, and preferences? How did they calibrate their own and others' social statuses based on their moviegoing habits, and what did this mean for moviegoers' sense of place in the city?

This chapter analyzes how moviegoers' experiences varied according to intersections of gender, class, and race, and how these differences were expressed spatially in the city of São Paulo. For a diverse cross section of moviegoers, the movie theater was an important site to negotiate social status and to hash out new rules of romance and respectability—rules that varied by moviegoers' class and gender. While the scope of this chapter cannot provide an exhaustive portrait of the complex social hierarchies embedded in the landscape of São Paulo, it does reveal how people used movie theaters as part of finding their—paradoxically both precise and unfixed—place in the growing urban society. A fine-grained approach to the very commonplace habit of moviegoing reveals complex, multilayered hierarchies, sometimes in hyperlocal contexts within specific neighborhoods and communities. By focusing on the nexus of moviegoing, gender, and sexuality, this chapter demonstrates alternative motivations for how people moved about the city, arguing that social status was not the sole determining factor in moviegoing habits. Rather, this chapter explores the importance of love, romance, and fandom in paulistanos' interactions with the city.

As evidenced in several types of sources across literature, periodicals, and municipal documents, moviegoers represented moviegoing as intimately tied to the ways in which they navigated São Paulo. This chapter also includes several oral histories that I conducted in 2011, from women who were able to reflect on personal memories of moviegoing, even as far back as the 1920s. Integrating these various sources creates a colorful portrait of São Paulo in the time period. Each individual story or memory provides both extremely personal accounts of moviegoing and insight into the social rules and expectations that governed this experience.¹ The focus on moviegoing and leisure opens up another avenue to look at paulistanos' lives, especially women's, outside of work and family. Through moviegoing, we see how urban-dwellers' experiences of the city reflected but were not reducible to questions of power and status, but also depended on affective motivations of desire and romance, and of course, attraction to the films themselves.

São Paulo City and Moviegoing in the 1920s

In this time period, São Paulo city's population was expanding exponentially with dramatic shifts in demography. A town of 35,000 people in 1880, it grew to 600,000 in 1920, and 2.2 million by 1950.² One of the largest cities in the world, the population hovers around 20 million today. Between 1870 and 1930, two to three million immigrants came to Brazil to fill the labor vacuum in Brazil's post-abolition period. In adherence to the ideology of whitening, São Paulo state actively encouraged and even sponsored European immigrants, especially from Portugal, Italy, and Spain, to work on its vast coffee plantations. Along with Asian immigrants, notably from Japan and the Middle East, many newcomers eventually followed shifting labor needs and increasing industrialization to settle in the city of São Paulo.³ By 1922 one in three persons in the city was classified as foreign.⁴ At the same time, even while the absolute number of Black paulistanos grew, their percentage within the city's population was shrinking, falling from 37 percent to 8 percent from 1872 to 1940.⁵ As São Paulo city rose in national prominence to be the second-largest city in Brazil, it also became a city with large segments of European immigrants, Asian immigrants, and an increasingly minoritized Black population.

As the city grew, São Paulo also gained a particular reputation as a hub of cinema in Brazil. According to the Rio de Janeiro–based film critics at *Cinearte*, São Paulo had movie theaters and film selections that increasingly outrivaled other Brazilian cities. For example, when the technology of sound film, which rippled through the cinematic world in the 1920s, reached Brazil in 1929, it first premiered in São Paulo, not in Rio de Janeiro. In response, a critic at *Cinearte* lamented, "S. Paulo represents one of the greatest cinematic centers of the country that day to day gains an advantage over Rio de Janeiro, even as the paulista capital has only half the population."⁶ Much of the growth in film exhibition, in both Rio de Janeiro and São Paulo, was in part due to the success of immigrant entrepreneurs who became prominent in the industry. For example, Paschoal Segreto, an Italian immigrant, founded the Cinema Parisiense in Rio de Janeiro and was foundational to the early exhibition circuit, and Francisco Serrador, a Spanish immigrant, established some of the largest and most prominent theaters in both Rio de Janeiro and São Paulo.[7]

Yet as film exhibition grew, the Rio de Janeiro–based film critics at *Cinearte* characterized the São Paulo moviegoing scene and film industry as less refined and dominated by mercenary film entrepreneurs. For example, according to Pedro Lima, São Paulo had the highest number of fans of Brazilian cinema, and the largest number of people who wanted to participate in the industry. Yet by "extraordinary contrast," São Paulo was also the "preferred paradise for conmen and those with bad intentions" who sought to exploit the "good faith and ignorance" of these eager movie fans.[8] Posing as producers and acting coaches with false careers in European cinema, these conmen convinced movie fans to sign up for expensive acting classes. Lima complained that "foreign adventurers, without a penny to their name, who claimed to hail from famous foreign studios, generally German or Italian, where they were employees or where they had actually never even stepped foot in" were the perpetrators of such crimes.[9] Because of them, fake film schools "proliferated at a shocking rate." Lima saw these paulistano conmen as sexual predators as well, claiming, "And if it is a young woman [who gets scammed by the fake school] we know the result that many have had when they are too trusting of the promises and lessons of these 'teachers.'"[10] While Lima lamented the familiar trope of the "movie-struck girl," he also located the dangers that threatened her to be particularly germane to São Paulo and, with xenophobic undertones, even to the "foreign adventurers" that he associated with the city. In the eyes of the Rio de Janeiro critics, São Paulo was a particularly exciting, but somewhat tumultuous hub for cinema's growth—a portrait that reverberated in *Cinearte*'s coverage of São Paulo films like *Fragments of Life* and *Traffic*, discussed in chapter 2.

The Geography of Moviegoing in São Paulo: Center Versus Periphery

In the 1900s, as moviegoing began, an early concentration of cinemas appeared as extensions of theaters and could be found alongside bars, restaurants, and other places of amusement in the "Triangle," a group of blocks in the "old center" of the city. By 1920 in the state (not just the city) of São Paulo, there were 259 theaters and cinemas, but already 32,006 film screenings,

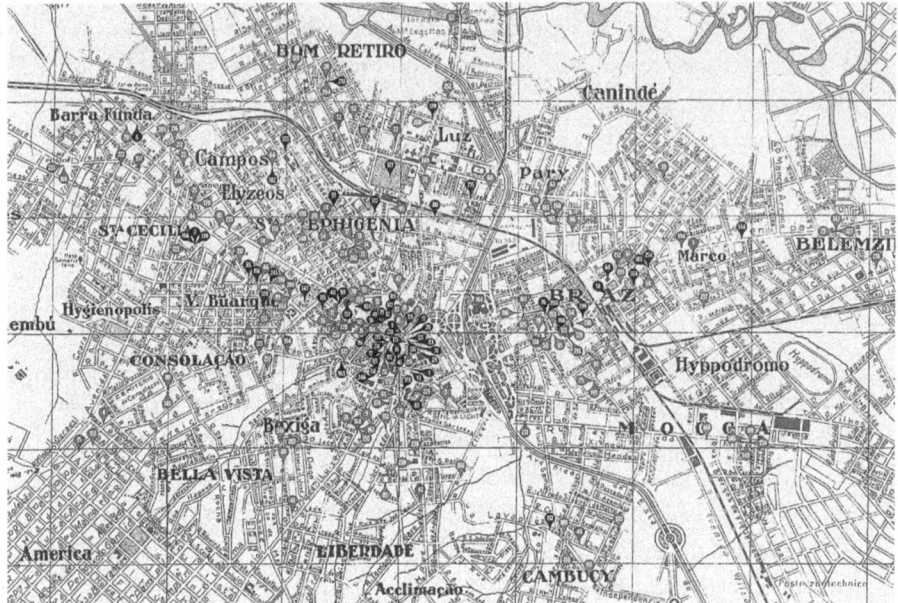

Figure 4.2. Map of cinemas in São Paulo, 1895–1929. This map is of cinemas over time, not cinemas concurrently operating. "Memória do Cinema no Acervo do Arquivo Histórico de São Paulo," Arquivo Histórico de São Paulo, *Salas de cinema em São Paulo 1895–1929*, exhibition, September 17, 2012, http://www.arquiamigos.org.br/bases/cine.htm.

over 90 percent of all accounted theater spectacles (including plays, operas, etc.).[11] Although the São Paulo state census likely undercounted both film screenings and live theatrical plays, cinema was clearly a dominant force at the beginning of the decade, and it continued to grow in the state and the city. As evidenced in the map of São Paulo city cinemas, there were 185 movie theaters that opened in the city between 1916 and 1930, though some of these were fleeting establishments that closed and reopened with different names and management.[12] These cinemas proliferated through São Paulo, and in contrast to Rio de Janeiro, some of the most prominent cinemas were in working-class neighborhoods outside of the city center.

Although from the 1910s to the 1920s, exhibition contracted as technologies and expectations for quality advanced, there was a resurgence beginning in 1925, so that by 1927, movie theaters had expanded from at least twenty-seven to thirty-five concurrently operating cinemas, eight in the city center and seven just in Brás, which was home to a large working-class population.[13] In the center, the concentration of central leisure and consumption had shifted westward from the Triangle to across the Viaduto do Chá, around the Praça

República. This westward push in the 1920s continued, resulting in a spray of cinemas that radiated in a northwest axis along Rua São João toward the tonier neighborhoods of Santa Cecilia and Higienópolis. Relevant to the social inequality in the city, the neighborhood of Higienópolis, or "Hygiene city," was developed and named as part of early twentieth-century urban reform—a clear marker of the neighborhood's distinction from the swampier, supposedly less "sanitary" neighborhoods further east. In the opposite direction, another hub of cinemas catered to the eastern side of the city, primarily in Brás. Even neighborhoods considered "suburban" or even rural, like Cambucí, Santana, and Vila Mariana, had at least a movie theater each.[14]

As in other cities, movie theaters were not all equal. Across cities in Latin America, the best movie theaters in the center of the city served the most elite clientele, while the cinemas in the "outskirts" tended to be more run-down, screening older films. For example, historians have found this dynamic in Rio de Janeiro, Buenos Aires, and Santiago de Chile, where the movie theaters downtown were the premier theaters, attracting crowds from the suburbs, and the "neighborhood cinemas" charged lower prices and exhibited older films.[15] Camila Gatica Mizala finds that cinema businessmen in Santiago de Chile changed prices according to geography, but also economic factors, the type of film being exhibited, and even the weather.[16]

While a rough division between center and periphery existed in São Paulo as well, literature from the time period in São Paulo paints a picture of moviegoing that was much more dynamic. Indeed, this perspective on the city reveals the many contours of the city and how the division between center and periphery was not so simplistic or dyadic. While literature and poetry are fictional, they reveal insight into quotidian habits and the complex uses of movie theaters in the collective imagination of the city's chroniclers. In their varied work, three writers from different ideological and political spectrums illustrate the complexity of social hierarchies in the moviegoing scene, and how a moviegoer's choice to attend one movie theater over another was an act of social positioning, relevant to their understanding of São Paulo's class hierarchies.

In the Rio de Janeiro film magazine *Cinearte*, the film critic Gabus Mendes covered the moviegoing scene in São Paulo. In the magazine's weekly reviews of films, he reported on the films premiering in the paulista capital. While he himself criticized the run-down "cinema of the outskirts" in São Paulo, he also complained that movie theaters in São Paulo's peripheral neighborhoods had better films than the ones downtown.[17] "Those who live in the center of the city or in good neighborhoods must take a less than comfortable trip, forty minutes long, in a streetcar. It is absurd!"[18] His indignation was not just because "the select crowd had to travel and risk hearing jeers," but because they had to attend "deficient cinemas, maybe not in size, but in the public that is in attendance."[19] Mendes lamented, "It is ridiculous that such good films be exhibited in such improper neighborhoods," which, according to him, were wasted on the people in the eastern neighborhoods of "Cambuci, Bom Retiro, Brás, and Barra Funda," who would be happy with any low-quality western or comedy film.[20] While most of the newest Hollywood films usually premiered in the "good" central neighborhoods, Mendes rued even the occasional need to visit a movie theater in the periphery.

Mendes laid out clear geographical and social hierarchies within the "select public" in "good neighborhoods" who had a true appreciation for films, and those in the "improper" neighborhoods who could not even differentiate between "any far-west film and something as superior as 'Cytherea'" (a 1924 silent film that used innovative color film technology). Mendes described this hierarchy in language inflected with eugenic ideology. Terms like "deficient" and "improper" referred directly to the type of racial degeneracy that eugenicists claimed would affect Brazilians exposed to poverty, vice, and disease. Mendes associated these neighborhoods with a vague sense of tastelessness and inferiority. Yet people in peripheral neighborhoods were also avid moviegoers, and Mendes found that sometimes the "best films," such as the newest Hollywood releases, were in these less-than-desirable locations. As Sheila Schvarzman points out, Mendes's comments must be contextualized as a perspective that was "elitist, conservative, and one that despised anything that deviated from the norm or the center that he believed he represented."[21]

Mendes made a neat, dyadic division between the "good" and "improper" neighborhoods, but was not above using the streetcar to arrive at one of these "improper" cinemas. Through his own spatial practices, he traversed the division between "good" and "improper," the fault lines between what he considered the respectable center and the inferior outskirts. He even reversed the stereotypical gendering of the woman who is harassed in public, such as the unsuspecting woman who is "honked" in the streetcar in the song "Fried Fish," discussed in the introduction. In his film review, Mendes is the aggrieved passenger who "risks hearing jeers." Though he lamented the situation, Mendes nevertheless participated in these social inversions of gender and class, driven by his cinephilia, even if it meant leaving his social milieu.

The modernist writer Ribeiro Couto's beautiful poem "Cinema on the Outskirts" also describes moviegoers traversing the city to see films, focusing on the fluid microhierarchies among people living in peripheral neighborhoods. In these "modest" cinemas, "all of the bourgeois families of the neighborhood come," whereas others fill up streetcars riding to the cinemas in the center of the city, "so that they can be the aristocracy of the outskirts."[22] Writing in the art magazine *Klaxon*, Couto was part of the São Paulo modernist art scene, a group that, in general, lauded the potential of cinema as a form of modern art.[23] While Couto was writing for a select audience in a magazine with limited circulation, his poem addresses the everyday social aspects of moviegoing. Couto describes two levels of social hierarchy and how moviegoers organize themselves in different groups according to where they attend or even sit at the movies. There is the hyperlocal hierarchy within the neighborhood, in which the "modest" cinema is attended by the local "bourgeois" families. The "modest" cinema might be incrementally nicer than other movie theaters nearby, or moviegoing itself might be a more respectable social activity than other local amusements like drinking or dancing. In either situation, certain families attend the movie theater to assert their status as the "bourgeois" families of the neighborhood. On another social level, Couto describes the "aristocracy of the outskirts" who demonstrate their social aspirations by eschewing the neighborhood theater and only attending cinemas in the center of the city. Showing a gap between the "aristocracy of the outskirts" versus the city's true elite, who live in the center of the city, Couto points out that in the outskirts, young girls are "proudly dressed in bad taste." The streetcar that Mendes rode in one direction, they take in the opposite—a symbol of social as well as geographic mobility—crisscrossing both the city and the spatialized divisions of class.

Patrícia Galvão, or Pagú, whose essays on cinema were briefly analyzed in chapter 1, also commented on the social and geographic weavings of women in São Paulo. Galvão lived in the neighborhood of Brás in the industrialized east side of São Paulo. Though living in a diverse neighborhood that was home to many industrial workers, her own family was part of what Couto might have called "the aristocracy of the outskirts." She was educated to be a teacher in the Brás Normal School, demonstrative of her family's bourgeois aspirations. Galvão's moorings are apparent in her most famous work, the 1933 novel *Industrial Park*, a brutal story of women workers and exploitation set in her home neighborhood of Brás. Moviegoing weaves in and out of the novel, making the movie theater a setting for romance and politicization and, at times, an indicator of the social and moral status of the fictional characters.

The novel follows the stories of several women from Brás, all of whom follow a trajectory of social (both upward and downward) mobility. Eleanora, in some ways fashioned after Pagú herself, attends the Brás Normal School as Galvão did, and she ends up marrying rich (also as Galvão did when she married writer Oswald de Andrade), but leads a life of idleness and corruption. Eleanora is condemned for her excesses in consumption, which in the novel is signaled through alcoholism and her predatory, homosexual relationship with a former schoolmate. Corina, possibly the most tragic figure, is a beautiful *mulata*, or mixed-race, Afro-descendant woman, who occupies a somewhat "in-between" class status as a seamstress in a small atelier. Although classified as industrial workers in national censuses, seamstresses who worked outside of factory settings had lower job stability than female textile factory workers.[24] Although Corina dreams of romance, marriage, and ascending from her life as a seamstress, these bourgeois aspirations lead to her moral and social downfall. Corina falls in love with a rich lover, but becomes pregnant and is promptly abandoned by him. She becomes a sex worker, gets sick from venereal disease, and in the novel's most shocking scene, gives birth to a deformed, skinless baby—the result of prostituting herself while pregnant in order to satisfy her bourgeois dreams of buying a crib. Corina's exploitation—a condition of her race, class, and gender—is amplified in the next generation. In contrast to Corina, the character of Octavia represents Galvão's ideal of modern womanhood. Like the other characters in the novel, Octavia is a working woman in Brás, but she is politically engaged, and in control of her body and her sexuality. Throughout the novel, Octavia becomes more politicized, and her final act in the novel is leading a workers' strike in the streets. Octavia is the only character to experience a consensual and romantic sexual relationship with Alfredo. At first married to Eleanora, Alfredo becomes disgusted with her corruption, and he moves to Brás to become an industrial worker and proletariat.

Galvão maps the trajectory of these characters across different neighborhoods in São Paulo and punctuates the symbolic difference between city center and periphery with incidents in and around movie theaters in the city. She focuses on the area around Centro and Brás as geographical symbols of bourgeois wealth versus working poor. Symbolizing their social mobility or lack thereof, characters traverse the boundary in automobiles and streetcars. The elite drive their automobiles to the outskirts, and workers take streetcars into the city center. In the moral universe of *Industrial Park*, the elite prey on workers of all genders and races, and workers who succumb to capitalist opiates are exploited and punished with sexual violence. In the opening scene of the novel, rich men drive from the Centro to Brás as a "chic" adventure during *carnaval* celebrations, where they cruise for men and women to seduce and exploit. Pepe, a male worker in Brás, is assaulted and raped by elites, who pick him up in their car. Corina, who dreams of romance and marriage, takes the #13 streetcar from Brás to see her rich boyfriend across town in the Centro.[25]

Movie theaters figure in the novel as indicators of class, moral, and ideological positioning of the characters. Galvão describes a microhierarchy of movie theaters within Brás, such as the Teatro Colombo, which was a real venue in the neighborhood that showcased theater performances but shifted to film screenings by the 1930s. Galvão's depiction of the Colombo recalls Ribeiro Couto's description of the "modest cinema of the outskirts," frequented by people from the neighborhood who were better off than others. The Teatro Colombo, "opaque and illuminated, indifferent to empty stomachs, receives Bras's aristocratic petty bourgeoisie that still have money for the cinema."[26] In the novel, the moviegoers of the Teatro Colombo are insulated from the poverty and the workers' revolt that are unfolding immediately outside. The door to the theater features a poster of "the pale enigma of Greta Garbo," a famous Hollywood actress in the 1920s and 1930s, whom Galvão calls "a prostitute feeding the imperialist pimp of America to distract the masses."[27]

In contrast to the Teatro Colombo, Galvão also writes of the Cine Mafalda, which was another real cinema in Brás, located on Avenida Rangel Pestana. Galvão depicts the Cine Mafalda as more affordable, a place that workers frequent when they can spare the money. At one point, Pepe offers to take Otávia on a date to the Cine Mafalda during "girls' night," when tickets would be half price for women. Symbolic of Otávia's preference for politics over popcorn, she declines his invitation. Yet Galvão homes in on the Cine Mafalda as a space that might realize the potential of cinema as a tool of proletariat awakening, a potential that Soviet filmmakers had been exploring for over a decade in films like *The Battleship of Potemkin*.[28] In contrast to the Teatro Colombo, which fed audiences Hollywood fare, Galvão depicts a night at the Cine Mafalda during a screening of a Soviet film. Galvão criticizes the members of the audience who ignore or do not understand the film's message: "A group of young women go out lamenting loudly the ten cents wasted on a film without love. . . . Fed on the imperialist opium of American films. Slaves tied to capitalist deception."[29] While condemning the stereotype of the "movie-struck girl" for idolizing Hollywood illusions and succumbing to its cultural and ideological imperialism, Galvão also plants seeds of proletariat awakening among the workers in the audience, as other moviegoers shout, "No one here understands this bombshell!"

Otávia, the proletariat heroine, is also in the audience at the Cine Mafalda with Alfredo, the formerly rich bourgeois. While inspired by the Soviet film, Otávia experiences her own Hollywood-style romance. "Otávia notices [Alfredo's] fleshy lower lip. His half-open shirt reveals a muscular, hairy chest."[30] In the darkness of the cinema, Otávia not only wants to "wrench from each still spectator's head . . . an allegiance to the emotional spasms that envelop her," but also "squeezes Alfredo's hand." Otávia's experience at the movie theater is thus multilayered, a place of politicization but also of budding love. In the moral universe of *Industrial Park*, in which the exploitation of the worker is often represented through sexual violence, Otávia is the only female character to express ownership of her sexual desires and romantic life. Unlike Corina, who was deluded and then abandoned by the promises of her rich boyfriend, Otávia maintains a relationship with Alfredo until she decides to end it. Again she chooses politics over romance, and she breaks with Alfredo when she decides that he is insufficiently radical. For Otávia, her multilayered experience at the Cine Mafalda represents the promises of a fully realized life of a modern woman, marked by political engagement, consensual, romantic love, and however briefly, a respite from the dire class and gender exploitation portrayed in the rest of the novel.

In *Industrial Park*, Galvão portrays cinema as a powerful influence on society—Hollywood films as an opiate of the masses, Soviet films as a tool to awaken proletarian consciousness. Movie theaters are symbolic of class hierarchy—represented in the contrast between the Teatro Colombo and the Cine Mafalda, but also of potential class solidarity—as seen in the budding politicization among the audience during the Soviet film. And yet even within Galvão's grim portrait of workers' lives, her characters still find space for romance and love at the movie theater, in Pepe's hopeful invitation to Otávia, in Otávia's realization of her attraction to Alfredo. These scenes are a glimmer of escape from the churn of class exploitation and violence, but they also reveal the complexity of moviegoing—that the decision to go to the movies was not dependent solely on material conditions, but instead intertwined with political ideology, class identity, romance, and sexual desire.

Mendes, Couto, and Galvão all comment on the ways in which class hierarchies were visible in the geographic distribution of movie theaters in São Paulo, but they also demonstrate how moviegoers were not bound by class when choosing a movie theater to attend. In their stories, these early twentieth-century writers ruminate on the divide between the geographic center and the periphery of São Paulo, between the Centro and the neighborhoods "of the outskirts" like Brás. While movie theaters from the time period roughly corresponded to this general divide, they also showed how this distinction was not absolute. In Mendes's essay, the "respectable" people of the Centro might leave the comfort of their elite neighborhoods, taking the long streetcar ride to see the latest movies in a suburban movie theater. Or, in Couto's poem, the "bourgeois" and "aristocracy" of the outskirts might assert their superiority to their neighbors by either attending the "modest" neighborhood theater or taking the streetcar to the Centro. Yet their decisions are not reducible to class positioning either, as "whispering lovers" sit together in the "shadowy corners," and audiences are "held rapt" by the film on screen.[31]

Microhierarchies Inside the Movie Theater

While the above writers elucidated distinctions between different movie theaters in the city, the interior of the movie theater was not a monolithic space. Rather, there were divisions of both class and gender inside movie theaters. While art deco movie "palaces" were appearing in North American cities in the 1920s, São Paulo's largest cinemas were built as "cine-teatros"—a portmanteau between "cinema" and "theater," as they both screened films and had a stage for theatrical and musical performances. Architecturally, they emulated nineteenth-century theaters and opera houses, with separate sections and prices for the floor, private boxes, and gallery seats. According to Alice Gonzaga, cinema owners in Rio de Janeiro used this tiered seating system to create social divisions within the moviegoing audience.[32] However, like the dynamics of center versus periphery, the hierarchical arrangement of seats was, in practice, not so rigid.

Inaugurated in 1921, the Cine-Teatro República exemplifies the system of tiered seating and how moviegoers imbued these spaces with nuanced and complicated meanings about class and decorum. In contrast to the ramshackle, ephemeral theaters discussed in the previous chapter, the name of the Cine República, named so for its location on the Praça República, but indirectly referential to the republican dream of order and progress, signaled compliance with state regulation and the municipal government's modernization projects.[33] The Cine República was a landmark of what was becoming São Paulo's "new" center around the Valley of Anhagabaú. By the 1930s other upscale cinemas appeared slightly further west around Avenida Ipiranga and São João, eventually forming the "Cinelândia" neighborhood discussed in the following chapter. Maria Rita Galvão has described the Cine República as "ultra-modern . . . whose elegant showings were the most refined that the city could imagine at the time."³⁴ This was in contrast to São Paulo's first large cine-teatro, "the old Bijou Theater, in which the red seats bled onto spectators' clothes."³⁵

Yet when the Cine República opened in 1921, cinema programs and news articles emphasized that it was "elite" and "traditional" as well as modern. As Aiala Levy points out, São Paulo cinema entrepreneurs in the 1910s utilized terms like "artistic," "elegant," and "elite," seeking to legitimize moviegoing among São Paulo's booming population and shifting social order.³⁶ Through the 1920s, cinema entrepreneurs depicted their movie theaters as both traditional and modern, gesturing to both the "traditional" respectability of the regional elite and the "modern" cosmopolitanism of the ever-expanding city. An article in the São Paulo newspaper *O Estado de S. Paulo* described the cinema as modern because it utilized new technology and represented the dynamic wealth of the region. The paper also deemed it traditional in that, as a respectable place of leisure, the cinema affirmed the status of the elites who frequented it. The article praised the cinema's "innovations" in lighting and the use of "incombustible" materials in its construction, descriptors that signaled the cinema's distinction from the cramped, enclosed, and makeshift cinemas of the previous decade.³⁷ *O Estado de S. Paulo* particularly commented on the connection between the cinema to a local sense of regional pride; the construction of the cinema "is in keeping with the great development of the city . . . [showing] the height of its great prosperity."³⁸

Even as advertisements and cinema programs lauded the Cine República as elite and luxurious, not all the spaces within the cinema had equal social status. In February 1922, just a few months after its inauguration, box seats in the Cine República were priced at 9$000, floor seats were 1$600, children had discounted entry at 1$100, and the gallery seats were $800, prices on par with other large cinemas.³⁹ Although it is tempting to read the physical and price distinctions of the theater as a straightforward division of "elite" people in the private boxes, "middle-class" people on the ground floor, and "working-class" people in the gallery, such a facile assumption disregards the complexities of both class and consumption. "Working class," "middle class," and "elite" are cultural constructions rather than standardized categories of socioeconomic or occupational status, and terms like "middle class" were not popularly used in the time period.⁴⁰ A combination of built space, social norms, and culturally constructed definitions of class contributed to the barriers between the seating sections. In newspaper articles, personal

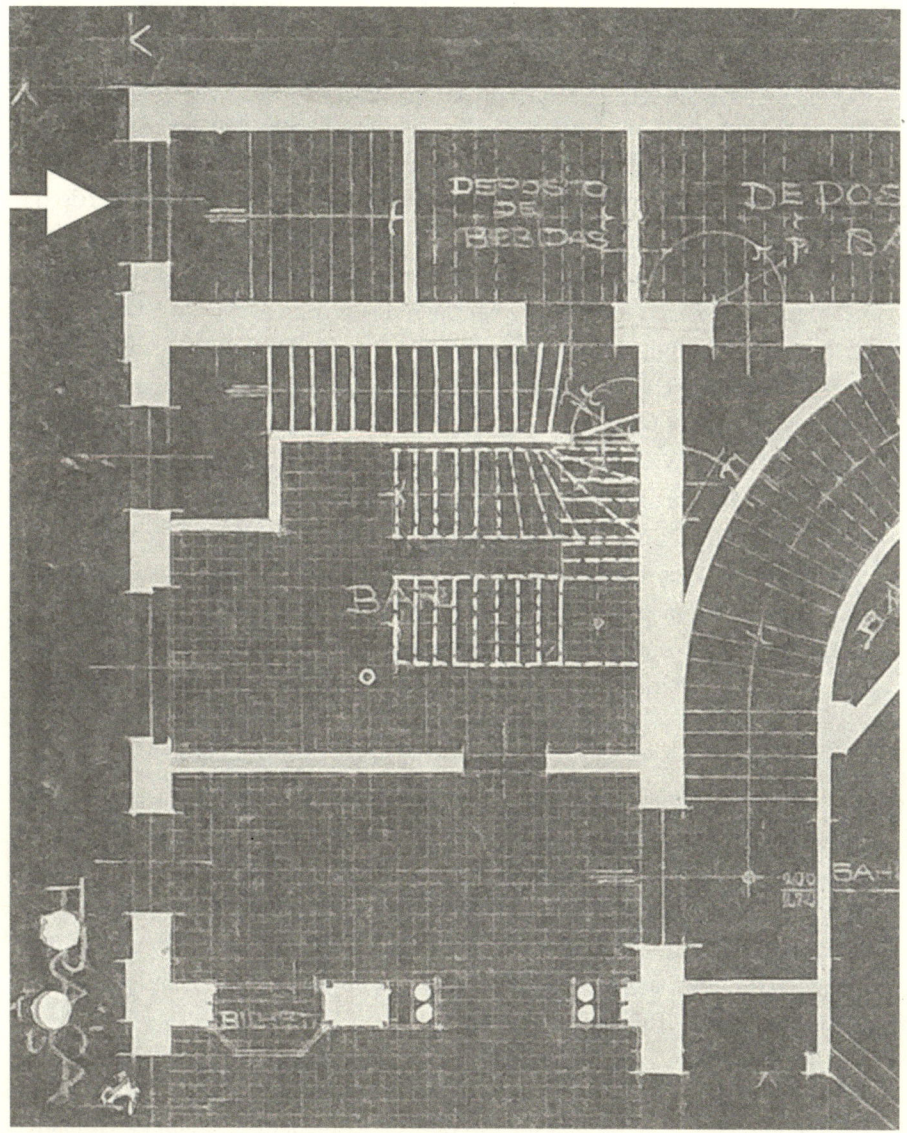

Figure 4.3. Detail from "Planta térreo," 1931 blueprint for ground floor of Cine-Teatro República. The arrow at the top left of the detail points out the separate entrance that went straight up to the third-floor gallery. "Cine República—Reforma do Predio," Cinemas caixa 1, Cinemas 1, processo 2007-0.273.665-8, número da capa 0.050.920-31, Arquivo Histórico de São Paulo.

accounts of moviegoing, and blueprints, moviegoers held divergent perspectives on the proper use of private boxes, and they developed shifting definitions of what "elite" meant in 1920s São Paulo.

In its coverage of the inauguration in 1921, the *Estado de S. Paulo* noted the construction of private boxes as an exclusive amenity, remarking, "The gallery and the private boxes on the upper and lower levels were constructed in such a way that one cannot trespass from these locations to any of the floors below."[41] The private boxes were made even more exclusive through the practice of reserving them ahead of time. Thus, although the cinema advertised the boxes as costing 9$000 a night, they were actually not even available to those who could afford them, since families reserved the boxes ahead of time. *O Estado de S. Paulo* commented that the inauguration of the Cine República "has been awaited with vibrant anxiety as a truly fashionable and artistic event" and mentioned that so many of the city's "most distinguished families" wanted to reserve boxes for the inaugural session of the cinema that its office decided to hold two sessions to accommodate the demand.[42]

However, there was some disagreement as to who constituted the "most distinguished families" in a city in which the wealthiest families came from both the rural, coffee-planting elite and the nouveau riche immigrant industrialists.[43] The coffee baron Joaquim Franco de Mello wrote a letter of complaint to the mayor of São Paulo in May 1923, a year and a half after the cinema's inauguration. In it, Mello accused the theater owners of "exploiting" and "shamefully abusing" the moviegoing public.[44] By renting private boxes on a monthly basis to "moneyed magnates," the cinema owners "only look at the money they make, only see the appeal of profits while they disregard the smallest rights of the public."[45] Rather than being available to anyone who wanted to buy a ticket, seats in these private boxes were only available for purchase at the last minute if the renters did not show up. Mello viewed this exclusion as a political matter. Not only did he write a letter to the mayor, he accused the cinema owners of failing to live up to the "luminous and pompous name of Cinema República."

Joaquim Franco de Mello evoked ideas of citizenship and republicanism to claim that renting private boxes was uncivilized and inegalitarian. Yet he was far from proposing that he and patrons of the gallery should sit mixed together. Rather than abolishing private boxes, he wanted to make sure that he had a seat in one of them. He reasserted class and cultural hierarchies in his letter, declaring the unavailability of private boxes a marker of bad taste. In referring to cinema owners as "shameful" exploiters and their friends in the private boxes as "moneyed magnates," he was referring to the nouveau riche status of cinema entrepreneurs, who were often first-generation immigrants in Brazil.[46] With an underlying xenophobic sneer, Mello accused the operators of the cinema of acting as if they were in "Morocco or Conchechina." The latter term was a reference to what is today Vietnam, but more colloquially, to a distant, foreign place.

In these references, Mello belittled cinema managers' wealth and entrepreneurship, recalling ambivalent stereotypes about the business acumen of certain immigrant communities. Ironically, the company that operated the Cine República was the Paulista Cinematographic Society (Sociedade Paulista Cinematográfica); its main associate and the sole proprietor of the building was Lupércio Teixeira de Camargo, a coffee baron who was politically active in the movement to increase coffee planters' hold on regional economy and politics.[47] While both Mello and Camargo were part of the elite rural oligarchy (though Mello's fortunes might be more ambiguous or on a downward trajectory), Mello depicted himself as the victim of class exploitation and Camargo as a nouveau riche foreigner. The letter does not reveal whether Mello knew that Camargo owned the Cine República, or whether he was making a pointed remark against Camargo's political or entrepreneurial endeavors. However, Mello attempted to buttress his moral superiority over people he perceived to be exploitative foreigners, focusing on the physical space of private boxes to assert the "proper place" of the rural elite versus the "moneyed magnates." Mello sent his letter directly to the municipal government, addressing the mayor, but aside from paperwork noting its receipt, the letter did not generate a paper trail or indication of an official response. Mello's sentiments reflect the contestations around the category of "elite" in this time period, and how sitting in the movie theaters' private boxes was a mark of class, taste, prominence, and even national belonging.

In addition to the complexities regarding who belonged to the "elite" audience in movie theaters, social expectations varied as to the appropriateness of women sitting in these private boxes. As historians have previously demonstrated for nineteenth-century Brazil, social expectations for proper ladies' behavior meant that, compared to working women, elite women enjoyed few public freedoms and limited geographic mobility.[48] In the 1920s the "private boxes" of movie theaters offered a degree of seclusion for elite women to attend the movie theater, but not enough to free women from needing a male chaperone. In 1927 the editor of *Cinearte*, Adhemar Gonzaga, lamented how moviegoers perpetuated what he considered to be dated gender norms. He complained, "A cinema is not an ordinary theater, with lines of despicable private boxes, in which ladies sit in the front with their heads tilted, and gentlemen standing on foot behind them." Yet he witnessed this behavior in São Paulo cinemas, and thus he preferred the cinemas of New York and even of Rio de Janeiro. In his special report on the "cathedrals of cinema" in New York, Gonzaga visited and praised the art deco movie palaces like the Roxy, the Paramount, and the Capitol.[49] Praising New York's Capitol Cinema as "a modern cinema," he pointed out its "grandiose" staircase and lobby, enormous seating area, and lack of private boxes. The theater-like structure that made the Cine República an "elite" and "aristocratic" space in 1921, according to Gonzaga, marked it as outdated by 1927. And while Gonzaga believed the practice to be passé, he noted that ladies, or senhoras, were still accompanied by gentlemen or *cavalheiros* on foot behind them.

In one woman's memories of moviegoing, a male chaperone was essential to moviegoing, even into the mid-century. In an interview conducted by anthropologist Heloísa Buarque de Almeida in the early 1990s, a woman named "Mariana" remembered that growing up in rural São Paulo state in the mid-century, her family rented a private box at their local cinema. Yet she was not able to enjoy it often because her father was a doctor. When called to a patient, he would have to leave the cinema and would not allow her to stay alone with only her mother.[50] In her household, her father did not consider the movie theater to be respectable enough for women to attend by themselves. Although the private box was an exclusive space, it was also a constraint, setting higher standards of gendered propriety for girls and women like Mariana.

The social rules that governed the separate seating sections were by no means uniform or absolute. For example, some moviegoers took joy in flouting the prim divisions between balconies and private boxes. Gabus Mendes groused about "the athletic activities of hysterical boys," who skirted rules to enter the movie theater ahead of others, "jumping from the private boxes to enter the second session, sometimes even pushing those coming out of the first [film screening]."[51] While Mendes avoided specifics about the social background of these "hysterical boys," they certainly were not the "gentlemen" who chaperoned senhoras, and likely claimed some combination of youth, lower social status, and disregard for propriety that drew Mendes's scorn. In addition, even as women sat in private boxes, this was not a guarantee that they were screened from all temptations of the cinema. In fact, one woman claimed that private boxes were the best seats in the house, not because they protected her modesty, but because they allowed her to be seen by the boys she had flirted with in the lobby. Even the mirrors that adorned the opulent lobby of the Cine Central provided her with the opportunity to catch the eyes of boys without her mother noticing.[52]

In 2011 I conducted my own interviews with women who had memories of moviegoing, even as far back as the 1920s. Because of the difficulty of finding interviewees who were then over ninety years old, I relied on personal connections to locate several grandmothers, neighbors, and aunts. We reminisced over coffee and cake, and I showed them photographs of old movie theaters to encourage their stories. A friend's grandmother, "Julia," had many fond memories of growing up as a child in 1920s São Paulo, including seeing an elephant escape the circus and run into the street. Julia, whose father was a carpenter and mother a factory worker, had grown up "humble," according to her granddaughter. Poring over an old photograph of a movie theater interior, she said that those who sat in the gallery were the "poorest" people. Yet Julia said that she never sat in the gallery herself because of her little "trick." As a child, she would lie to the ticket taker that her father would be there shortly to pay for her. Once she entered, she sat where she pleased, typically in the floor seats, but never in the balcony. In Brazil, tricks and shortcuts like these are called *jeitinhos*, and are the little ways, from bribery to smiles, that people get things done. Yet when I asked whether she had ever used the same trick to sit in the private boxes, Julia replied that she had not, as she would probably attract attention and looks.[53]

Julia's trick displayed less bravado than the "athletic activities" of boys who jumped over seating sections, and was more in line with gendered expectations for a young girl's behavior. It exemplifies how even young children toyed with nuanced understandings of social positioning within the movie theater, and how moviegoers adhered to subtle social cues to govern their behavior. Julia precociously avoided sitting in the hot, uncomfortable balcony crowded in with the "poorest people." Yet even if Julia could use her trick to sit where she pleased in the movie theater, disapproving looks deterred her from sneaking into the private boxes. Rather than the physical or financial barriers like the low wall separating the boxes from the main audience, or the price difference, social cues like looks and glances could also subtly maintain social distinctions in the movie theater.

Michel de Certeau's framework of "walking the city," briefly introduced in the previous chapter, presents an opposition between those who plan the city from above versus those who walk the city from below—each contributing to the construction of urban space. If the previous chapter examined the aspirations of the municipal legislators and officials to regulate the unruly city, this chapter demonstrates that moviegoers had their own tactics and maneuvers for using city spaces like the cinema. However, unlike de Certeau's dichotomous framework, those who "walked the city" from below sometimes challenged, and other times actively constructed, their own social hierarchies.

Moviegoing in Black and Immigrant Communities of São Paulo

Considering that in the home of Hollywood, movie theaters were rigidly segregated by race, the divided structure of São Paulo's "cine-teatros" begs the question of the dynamics of race in Brazilian movie theaters. While the previous section focused on the expression of class difference in the São Paulo moviegoing scene, this section shifts to the overlapping arenas of race and ethnicity. Among many differences from the US context, the Brazilian moviegoing scene provides no straightforward "rule" regarding moviegoing habits. Rather, this section focuses on glimpses of moviegoing from within Black and immigrant communities, gathering perspectives on how these moviegoers interpreted the cinematic experience, and how they utilized cinema and moviegoing to ruminate on their place in the multiracial, multicultural city of São Paulo.

In the US, separate seating sections, whether in theaters or movie theaters, have a long history of segregating people by race, class, or even gender and moral status. In the nineteenth century, some theater balconies were reserved for sex workers, where they attracted and set up meetings with clients.[54] In the twentieth century, movie theaters in the US Jim Crow south could be wholly segregated—refusing any Black patrons at all. Many, however, were segregated by time or space—for example, white audiences earlier in the evening and then Black audiences at a later, even midnight showing. Other theaters reserved the balcony area, derogatorily called "buzzards' roosts," for Black moviegoers. The distribution of films was also racially differentiated, as Black theaters and screenings received independent and second-run films, or those thought to have so-called "Negro appeal."[55] In addition, itinerant African American film exhibitors and even religious preachers creatively edited white-produced films to create unique multimedia productions for Black audiences in the US.[56] Though the circumstances were borne of systematic, racist exclusion, Black moviegoing audiences in the US found creative means to develop their own film exhibition and reception practices, including "laughing back" at negative portrayals of Black characters on screen.[57]

In contrast to the US context, racial segregation was never a legal mandate in Brazil. Though legislation and urban reforms that resulted in segregation and displacement are well documented in Rio de Janeiro and São Paulo,

Brazilian movie theaters did not employ the extreme methods of social exclusion found in US theaters.[58] Regarding the Afro-Brazilian moviegoing experience, the mainstream film publications that I have used throughout this book were largely silent, likely from a combination of pointed exclusion and indifference. Unsurprisingly, *Cinearte* and other film publications lacked specific commentary on the ways in which the moviegoing experience might vary by race and ethnicity, a type of omission largely consistent with the elite, white perspectives that appeared in mainstream press and politics in the time period. Though evidence is scant, it does not appear that the Black population of São Paulo had access to films produced specifically for Black audiences, whether by Black-identifying filmmakers in Brazil or elsewhere. Whereas in the US, the "race films" of Oscar Micheaux made their rounds among Black audiences in urban centers. While examples of itinerant Black film exhibitors similar to those in the US might be possible, this is an arena yet to be explored for early twentieth-century Brazil.

My own small network of family, friends, and neighbors had similar limits as to perspectives on and from communities of color. The several oral history interviews that I conducted on this subject were all with white-presenting women, and in response to my questions, they carefully relayed that segregation and racism were not problems in Brazil or in movie theaters, an answer typical of the myth of Brazil as a "racial democracy."[59] The closest any interviewee came to mentioning race is when one woman named "Laura" pointed to a few blurred, dark figures in a photo and remarked that children might go to the movies on their own, "or you could go with a household servant (*empregada*), see?"[60] To my eye, she had not pointed to a specific person, but to a grouping of figures that appeared dark because of a combination of skin tone, dark clothing, and poor picture quality. Yet these signifiers were enough to connote a conflation of Blackness and servitude to Laura—an unscripted reaction that betrayed the systemic and historical prejudices facing Black people in Brazil.

As a result of these lacunae in film magazines and oral histories, there are silences and erasures regarding the Black moviegoing experience. However, beyond the mainstream publications that elided the topic, the local Afro-Brazilian press, in gossip columns and news, made clear that Black paulistanos went to the movies as well as other urban places of leisure. In addition to circulating in parks, eateries, and dance halls, they forged spaces of political and cultural solidarity in the city.[61] As detailed by both Kim Butler and Paulina Alberto, the São Paulo Black press was a forum for intellectuals to ruminate on Afro-Brazilian identity, national belonging, and politics from

Aspecto do Theatro S. Paulo, por occasião de um dos ultimos espectaculos realisados e que attrahiu uma enorme concorrencia.

Figure 4.4. I used a printed version of this photograph during interviews that was slightly blurrier and darker than this digital copy. Laura pointed to a dark grouping of people when she said that a moviegoer could go to the cinemas accompanied by their maid. Photo from A Cigarra, 1929, reprinted in Souza, *Salas de cinema em São Paulo* (database).

a range of ideological perspectives. The founders and contributors of these newspapers were generally well-educated, literate Black men in a variety of skilled professions, from law clerks and public employees to cooks and electricians. Far from monolithic, newspapers emerged from competing social clubs and factions. They sometimes clashed over the methods and means for the uplift of the Black community, even as they converged on the need to assert the citizenship and full participation of Black Brazilians in public life. Directed primarily to the São Paulo Black community, the newspapers were also read by "curious" white readers.[62] Brief mentions of cinema in these newspapers demonstrate how Black intellectuals varied in their interpretations of cinema—for instance, in their views on Hollywood's racism and cinema's potential corruption of youth.

For example, several writers pushed back on the representation of Black characters in films from around the world, evidence of the writers' critical reception of cinema and of the transnational cultural production present in the city. Historian Kim Butler describes a review of the Franco-Spanish film *The Black Man Who Had a White Soul* (*El Negro que tenía el alma blanca*, Goya Producciones, 1927) that appeared in the Afro-paulista newspaper *O Progresso*. The film's story, centering on a Black dancer (portrayed by a white actor in blackface) and his unrequited love and sacrifice for a white woman, was intended to showcase the humanity of its Black protagonist. However, its premise, as well as that of the 1922 Spanish novel from which it was adapted, was rooted in the supposed misfortune of Blackness. In the logic of the story, if one's soul was noble, it was therefore "white." The reviewer in *O Progresso* criticized the inherent racism of the film, commenting that the Black protagonist's final act of love, in which he bequeaths his fortune, was "a beautiful gesture from a beautiful soul, a philanthropic soul, a great soul, but never, never, a white soul."[63]

Another column in *O Progresso*, written by Aristeu de Moraes, took such film criticism a step further by rejecting cinema altogether. Moraes saw cinema, particularly Hollywood films, as a medium of white racial supremacy because of the racist depictions of Black people. Film historians have extensively documented the negative stereotypes of Black characters in Hollywood films, from servile maids to villainous fools, often represented in the early twentieth century through caricaturized blackface.[64] In recognition of this standard, Moraes turned to theater as a potential tool of Black artistic expression and pride. He wrote, "The theater of today, in contrast to North American films, does not expose the Black man to ridicule. No. [Theater] gives the Black man the same role in the ephemeral life of the limelight that he plays in his life of struggle." Moraes then praised the production of local plays that were adapted from "sainetes," a genre of plays that were popular in Argentina, which often featured stories about the struggle of immigrants.[65] Moraes remarked, "The 'sainetes' that were put on at the Apollo, all of them were adopted from French, Spanish, and Argentine theater. In them, we find a champion of our richness. Human and real. Photographic. Nothing like a caricature."[66] Moraes played on the concept of film as a medium technically based on photography, but pointed out that for him, it represented only ridiculous, cartoonish representations of Black people. In contrast, theater, while not photographic, was nevertheless more realistic to Moraes, presenting characters with true-to-life human concerns and struggles. It is unclear whether Moraes found the realism and humanity in the sometimes stock Afro-Argentine characters who appeared in sainetes, or whether by casting Black actors in the roles, the theater group was able to interpret and perform the sainetes as relevant to their personal or communal experiences. The praise of sainetes and their stories of immigrant struggles also spoke to the complicated perspectives of Black intellectuals toward São Paulo's immigrant communities, which ranged from critiques of their anti-Black racism to admiration of immigrants' efforts at community solidarity.[67] In the late 1920s, *O Progresso* leaned to the latter perspective, praising, for example, the Syrian-Lebanese community's establishment of a city monument.[68] In Moraes's interpretation of transnational American films and European and Argentine theater, he touched on the highly local question of Black cultural expression within São Paulo's complicated racial and ethnic dynamics.

In a slightly different vein, one intellectual writing for *O Clarim da Alvorada* also criticized Hollywood films, but less on the basis of race than of gender. In an opinion piece on "Marriage," L. Asobrac lumped together male fashion, Rudolph Valentino, and moviegoing in a larger conversation of the negative influence of cinema on youth culture, and how the youth did not understand the true responsibilities of marriage. According to Asobrac, girls and boys (*meninas e rapazes*) of nineteen or twenty years had a natural inclination to marry, but in "the old days . . . a boy would want to know a girl's character and her moral and intellectual qualities. . . . In the current era of progress and speed, in which everything is undergoing a great metamorphosis, this is all in the past." Rather, in this day and age, "Girls no longer want to know about sly, old-fashioned Romeos, nor about their social or moral status. They ask about long pants . . . , striped ties, and the sideburns of Rodolpho Valentino, the extinct emperor of futility." In the end, women who married out of desire with little thought on the practicalities of establishing a home, would end up "going through hardships, not even guaranteeing a daily ticket to the movies."[69] Writing for *O Clarim da Alvorada*, which was strongly invested in the politics of respectability, Asobrac viewed cinema less as a symbol of racial injustice than a threat to gendered propriety and the sanctity of marriage. In his interpretation, the "movie-struck girl," seduced by the romance of Hollywood, was a social problem that also plagued the Afro-Paulista community, and he echoed the concerns of writers speaking to largely white audiences in the illustrated magazines discussed in chapter 1.

On the other hand, another writer for *O Clarim da Alvorada* reflected the more common perspective on moviegoing, mentioning it in passing as a social activity that, whatever its offenses, was entrenched in contemporary leisure culture. In fact, Horacio da Cunha saw moviegoing to be in some ways superior to other forms of urban leisure. Upon witnessing a group of young Black men and women flirting in a specific area of a public park, he criticized their behavior as a form of self-segregation, symbolic of the Black community's need for greater participation in public life and urban space. In an ambiguous tone, he especially counseled Black women to avoid such activities in the park, remarking, "It is preferable that before going to the garden to watch the concert, that they go to watch a movie or play. They will find more respect in these theaters than in the gardens."[70] Whether he was really pointing to cinemas and theaters as spaces that were more socially acceptable than public parks, or whether his advice was a sarcastic reference to the impropriety that these spaces held, is ambiguous. Whatever his thoughts were about moviegoing, it is clear he saw it as a social activity that was part of the urban leisure scene, an option among others for Black urban Brazilians. The varying perspectives on cinema and moviegoing reflect the range of ideological perspectives within the São Paulo Black press, including issues such as Black representation, artistic expression, and the politics of respectability.

In addition to news, essays, and opinion pieces, Afro-Paulistano newspapers often featured a section called "Criticisms" (*Críticas*) that functioned as both a gossip column and a guide on social etiquette. Written by anonymous gossip columnists or compiled from reader submissions, the "Criticisms" sections playfully chastised men and women in their community, yet still adhered to the larger, more politicized goals of community education and assertion of the Black community's respectability and status in Brazil.[71] They commented on who went about arm and arm in public, the actions of youths with unrequited love, people who wore ridiculous clothing, and girls who giggled too much as they came out of work, for example. "Certain girls of the 'S-das' Factory can't stop laughing when they see me in the street (could it be because I am handsome?)," joked one writer.[72] In addition, the Afro-Paulista commentaries reflect the racially and ethnically diverse community of São Paulo, with sightings of "Portuguese," "Turkish," and other immigrant men and women in the arms of people described as Black, brown, and light brown. For example, one criticism in *A Liberdade* called out the actions of a certain "Izaura do Carmo, walking arm in arm with a whitey [*neve* or 'snow'] on Rua Tamandaré on Saturday . . . then walking with a young colored guy [*rapaz de cor*] on Sunday."[73] Izaura's choice of white and Afro-descendant boyfriends was at least as interesting to the writer as her two-timing of them.

The scandals of love and romance in Afro-Paulista newspapers were similar in some ways to humorous articles like "The Cinema in the Dark and the Light" that appeared in mainstream newspapers, pointing to couples caught kissing in the dark or cheating on their spouses. One reader at *A Liberdade* used the pseudonym "In the Dark," which alluded to the improper actions hidden in the movie theater, to poke fun at "Lazinho, who has invited Filhinha to the movies."[74] In another *crítica* in *A Rua* in 1916, a writer called out to one unlucky couple, "A certain gaucho [person from the southern state of Rio Grande do Sul] in the movies waits until the lights go off to kiss the little lady. And how does she like it? *A Rua* was in the aisle behind and saw everything."[75] The reference to the "gaucho" man, or someone from the southern Brazilian state of Rio Grande do Sul, is racially ambiguous, but could refer to a fair-skinned white person, the stereotypical phenotype of the southern state. Mirroring the illicit sexual acts in "The Cinema in the Dark and the Light," the man "waits until the lights go off" to kiss a woman. From the phrasing, it is not clear whether this is another example of the sexually predatory "bolina" or a couple consensually seeking a dark space for romance. In either case, it similarly points out the cinema as a space both public and private, where furtive sexual relations could come to light. However, it adds another layer of meaning through the possible insinuation that the cinema was not just metaphorically a place of "dark" and "light" for men and women, but also where Black and white Brazilians came together in hidden embraces. These brief criticisms cannot reveal the complex inequalities related to race, class, and power, and there is not enough evidence to suggest that interracial romance was either more or less prevalent or controversial at the movies than in other spaces of leisure. The lightheartedness of these rumors should also not feed the myth of racial democracy, which has obscured the histories of sexual violence against Black men and women in Brazil.[76] However, they do provide a glimpse into an urban society that was diverse but far from color blind, and one in which interracial romance attracted attention but not outright condemnation. Moreover, while mainstream film publications made Afro-Brazilians invisible, the São Paulo Black press did quite the opposite—calling (perhaps unwanted) attention to members of the Black community and their presence within São Paulo's moviegoing spaces. In an indirect and humorous way, the criticisms presented an opportunity to "laugh back" at the elision of Black Brazilians in white-dominated film magazines, and further asserted their presence in a diverse but oppressive city.

These "criticisms" also provided a nuanced perspective on the tenuous boundary between harmless scandal and immoral act. As Sueann Caulfield has shown, the concepts of female chastity and gendered honor still held immense sway—both social and legal—for women in the 1920s, and violations of honor meant social condemnation for victims and criminal trials for perpetrators. Yet the Criticisms section points to a different set of social rituals involving romance and flirtation. While these community scandals were "criticized," it was done so with tongue-in-cheek humor. Similar to the stories of cheating husbands and secretive lovers in illustrated magazines like *Para Todos* and *A Cigarra* discussed in chapter 1, the Criticisms section approached the foibles of dating and romance with a mixture of disapproval, fascination, and amusement, showing that the movies were a place where romance, flirtation, and scandal might be criticized, but not necessarily condemned.

While Afro-Paulista newspapers reveal that Black moviegoers were integrated within the São Paulo moviegoing scene, paratextual sources indicate that immigrant communities in São Paulo had opportunities to create diasporic experiences through moviegoing. Part of this was because some immigrant communities had the opportunity to watch films from their native countries, sometimes imported or exhibited by film entrepreneurs who were themselves immigrants. There was no strict segregation of moviegoers based on ethnic identity, and in fact, as the Afro-Paulista papers point out, opportunities for racial and ethnic mixing were common. In his personal memories, essayist Jacob Penteado confirms this in his descriptions of moviegoing in the suburban neighborhood of Belénzinho. According to Penteado, movie theaters were a place where many diverse paulistanos came into contact, old and young, and also racially and ethnically diverse. Italian performers, Middle Eastern merchants, and native Brazilians all congregated in cinemas that played a mix of European and Brazilian music in between European and American films. Like the Black press's *críticas*, Penteado recalls the scandalous romances between people of different ethnic backgrounds, including one "Syrian" merchant who fell in love with an "Italian" dancer (though these descriptors may have belied their actual ethnic identities), eventually going mad from his unrequited affections.[77] Amid the film, the gossip, and the neighborhood intrigues, the cinema was a place of fluid racial and ethnic mixing even as it simultaneously created opportunities for immigrant groups to enjoy music and nostalgia from their home countries.[78]

Through the origin of the films on screen, the people in attendance, or the location of the theater, movie theaters in early and mid-twentieth-century São Paulo could become associated with specific ethnic communities. For example, in the 1940s, the neighborhood of Liberdade was known as the "Japanese" neighborhood (though the ethnic moniker belies the diversity of the residents who lived there). Liberdade's movie theaters specialized in exhibiting Japanese films for the Nipo-Brasiliero community and for cinephiles interested in foreign art cinema.[79] Immigrant mutual aid societies could also be fixed venues for immigrants to watch films and theater performances in members' native languages. For example, Italian mutual aid societies in the late nineteenth century put on Italian plays and operettas.[80] Or, mutual aid and cultural societies could provide the venue for films of diverse languages and countries, but moviegoers might congregate there based on their affiliation with an immigrant or ethnic community. The Cine Oberdan discussed in the previous chapter was one of the largest cinema venues of São Paulo, and aside from its Italian name, it also had ties to the large Italian Brazilian community. Although the Cine Oberdan did not specialize in exhibiting Italian films, the Italian "Leale Oberdan" society maintained its offices and a meeting space on the top floor, so that the movie theater remained a spatial and social focal point for Italian Brazilian gatherings. In one oral history, a woman remembered forming a "cine-club" with her friends in the basement of their synagogue, where they projected rented films and used a bedsheet as a makeshift screen. At the same time, she also remembered getting introduced to Japanese cinema through her Japanese Brazilian schoolmates, who took her to Liberdade to see subtitled films.[81]

Occasionally, film exhibitors utilized targeted advertisements to promote certain films as relevant to specific ethnic groups. In contrast to the case of Japanese-language films in 1940s Liberdade, these film screenings were not fixed in a certain location or theater. Rather, local exhibitors capitalized on certain elements of films, like language, country of production, or "immigrant" themes, to appeal to diasporic identities. For example, the film *A Rosa da Irlanda* (*Abie's Irish Rose*, Paramount, 1928) provides an example of advertising targeted to Jewish Brazilians. As a product of the Hollywood-based Paramount Studios, the film premiered in São Paulo at the Cine Paramount, the first of Hollywood's proprietary movie theaters in the city. Located on the western edge of the Centro neighborhood, the Cine Paramount opened to great fanfare in 1928. Hailed by local reporters as a truly "modern" cinema, the cinema featured an art deco design, without the private boxes and theater-like structure of São Paulo's earlier cine-teatros. Originally titled *Abie's Irish Rose*, the film was about Abie, a Jewish American World War I soldier who marries Rose, an Irish American, Catholic woman. Knowing of their families' disapproval, the couple hide their religious identities from their respective in-laws, marrying in separate Christian, Jewish, and eventually Catholic ceremonies. When the families uncover the truth, they are first incensed, but eventually approve of the couple and their children. The subject of assimilation and ethnic identity was a common thematic strain of early twentieth-century films that explored the struggles of working-class Jewish immigrants, often set in New York City.[82]

Because of the content of the film, local newspapers ran advertisements in both Portuguese and Yiddish, the latter aimed at the Yiddish-speaking Jewish community. Alluding to the representation of multiple religions and possibly the multiple wedding scenes and their attending religious leaders (quite literally a rabbi, a priest, and a minister), the Portuguese language advertisement praised *Abie's Irish Rose* as "the first film made to please all the social and religious orders."[83] The Yiddish version, however, emphasized the representation of Jewishness in the film, claiming that it would speak to "the soul of all Jews."[84] Such appeals to diasporic identity were slightly ironic, given that the film's subject matter featured interethnic marriage, ending with the immigrant sons and daughters affirming their American values over their families' cultural expectations for marriage.[85]

The premiere of the German movie *Varieté* (UFA, 1925) in São Paulo's Cine República also generated German-language advertisements, some showcasing local German Brazilian businesses. Upscale cinemas like the Cine República produced nightly programs, little booklets with information about the featured films, along with songs and advertisements. On a typical night, the Cine República had no discernable link to Germany or German identity (in contrast to the UFA Palace, which opened in 1936 and screened films produced by the German UFA Studios). However, for this specific film, the Cine República produced a bilingual program with a film synopsis and advertisements in both Portuguese and German.[86] Local businesses like the "Teutonia Bar" might have had some connection (either real or imagined) to Germany, but others like the Casa Moraes, which sold eyewear, might have simply decided to produce a German advertisement for this specific program.

Unlike *Abie's Irish Rose*, which exhibitors claimed would appeal to different religious groups, *Varieté* offered a less wholesome story. The film starred Lya de Putti, a Hungarian-born actress, in the role of Berta-Marie, "an exotic-looking" performer.[87] Boss Huller, a down-and-out former trapeze artist, hires Berta-Marie to dance in his peep show. Berta-Marie's revealing "hoochie-coochie dance" (illustrated on the cover of the *Varieté* program), entrances Boss Huller, who leaves his wife and child to run off with Berta-Marie. Lya de Putti's character is consistent with other "vamp" figures, including a hypersexualized persona, suggestion of racial or ethnic otherness, and seductive powers that entrance male viewers to the point of near hypnosis.[88]

Figure 4.5. A cinema program in both German and Portuguese. "Varieté," Cine República program, n.d., Cinemateca Brasileira São Paulo, 1481-31.

While the Cine República claimed to be an upscale cinema for distinguished, "traditional" families, it still exhibited films like *Varieté* that prominently featured images of seduction and storylines of adultery and violence.

These themes were as much a part of the moviegoing experience as the advertisements that claimed movie theaters to be upright institutions for the elite. And films from Hollywood, Germany, Spain, and other countries brought these images to audiences in Brazil, both immigrant and native-born.

The Cine Odeon provides yet another example of a moviegoing experience that was simultaneously diasporic and interethnic. Located on Rua Domingos de Morais in the then peripheral neighborhood of Vila Mariana, the Odeon existed on the fringes of the city as well as the law. Like other cinemas discussed in the preceding chapter, the Cine Odeon attempted to evade the municipal regulations that sought to reform cinemas and develop a safe, sanitary city. The Cine Odeon did so by dropping its former name, the Cine Apollo, which authorities had found to be severely out of step with building codes. The São Paulo city government ultimately caught up with the ruse when the Cine Odeon handed out flyers for a Portuguese film called *O Condemnado* (1921). Appealing directly to Portuguese immigrants, the flyer invited viewers to watch "the most Portuguese film ever produced," replete with "regional customs, clothing, dances, and Portuguese music." By watching the film, "every Portuguese will have the opportunity to re-live a corner of his land and a bit of his customs." At the same time, the flyer invited all "Europeans and Brazilians" to enjoy the show, alluding to multiple identities and perspectives that might simultaneously exist within the same space. Anyone might enjoy the promise of an exciting love story starring a beautiful woman. A poem on the flyer teased audiences to see "how different love is in Portugal . . . sentimental love / delicate love / Ai! How the Portuguese people / know how to love!"[89] While the flyer claimed the film would "speak to the soul of Portuguese and Brazilians," it also characterized the film specifically as a Portuguese one wherein one could observe "how different love is in Portugal." In the case of *O Condemnado*, the screening temporarily created an ethnic space, but moviegoers may not have interpreted it as such. Some Portuguese Brazilians may have come to see their "homeland," others to see a great love story. Other paulistanos might not have even recognized the Portuguese origin of the film and instead went for the social experience. As a polyvalent space, the movie theater could be simultaneously interpreted in different ways.

Finding Love in Personal Ads

As many of the magazines of the time period showed, the themes of love, romance, and desire were not just limited to the images on screen. Similar to the críticas in the Afro-paulista press, other magazines in São Paulo included sections for gossip columns, letters to the editor, and personal ads, all of which provide insight into readers' daily practices and interactions in their local neighborhoods. In 1920 *A Cigarra* was the most popular magazine in São Paulo, circulating among elite families as well as women of "more modest means," who were seamstresses, telephone operators, and white-collar workers like secretaries.[90] Nearly half of the magazine was dedicated to "letters from our readers," wherein readers wrote anonymously to joke about friends, advertise projects (even amateur film productions), and seek information about "missed chances" with attractive strangers. One edition from March 1929 contained sixty pages (including the cover and back), of which twenty-three were dedicated to letters from readers.[91] Readers wrote in with pseudonyms and nicknames, sometimes writing open letters to ask, for example, if "anybody" knew if a desired person already had a boyfriend. Within the context of 1920s São Paulo society, these personal ads were surprisingly candid in their expression of desire, admiration, or even sexual availability. For example, "Flor de lotus" sent a frank open letter to the general readership of *A Cigarra*: "Searching for a rich, intelligent, sincere, and good-looking boyfriend that has not yet loved."[92] Writing to "whoever desires," three sisters wrote in, "We come offering our little hearts. We are 3 sisters, one light ["clara"] and two dark ["morenas," referring to possibly eye/hair color or skin tone]. We desire three young men that are understanding and older than twenty years old. We will trace our profiles, if necessary."[93] They signed their ad "Three little hearts of gold." Readers received responses to their posts via the magazine as well. "Meiranita," a frequent contributor to the magazine, wrote a response to the reader "B. do Rei": "Great, I want a boyfriend! Give me your address. I want to meet my future 'half,' hoping that you will be a lovely 'piece.'"[94]

In "missed chances" and personal ads, cinemas could function as a meeting spot for strangers. For example, one reader asked, "I'd be very thankful to someone who could tell me if the heart of a certain boy is already taken.... He goes to the Cine Penha and, during the intervals, usually stands up, front towards his seat, his back to the screen. —Me."[95] This ad emphasizes the way in which people and bodies, both male and female, were publicly on display during the periods of "light" inside the cinema. With his back to the screen, facing the audience, the mystery moviegoer visually supplanted the film itself, and for "Me," he was the feature attraction at the cinema.

Readers wrote in stating their preferences for blondes, brunettes, and persons of light or dark complexion, adding another layer to the idea of cinema as a place that brought together different physical types. For example,

"Whitey" ("Branco") pledged his interest to "Moreninha" ("Little Brown/Brunette") and sought "three little girlfriends" for himself and his friends. He humorously described himself: "I present myself as a candidate to the hand of 'Moreninha.' I am tall, fair [claro], brown hair and eyes. I am 25 years old, single, vaccinated, independent, etc. I go to the [Cine] Odeon on Sundays with two friends who can be introduced to your friends. Sound good?" "Moreninha," the diminutive of "morena," means small with either dark hair or a dark complexion, and thus can be a racially ambiguous term. In the same edition, a woman with the pseudonym "Looking for Love" seemed to be a perfect match. She wrote in, "I'm looking for a good-looking boyfriend who likes me. Now my profile: I am 17 years old, 'morena,' the cutesy type, black eyes, wavy black hair, small mouth. I like the matinees at the Odeon." Unfortunately for "Whitey," who described himself as "fair," she also wrote that she liked "boys who are 'brown [Moreno].'" Although they were both seeking love at the "Odeon" on Sunday, "Whitey" did not quite fit the bill. In the following issue, however, "Arth" responded to "Looking for Love" with the following ad: "I put myself forth as a candidate. My profile: I am 'Moreno,' not handsome or ugly. I'm 23 years old, wavy black hair, brown eyes. I go to the matinees at the Capitólio."[96]

"Whitey," "Looking for Love," and "Arth" described their own appearances and their romantic preferences with explicit terms for light or dark eyes, hair, and skin tone. However, each of these ads was racially ambiguous. Aside from occasional references to European nationalities (like one reader who wanted to know the name of a French woman), the personal ads in *A Cigarra* avoided specific reference to racial categories. This was consistent with two broader trends; one was a Brazilian tendency to describe race based on phenotype and skin tone (black, white, brown) rather than a North American system based on heredity. This meant that people seeking someone brown (*moreno*) or fair (*claro*) could be referring to hair/eye color, or skin tone, but with potential ambiguity in terms of African descent. However, readers of *A Cigarra* were also addressing a limited audience with the possible assumption that most other readers would self-identify as white or near-white.[97]

Moviegoers used movie theaters as a space to find and meet people they desired but did not know. It was a place where transactions of love and romance could be made, where people from different family circles, racial and class backgrounds might see each other and even fall in love. Moviegoers, both male and female, positioned themselves as sexually desiring individuals who anonymously but publicly declared romantic interests for specific types of bodies and people. While the stated preferences for "light" and "dark" peoples only vaguely recalled the racial mixing that has characterized Brazilian demographic history, these ads announced readers' physical attractions and romantic desires. In a society where chastity was still important to gendered honor, the open flirtations in personal ads reveal spaces (both in the public forum of the magazine pages and in the physical spaces of movie theaters) that destabilized these standards.

Moviegoers navigated their place in the city's hierarchies of race, class, and gendered respectability through their spatial practices inside and around cinemas. Moviegoers contributed to the social construction of cinemas as elite, respectable, working class, disreputable, or even as diasporic ethnic spaces. If the previous chapter examined the hopes and plans of legislators and municipal officials to regulate movie theaters according to ideals of health and hygiene, this chapter demonstrates how regulation did not dictate everyday use. And while moviegoing reveals how quotidian social habits varied by gender, race, and class, it also reveals the strong motivation of desire, romance, and fandom in paulistanos' daily lives—determining where they went to the movies, where they sat, and who they met in the darkness. In moviegoers' social practices, they participated in the construction of São Paulo through its movie theaters, centering gender and sexuality in the production of urban space.

As demonstrated in the following chapter, movie theaters continued to function in a similar way into later time periods through the mid- and late twentieth century. Following these social threads in São Paulo reveals that moviegoers continued to use moviegoing as an act of social positioning, and they developed new rituals of romance and love. However, shifting to this later time period delves into the deep scars that social inequality, coupled with moral panic surrounding sexual liberation, left on the city.

5

DREAMS AND MEMORIES OF A RESPECTABLE CITY

São Paulo Moviegoing in the Mid and Late Twentieth Century

"In the darkness of the cinema . . . close to a happy ending," sings the famed São Paulo musician Rita Lee in her 1982 hit song "Flagra," or "Caught Red-Handed." In the song, Lee appropriates Hollywood symbols to narrate the limits between respectable romance and illicit sex in a movie theater. Referring to stars of the mid-century Hollywood golden age, Deborah Kerr and Gregory Peck, she teases, "Se a Deborah Kerr que o Gregory Peck," a play on words that, when spoken, sounds like "Se a Deborah quer que o Gregory peque," or "If Deborah wants Gregory to sin." Lee then pronounces herself to be "the sheik Valentino," the 1920s Latin lover representative of illicit, exotic sexuality, and says her "girl is Mae West," the 1930s fast-talking, sexually provocative comedian. In Lee's song, moviegoers in the audience mediate their sexual identities through images from Hollywood, from the glamorous romance of the 1950s to the subversive sexuality of the 1920s and 1930s. Writing in 1982, Lee looks back on moviegoing as sexually charged but relatively innocent. Although the "kids" in the movie theater imagine themselves as Latin lovers, when the lights come on, they realize, "Damn, we've been caught!"[1] Lee's song mirrors the 1925 story of "Cinema in the Light and the Dark," discussed in the introduction, wherein sexual predators and adulterous husbands are caught when the lights flicker back on. Whereas the 1925 story worried that the darkness of the movie theater threatened the stability of the Brazilian family, Lee's version of the "darkness of the cinema" represents semilicit flirtations as a nostalgic take on youth culture.

Lee's song illustrates new narratives of moviegoing that emerged during and after the mid-twentieth century. In the 1920s, commentators of moviegoing imagined how movie theaters symbolized the potential of a changing city, for better or for worse. They imagined how gender roles would evolve, how men and women would mix and mingle, and what this meant for the reconfiguration of urban spaces in the present and future. In contrast, by the late twentieth century, commentators looked back on the late 1930s–1950s and lamented the loss of the city as it once was. As remembered through nostalgic lenses, dating and romance in the mid-century became acceptable habits of sociability rather than illicit threats to Brazil's social fabric. Women who went to the cinema—as long as they dressed a certain way and went to the right type of cinema—did so in transit between work and home. Their presence in the street did not necessarily signify their proximity to prostitution or their abandonment of the domestic sphere. These narratives of respectable consumption and leisure painted dating and flirtation as youthful rites of passage, often leading to, rather than obstructing, eventual marriage and family.

In memoirs and oral histories recorded in the 1980s, 1990s, and into 2010 and 2011, paulistano moviegoers and film critics contrasted their memories of the glamour and romance of the mid-century with what they perceived as the city's decadence in the late twentieth century. Moviegoers tied their memories of a vibrant moviegoing scene to an idealized version of mid-century São Paulo that was respectable, civilized, and vaguely "middle class"—values inextricably bound with notions of gendered propriety and sexual morality. In contrast, moviegoers characterized the late twentieth-century city as "decadent"—socially, morally, sexually, and even racially. They mediated these narratives through a small cluster of cinemas designated as "Cinelândia," which spatially and symbolically represented the century's broader social shifts. Filtered through decades, these memoirs and oral histories belie the continuities from the early to the mid-twentieth century, and the ways in which the cinema remained a space of both the dark and the light in both time periods. Across these decades, moviegoing illuminates the centrality of women's sexual mores to constructing hopes, dreams, and memories of urban Brazil.

Cinema and Moralism in the Mid-Twentieth Century

While previous chapters have focused on the 1920s, this chapter assesses shifts in moviegoing across two broad time periods in the city of São Paulo: the "golden age" of moviegoing from the late 1930s to the mid-1950s, and the transformation of moviegoing in the 1970s and 1980s. Rather than two distinct and clearly defined eras, this periodization does not adhere to traditional shifts in Brazilian political history, which might locate a more precise break in the beginning of Brazil's military dictatorship in 1964. Instead, this chapter follows the contours of moviegoers' memories, including nostalgic definitions of an idealized mid-century past versus a less rosy view of the decades after. This periodization also follows a general timeline in the Brazilian film industry and global moviegoing that locates a "golden age" in the mid-century.

After the end of the Old Republic in 1930, Brazilian politics underwent multiple transformations, from the rise of dictator-president Getúlio Vargas to a post–World War II return to republicanism and tenuous democracy from 1945 to 1964. Vargas represented many political trends of Latin America in the 1930s and 1940s, mixing popular social welfare policies and a paternalistic image with authoritarianism and an embrace of fascist ideology.[2] With the establishment of the "Estado Novo" in 1937, the federal government reached new heights of power, including the creation of powerful units of state surveillance, political repression, and media censorship. Although less charismatic than his contemporary in Argentina, Juan Perón, Vargas similarly made use of media technologies to broadcast patriotic messages surrounding his cult of personality.[3] Vargas was ousted from power in 1945, but he returned as a democratically elected president from 1951 to 1954, until he died by suicide while in office. The following presidential elections led to the presidency of Juscelino Kubitschek, who campaigned with the message of developmentalism and the slogan of "fifty years of progress in five." Kubitschek's government oversaw large-scale national projects, most notably the construction of the new capital in Brasilia in the interior of the country, which was intended to symbolize the integration of Brazil's vast regions into a unified and developed nation.[4]

Cinema and media in this time period increased in legitimacy, with national cinemas in Brazil and beyond ascending in production quality and popularity. In the 1930s Adhemar Gonzaga, one of the original editors of *Cinearte*, became a "founding father" of Brazilian cinema when he produced a bevy of successful *chanchadas*, or popular musical comedies.[5] Chanchadas brought forth iconic Brazilian stars such as Grande Otelo and Carmen Miranda, the latter of whom gained international acclaim for her appropriation of quintessential "Brazilian" imagery.[6] By the 1940s the establishment of the film studio Companhia Cinematográfica Vera Cruz, often referred to as just "Vera Cruz," represented a new movement of domestic film production. Dubbed the "Hollywood of Brazil," Vera Cruz was a homegrown Brazilian studio, but it was promoted as capable of creating films resembling those of Hollywood and Europe, even importing equipment and hiring personnel from abroad.[7] Hollywood, Mexican, and Argentine national cinemas also entered their respective "golden ages," characterized by the rise of famous movie stars, marquee productions, impressive cinematography, and eager audiences.[8] The 1939 blockbuster *Gone with the Wind*, the highest-grossing film for decades after, serves as a premier example of Hollywood's golden age and its popularity around the world.[9] In Mexico, films featuring stars such as Dolores del Río, María Félix, and Pedro Infante demonstrated the growth and artistry of mid-century Mexican cinema.[10] These mid-century films from Hollywood, Brazil, and abroad were shown to eager audiences in São Paulo, and their high quality and magnetic stars contributed to the glamour of moviegoing in this time period.

Along with the growth of various film industries, the federal and state governments in Brazil sought to utilize the power and popularity of cinema and visual media. Although the Vargas regime stopped far short of developing a national film industry, it established the foundation for regulation and investment that grew in later decades.[11] In essence, the federal government adopted theories that had originated in film magazines and treatises of the 1920s and 1930s, namely that the development of "good," rational, and morally upright cinema was necessary to combat the influence of "bad," or overly dramatic, captivating, and morally bankrupt cinema.[12] Thus the Vargas regime set the stage to invest in Brazilian films and newsreels that encouraged patriotism and productive citizenship.[13] In contrast to the "exploitation/exploration" films featuring "naked Indians" that Adhemar Gonzaga lamented in 1930, the short films played during a night at the cinema in the mid-century became state-approved newsreels, even after the end of the Vargas regime.

For example, during the era of the fourth republic in São Paulo, the state government did not directly sponsor the production company "Bandeirantes da Tela," but it distributed and promoted its films about the work of the São Paulo first family.[14] Visions of Governor Adhemar de Barros and his wife, "Dona Leonor" Mendes de Barros, appeared frequently in these newsreels, which explored "wholesome" fare like social welfare programs, public health needs, and the work of private, charitable organizations. According to Rodrigo Archangelo, Dona Leonor was the featured subject of several newsreels in which she appeared as a maternal, nurturing woman who cared for indigent and sick children.[15] Adhemar de Barros was himself somewhat of a cinephile, as was Dona Leonor, and they both enjoyed going to the movies as a couple. Leonor Mendes de Barros also partook in moviegoing as a respite from childcare.[16] Their enjoyment of cinema was tangential to their canny use of state media for political purposes, but it serves as a noteworthy symbol of the broadening legitimacy of cinema in the mid-century.

Sections of the Catholic Church in Brazil echoed the discourse of the good and bad potential of cinema. There were some extreme corners of Catholic activists who soundly rejected cinema as symptomatic of degenerate social mores in Brazil, but they found little political support during the Vargas era (though their conservatism informed the moral politics of later decades).[17] At least one local priest in São Paulo presented a less extreme point of view, but nevertheless preached on the perceived dangers of cinema, many of which had persisted from the earlier twentieth century, such as the insalubriousness of movie theater airflow and the particular harm that films might have on young women. Speaking to a group of young women affiliated with the League of Catholic Women in São Paulo, a local priest named Father Roberto cautioned, "Do not shut yourselves up in cinemas or theaters where the air is poisonous [*viciado*—the same term that Rio de Janeiro public health practitioners had used in 1916], but seek contact with nature, which will yield much more for your health and for your spirit. God is in nature, but it is difficult to find God in a reel of film."[18]

In the 1950s a unique effort within the Catholic Church challenged this notion that God could not be found in film—even in Hollywood films. This effort reflected a conciliatory attitude that sought to utilize rather than excise cinema's popularity, especially among youths and women.[19] It also echoed the philosophy of "educational cinema," whose proponents had lobbied for moral films that, through alliances with the Catholic Church and government, would counter the negative influence of overly dramatic Hollywood films.[20] By the late 1950s, "Catholic Action," a lay Catholic organization with gender-separated units dedicated to youth, students, and workers, implemented its own moral guidance for cinemas. Sections of Catholic Action, such as its university students' and workers' groups, were socially and politically progressive, and although not representative of mainstream Catholic thought, developed commitments to leftist social justice in resistance to Brazil's military dictatorship.[21] Catholic Action maintained a specialized "Cinematic Information Service" that recommended the censorship of films based on "moral and artistic" criteria that they printed in monthly bulletins. Surprisingly, Catholic Action went beyond labeling Hollywood films "bad" and propaganda films "good," and explored cinema's potential as a form of art, so that even commercial filmmaking might be interpreted as a positive cultural force. The organization developed a "prayer for cinema," beseeching that films, "in virtue of the progress of science," might "work always for the greater spiritual and moral progress of humanity, and for the glory of the Holy Name."[22]

In the 1950s, Catholic Action initiated the rather exceptional offer of a written film course to its female adolescent student wing, the Female Catholic Student Youth (Juventude Estudantíl Católica Feminina, JECF). The written lessons were distributed via the Catholic Action's bulletins, with the suggestion that groups of six to ten students gather weekly to discuss. Each lesson presented a mix of moralism and film appreciation, so that students might glean good morals from the entertainment and appreciate the artistry of film production. The course meant to correct alarming behaviors that JECF had discovered in a survey of members, including that female students went to the cinema at least three times a week, and that in choosing films, they almost always based their decision on their favorite movie stars rather than "the moral, artistic, and cultural value of the film." The worry was that "the attitudes of our students, their reactions to grave problems such as divorce and marriage, reveal the prodigious influence of consuming [cinema]."[23]

In their alarm, Catholic Action echoed the critics of the 1920s, discussed in chapter 1, who lamented the "movie-struck girls" who filled their heads with Hollywood romance to the detriment of marriage and family. However, Catholic Action's antidote for the "movie-struck girl" was to train the moviegoer to be more discerning rather than discourage movie-watching completely. One lesson thus challenged students to guess the title of a film based on a picture and an accompanying description that read, "a neo-realist film that addresses a social problem." The answer was the Italian neorealist *Bicycle Thieves* (Produzioni De Sica, 1948)—a surprising choice for both its secular origins and art film status. Apparently, Catholic Action interpreted its raw exploration of poverty and desperation as more moral and artistic than standard Hollywood fare.[24] Another lesson asked students to rationally critique films with questions like, "What is the central message of the film? . . . What is its moral value? . . . What individual and social influence does it exert?"[25]

The need to educate viewers reveals that Catholic Action still considered cinema to be somewhat of a threat to young girls. If they had thought of it as wholly benign, there would have been no urgency to train adolescents to view films critically. Nevertheless, the program to find a film's moral and artistic merits reveals Catholic Action's acceptance that "good cinema," or good viewing habits, could counteract the negative effects of "bad cinema." Rather than eradicating the presence of cinema in Brazilian society, Catholic Action sought to harness and shape its influence. This approach was recognition of the extent to which cinema was both ingrained in and legitimate in mid-century society, but also how it maintained an ambivalent moral status—with shades of both the dark and the light that could serve to pollute or uplift young minds.

The Vargas regime was heavily involved in defining gender and family roles, imagining women as key to strong Brazilian families and nationhood.[26] Consistent with the Vargas regime's inclusion of women in nation-building mythos, new types of "respectable" women increased in public visibility, from women who utilized "scientific mothering" to cultivate healthy Brazilian citizens, to middle-class, productive workers who provided income for their families (albeit the latter was not without controversy).[27] The first lady of Brazil, Darcy Vargas, though not as famous or magnetic as her Argentine counterpart Eva Perón, provided an aspirational example for public service, especially in the sectors of infant welfare and motherhood.[28] Elite and middle-class wives and mothers joined civic organizations, some of which were right-wing and claimed to uphold traditional institutions of family and marriage.[29] Young, unmarried women had opportunities to join public institutions like domestic and puericulture schools that educated them as the future mothers of Brazil.[30] In general, there were ways for women to inhabit public spaces, though often treading a fine line to demonstrate how these acts did not contradict their commitment to the traditional Brazilian family.

Consumption habits were another way in which women might publicly demonstrate respectability, particularly in affirming their belonging to the ambiguous but beguiling category of the "middle class." By the mid-twentieth century, government censuses, print publications, and politicians used language to refer to the "middle class," even if they did not always agree with what it meant. There was little in terms of socioeconomic status, profession, income level, or ideology to unify or concretely define the term. As Brian Owensby writes, the middle class was more of an aspirational category than a defined sector of society.[31] In Brazil, as in many nations outside of the US and

Figure 5.1. "Barbeando-se em Casa!" Gillette advertisement, *A Careta*, no. 1554, April 2, 1938, p. 11, Acervo da Fundação Biblioteca Nacional–Brasil.

Europe, the existence of a middle class was tied up with the achievement of modernity.[32] Barbara Weinstein states that while it is problematic to assume there were "stable, empirical measurements of what it meant to be middle class in São Paulo in the early 1930s," the middle class was a principal characteristic of regional identity. For example, journalists, writers, and veterans depicted São Paulo's unsuccessful 1932 revolt against the federal government as a middle-class effort that mobilized "respectable" people.[33] If understanding how certain "desirable" characteristics were proxy terms for whiteness in Brazil, especially in São Paulo, then "middle class" aligned with the cultural markers associated with whiteness—respectability, cleanliness, and gendered propriety.[34]

The mid-century was a period of a growing consumer culture in Brazil,[35] and consumption habits could reinforce or signal aspirational status and middle-classness.[36] The bourgeois woman consumer, as long as her habits of consumption were for domestic happiness and comfort, was a boon, not a threat, to the traditional Brazilian family.[37] Mid-century advertisements and sources reinforced the triangulation between gendered propriety, middle-classness, and moviegoing. For example, an advertisement for Gillette razors tied together courtship, gendered beauty, appropriate spending habits, and moviegoing. In the ad, a white-presenting man and woman buy movie tickets, and the slogan reads, "Save money for the movies by shaving at home!" ostensibly by purchasing Gillette razors. Significantly, the illustration makes clear that the man is the one paying for the tickets.

The advertisement promotes the idea that a man would fulfill multiple duties appropriate to his gender through acts of consumption—maintaining a masculine ideal of beauty and hygiene, living responsibly and economically, and thus providing for his date to go to the movies. The act of buying movie tickets reinforces the idea that this man is heteronormative, a capable provider, as well as clean and attractive. These were also racialized concepts associated with whiteness, and the white-presenting figures were consistent with other depictions of middle-class consumers of soda, automobiles, or appliances in mid-century Brazilian advertising, which typically only represented Black figures in the context of labor or servitude rather than consumption.[38] The heteronormative masculine ideal additionally contrasts with the philandering or predatory man of the 1920s, who went to the movies with his lover, or worse, went alone to prey on innocent women. It also contrasts with the dandyish *almofadinha*, whose exaggerated grooming habits marked him as effeminate and juvenile, or the degenerate and irresponsible *viado* discussed in chapter two. Rather, this advertisement presents moviegoing as a practice consistent with, rather than aberrant from, the path toward domestic happiness and a nuclear Brazilian family.

Another version of the mid-century moviegoing woman was presented very differently from the melindrosa of the 1920s. In the inaugural program of the Cine Metro, the front cover featured an image of the facade of the cinema. Foregrounded is the figure of a woman, standing alone in the street. Instead of a symbol of the "specter of prostitution," as the 1920s melindrosa, this single moviegoing woman walks among other respectable moviegoers. A family with a young child is visible across the street from her, ready to go inside. No man is approaching her or offering to buy her company as was depicted in earlier cartoons. In fact, the Cine Metro took a similar marketing approach as the Cine Odeon did in the 1910s when they featured "elegant" women in promotional ads to signal the legitimacy and respectability of cinema.[39]

While such promotional materials signaled that moviegoing was a respectable act of consumption and leisure for men and women, the association with "middle-classness" was as tenuous as the term itself. For example, when the municipal government attempted to regulate the cost of movie tickets in 1946, claiming cinema as a "basic necessity of the middle class," it set off a public and legal debate about the meanings of this elusive term. In a legal challenge to the regulation, cinema owners claimed movie theaters were "elite" and "luxurious," rather than "middle class." The municipal government countered that, with nearly a million tickets being sold in the center

Figure 5.2. Inaugural program for the Cine Metro, December 16, 1938. Cinemateca Brasileira, D1466-1.

of the city, moviegoing was too popular to be considered "elite." When a handful of movie theater owners protested the regulation by shuttering their cinemas, they inadvertently provided fodder for the municipal government's arguments. Journalists in São Paulo and Rio de Janeiro, who in the era of heavy state oversight would be wary of criticizing the government, blamed the movie theater owners for their outrageous actions.

In the *Correio Paulistano*, a journalist described "hundreds of disappointed moviegoers" waiting outside of theater doors as if they had been denied their daily bread.[40] The article lamented the "sudden and radical decision of the managers of cinema companies . . . [that] directly hurt the population. . . . Nor does the population deserve to be deprived of a diversion that for us, paulistanos, can be considered a primary necessity."[41] In equally dramatic fashion, the Rio de Janeiro newspaper *Folha Carioca* referred to the residents of São Paulo as "cheated/injured people. . . . Brazil's most industrial state is deprived of its primary way of passing time, which is without doubt, the cinema. There are no words to express this."[42] The comment might reflect regional stereotypes of São Paulo as a drab, industrial city without the natural beauty of Rio de Janeiro's beaches, where paulistanos had only cinema to amuse themselves. While the journalists' comments may be a bit exaggerated, the dramatic episode of movie ticket regulation demonstrates the overall popularity of moviegoing in the city as well as cinema's relationship to "middle-class" identity. The shuttering of a few movie theaters merited fevered discussion in newspapers of supposed societal "injury." If movie theaters were "basic necessities" of the "middle class," could they also be elite and luxurious? Could they also be popular?

The uncertainty surrounding the status of movie theaters remains a theme in descriptions and promotional materials of the time period, even as moviegoing increased in social legitimacy from the 1920s. By the 1940s and 1950s, cinema was an established social activity. Both state and religious organizations recognized its popularity, and even sought to harness it as a positive force in Brazilian society. Women's participation in public work and consumption also became increasingly widespread, if not shielded from reproach. Women had to prove that their actions adhered to ideals of domesticated femininity, as well as to the values of a strong family and nation. Nevertheless, the social needle had shifted so that by the mid-century, the language to discuss women's acceptable participation in work and leisure had evolved from earlier decades. Activities that were deemed "middle class" signaled a broad social acceptability for men and for women. Women's presence waiting in line for the movie theater was not the social threat that it had been in the 1920s. However, cinema remained shaded as both "dark and light," bad and good, even as the proportion of bad and good had altered since the 1920s. Although in the late twentieth century, moviegoers looked back at mid-century moviegoing as a middle-class and respectable activity, sources show that the social boundaries of respectability were not so clearly defined.

The São Paulo Centro: Cinelândia and Social Status

This section addresses the constitution of Cinelândia, a section of the Centro neighborhood that was characterized by monumental, luxurious movie theaters, leading to the moniker of "movie-land." In the early twentieth century, high-end retail shopping had been concentrated in the "Triangle," a triangular-shaped group of blocks bordered by Rua Direita and the Viaduto do Chá. In the following decades, the hub of retail and leisure shifted slightly westward, punctuated by large movie theaters like the Cine Paramount on Avenida São João. Department stores like the English-branded Mappin, retail shops, and restaurants also migrated westward. By the 1930s this "new" Centro neighborhood fortified its position as a local destination for respectable consumption and leisure. Sociologist Lúcia Helena Gama describes the Centro in the 1940s as a vibrant space in which artists, intellectuals, and self-proclaimed middle-class consumers went to enjoy movies, theater, shopping, and public dining.[43]

Luxurious street cinemas populated the Centro neighborhood, especially around the intersection of Avenida São João and Avenida Ipiranga. These new cinemas featured ostentatious and fantastical designs, and being monumental in size, they seated thousands of spectators at once. In contrast to the nineteenth-century Beaux Arts style of the 1920s "cine-teatros," the mid-century cinemas were inspired by modernist and orientalist aesthetics. Cinemas like the Cine Paramount, which architectural historian Renato Anelli has called the first "modern" cinema, phased out the use of private boxes, galleries, and the nineteenth-century theater style that film intellectual Adhemar Gonzaga had deemed passé in 1929.[44] Symbolic of this transition, the Cine-Teatro República, the "traditional cinema of the elite" discussed in the previous chapter, shuttered its doors in 1937. In the same year, the Cine Art-Palácio opened with great fanfare just a few blocks away. Brazilian modernist architect Rino Levi designed the Art-Palácio with over 3,000 seats, marble finishing, and a modernist aesthetic. According to film historian Inimá Simões, it represented "a new concept of a movie theater" with curved columns, walls, and entrances that were both aesthetically innovative and designed to maximize acoustic reverberations.⁴⁵ One enthused reviewer in the state newspaper *Correio Paulistano* claimed that the cinema's innovative lighting not only perfectly illuminated the interior of the building, but also illuminated faces without any hint of shadow, heightening moviegoers' appearance and making them more attractive.⁴⁶ Aside from ascribing rather fantastical powers to a movie theater, the review hinted at an underlying ideology of urban reform—how the grandeur of a building might elevate its surroundings, beautifying the city and its inhabitants.

Along with the greater opulence and size of movie theaters in São Paulo, moviegoing reached a zenith of popularity. Simões refers to the decades after 1935 as a time when "the city was on a honeymoon with cinema."⁴⁷ Between 1940 and 1950, the population of the city increased by 60 percent while the moviegoing public increased by 83 percent.⁴⁸ Literally millions of moviegoers came to Cinelândia to watch movies. For example, in 1948, 1,824,477 tickets were sold in just the UFA Art-Palácio alone, which held over 3,000 seats.⁴⁹ To be sure, the entire city was not going to the movies every day. Moviegoing tickets were not accessible to the poorest citizens of the city. However, those who could afford the price and time might go to the movies several times a week.

On its surface, the movie theaters of Cinelândia materialized the dreams of the early twentieth-century film intellectuals who advocated for Brazilians to see movies in respectable and technologically advanced cinemas. Film technology such as sound film and industrial practices such as vertical integration (e.g., Hollywood studios owning their own movie theaters) squeezed out the would-be, casual film entrepreneurs of the early twentieth century. Although there were still run-down theaters, the "wooden shacks" and combination brew-bar-cinemas in the Centro had disappeared. Ramshackle movie theaters could no longer spontaneously pop up in the Centro, sharing spaces with restaurants and bars. Hollywood studios and Brazilian distributors had concentrated the circulation of films, and the cost and maintenance of film projection technology had evolved to the point that "cinema kings" had replaced the 1920s upstart entrepreneurs who had projected films from their bedrooms and basements.

On the other hand, movie theater owners still engaged with languages and gimmicks that spoke to the continued ambivalence surrounding moviegoing. For example, the Cine Metro movie theater demonstrates that even the most luxurious movie theaters still had not completely shed their association with dark, enclosed spaces. In fact, movie theaters continued to advertise specific technologies using language that reflected the continuous influence of the sanitation movement on popular and commercial concepts of hygiene and health. The Cine Metro's inaugural program from 1938 boasted the use of air-conditioning as an update to the old "automatic ventilators" of the early twentieth century. As intimated by its name, the Cine Metro was vertically integrated into Hollywood's Metro-Goldwyn-Mayer (MGM) Film Studios, meaning that the studio owned the theater and exhibited its own film there: "The directors of [Cinema] 'Metro,' not considering the enormous cost, wanted to give the theater an indispensable indulgence: the installation of ultra modern machines for the production of AIR CONDITIONING, appropriate for all seasons of the year, from the world famous brand Carrier. Inside of the theater of the 'Metro,' and in the lobby, the air will be cleaned, dehumidified, refreshed or heated as necessary, to always produce an agreeable, favorable temperature, and most importantly, stable, as it will be continually controlled by specialized technicians."[50]

Although it was technologically more advanced, the Cine Metro's air-conditioning was thematically a continuation of the Cine Capitólio's "Radio-San" from 1925, which the film impresario Francisco Serrador had employed to disperse perfumed air through the theater. In 1925 the Radio-San purportedly sanitized the air and by extension uplifted the moviegoing experience. Twelve years later, the Cine Metro hinted at the same phenomenon with the added novelties of a US-based brand and climate control. However, the program also specified that the air would be "cleaned" in addition to cooled or heated, harkening back to the earlier twentieth-century fears that dark, enclosed cinemas were prone to "poisoned air"—fears that had persisted, if somewhat abated.

The advent of 3D films provides another example of how hygiene and femininity intersected at the movie theater. When the first 3D movie opened in São Paulo in 1954 at the newly renovated and reopened Cine República (now an enormous cinema with the "largest screen in the world" rather than an antiquated "cine-teatro"), the cinema employed women in white uniforms to sanitize the glasses with an imported "Sanitron" machine after each use.[51] The "san" in "Sanitron," again like the 1925 "Radio-San," was meant to signify "sanitary," again evoking modernity via cleanliness.[52] Like the "female ushers" employed at the inauguration of the Cine Capitólio in 1923 Rio de Janeiro, the women who operated the Sanitron wore white uniforms like nurses, which meant to convey cleanliness, hygiene, and professionalism. The use of uniformed female employees signified a nonthreatening space in which respectable yet subservient femininity could be on display. Just like in the 1920s, some critics dismissed these displays of hygiene as merely cosmetic. Like the journalist who ridiculed the ineffective "ventilators with fancy names" in the 1920s, a Rio de Janeiro film critic in the 1950s similarly saw 3D technology as a new technology that was far from sanitary.[53] Waldemar Paiva painstakingly described a man with "eyes attacked by a contagious illness" who had to leave a 3D film screening "twisted in pain." He took off his 3D glasses on the way out, and then the usher promptly gave the glasses to an unsuspecting young woman who "possibly also left sick."[54]

The examples of the Cine Metro's air-conditioning and the Cine República's "Sanitron" machine point to the complicated layers in forging the social status of movie theaters. Did the Cine Metro have a brand-name air conditioner that "cleaned" the air because it was such a sanitary, luxurious theater? Or did it need to boast of the air conditioner because its presumably "poisoned" air needed such cleaning? Far from static, the status of movie theaters was in constant negotiation, even as cinemas reached wider social acceptance and respectability into the mid-twentieth century.

Sources from the time period hinted at the difficulty of fixing the social status of cinemas, and of middle-classness in general. However, oral history sources demonstrate how moviegoers utilized the idea of middle-classness, even if the term remained diffusely defined, to characterize the dating habits and rituals of mid-century moviegoing. Cinemas were an important arena for the display of shifting habits of gender performance, courtship, and dating. As in earlier decades, men and women continued to meet each other at the movies. But in contrast to the illicit sexual encounters of the 1920s, narratives of moviegoing in the 1940s emphasized dating as a normalized rite of passage. Men and women kissed and held hands in the dark, but they used a new taxonomy to describe acts like dating, flirting, and romance. In the 1920s, when cinema was still on the margins of respectability, political, religious, and moral authorities characterized moviegoing as a threat to the institution of marriage and the Brazilian family. In memories of 1940s Cinelândia, however, men and women remembered dating as an innocent activity that did not threaten their social status and in fact could be a precursor to married life.

As part of her master's thesis, anthropologist Heloísa Buarque de Almeida conducted a series of interviews with paulistanos in the 1990s on the topic of moviegoing in the 1940s. Almeida generously shared with me the transcripts of twenty-three interviews she had conducted for her ethnography on moviegoing.[55] I also rely on transcripts and audio recordings of interviews with

Figure 5.3. Facade of the Cine Ipiranga, designed by modernist architect Rino Levi. "Cine Ipiranga e Hotel Excelsior," *Acrópole*, February 1943, periodicos, Faculdade de Arquitetura e Urbanismo da Universidade de São Paulo (FAU USP).

film critics and filmmakers conducted for Inimá Simões's book on São Paulo movie theaters.[56] Almeida's and Simões's interviews were conducted in the 1980s and 1990s and provide insight on how moviegoing changed over time.

In addition, between 2010 and 2011 I conducted a series of group interviews with members of various social clubs for elderly people. In particular, I interviewed participants of a São Paulo state program that bussed seniors from all over the city to attend screenings of older and contemporary Brazilian films at the Cinemateca Brasileira, the state film archive. These group interviews, casual and conducted over coffee, gave me brief snippets and anecdotes about moviegoing, and a glimpse into social mores.[57] I conducted these group interviews about the mid-century separately from the individual interviews I did with the older women who shared memories of the 1920s, which were analyzed in chapter 4.

For these interviews about the mid-century, Buarque and I, both women, spoke to more women than men. In my own case, nearly all the participants in the social programs were women. One participant at the Cinemateca told me that her husband was "too macho" to attend such events, and he thought associations for the elderly were just for women. Buarque comments that female interviewees seemed comfortable speaking with her about dating in their youth. Some male interviewees, on the other hand, were slightly embarrassed to speak about dating, but in her interpretation, this was because they apologized for being too innocent and inexperienced, not because they had committed any immoral acts.[58] In the group interviews I conducted, I also found female interviewees speaking fondly of the topic, including stories of romance and dating. This may be because their memories were filtered through a contemporary perspective in which standards for women's public behavior were more liberal. The inherent nostalgia associated with the pleasures of youth also made moviegoing a relatively safe and even enjoyable topic of discussion among a homosocial group of older women. This, paired with the setting of the interviews, held in the afterglow of watching nostalgic, family-friendly programming, might have skewed memories to emphasize the fun and "light" side of cinema rather than the dangerous or "dark." In contrast to Buarque's and my own interviews with predominantly women, Inimá Simões interviewed mostly male individuals who were not just casual moviegoers but professional film critics, historians, and filmmakers. Simões thus elicits different perspectives, and being male himself and conversing with interviewees in a homosocial environment, he may have had the liberty of covering topics considered taboo for Buarque and me. Together, Simões's interviews from the early 1980s, Buarque's interviews from the 1990s, and my own interviews from 2010 to 2011, though separated by decades, carry forth a recurring theme of nostalgia for a more innocent era and stage of life.

Another recurring theme across these oral histories was an emphasis on legitimizing formerly illicit activities, such as flirting and meeting people of the opposite sex, by associating them with middle-classness. Most of Buarque's interviewees described themselves as "middle class." According to these interviewees, "everyone" was in the Centro on the weekends, the popular hub of leisure. When pressed to explain who "everyone" was, housewife "Lina" clarified that they were "well-dressed, fine people," suggesting that "everyone" was indeed limited to a particular group of people.[59] In addition to class, race was also a factor in defining "good" and "middle-class" people. The oral histories examined in this chapter elided issues of race and did not betray that the audience might be other than white and middle class. Yet instances of race-based discrimination did appear. For example, one of Simões's interviewees, who had been a projectionist at the Cine Metro, offhandedly commented that the cinema had such high standards that "blacks and men without ties" were never admitted.[60]

Interviewees reflected on the pains they took to perform gendered respectability through clothing and behavior, again begging the question as to exactly how acceptable moviegoing really was. Like the Cine Metro's air-conditioning system that "sanitized" the air, were these markers of respectability a performance to remediate the darkness of the cinema, or were they the visible symbols of a class standard that had to be upheld? In his interview with Inimá Simões, film historian Máximo Barro remembered the importance of clothing in cinemas, because people went to see each other as much as they went to see the films on screen.[61] Barro emphasized that while people of classes "B and C" (meaning in a tiered class system, the people who did not belong to the elite "A" and were thus considered middle and lower-middle class) went to the cinema, they had to dress up as well as they possibly could according to their means.[62] Barro particularly highlighted the importance of ties, stressing that men would be denied entry or kicked out of cinemas for not wearing one. He remembered that some of his friends carried a tie in their pockets just in case they needed one for the cinema. The Cine Marrocos, inaugurated in 1951, was the last cinema to demand that men wear ties, and Barro's friends, just to provoke others, would wear a tie to enter, and then showily take them out as soon as they entered the door, though they would risk being thrown out for doing so.[63] Barro also laughed, recalling the sculptor Flavio de Carvalho, who entered the Cinema Marrocos wearing a skirt as a kind of outlandish flouting of the rules. Filmmaker Jairo Ferreira echoed Barro, remembering that without the right clothes, he did not even dare to walk into the deluxe cinemas.[64] Ties were such a necessary accessory that one entrepreneur rented them outside of the Cinema Marrocos—a business idea that demonstrated the performativity of such dress codes, so that men rented what they did not own or normally wear, in order to present themselves a certain way at the movies.[65]

For women, the ideal moviegoing outfit was a far cry from the scantily clad and sometimes androgynous melindrosa of the 1920s. Rather, 1940s dress codes included layers upon layers of clothing, including accessories that were unnecessary for the climate. Various women recalled that hats, pantyhose, and gloves were de rigueur to go to the movies, and even in the summertime, they wore gloves made out of lace.[66] Film critic Rubem Biáfora attributed women's high standards of elegant dress to the movies themselves. Reminiscing about the mid-century, Biáfora claimed that women in the 1940s copied Hollywood actresses like Gene Tierney, famous for being a beautiful actress. According to Biáfora, women watched her films and emulated her entire "toilette" from her hairstyle to her social manners, even to the way she opened doors to visitors.[67] Implicit in his mention of Gene Tierney is the idealization of whiteness and affluence, the idea that one could be elegant like her if one were similarly white, rich, and diligent in copying her manners.

From the perspective of women speaking about the mid-twentieth century, the darkness of the cinema was not necessarily a threat to the institution of marriage. Rather, men and women developed codified dating practices that involved cinemas. In one memoir, a woman named Carolina remembered reconciling with her future husband inside a cinema. Her friends arranged an outing to the movie theater but secretly invited her ex-boyfriend. Stuck in the middle of the aisle, she had no choice but to speak to her ex-boyfriend, who apologized and eventually proposed marriage.[68] For some moviegoers like Carolina, the darkness and intimacy was not an impediment to marriage but was the place where she reconciled with her future husband and found marriage and family. In another kind of play on the dating rituals of how and where to sit in movie theaters, Barro recalled that in the 1940s, it became more standard that men would pay for their dates' movie tickets. In order to avoid this, men would sometimes tell their date to meet them inside the cinema, rather than outside, so that the woman would have to buy her own ticket.[69] One woman I interviewed, however, subverted this practice when she promised an annoying man who had been aggressively asking her for a date to meet him outside the cinema. While he waited outside, she met her real date inside. To her embarrassment, however, her tactic did not work very well because the stood-up man came inside during the middle of the movie, and to her embarrassment, peered into each row to find her.[70]

Moviegoers established methods to mitigate the "darkness of the cinema." Until they were married, couples had to bring along a chaperone, called a *vela*, meaning "candle," typically a younger sibling, a single aunt, or a maid. The "vela" served the purpose of allaying the romance that might happen in the dark.[71] Ushers were also called "lanterninhas" for the flashlights they used not only to lead people to their seats before the film, but to shine onto misbehaving moviegoers.[72] Although "flashlights" and "candles" policed behavior, class habitus governed the range of sexual acts that might actually occur in the cinema. *Namorar* was a sanctioned transgression, just scandalous enough to be hidden in the dark, but ultimately made safe by nostalgic interpretations of the moviegoing experience.

Moviegoers remembered certain cinemas and sections within cinemas as more romantic than others. The Cine Ipiranga included a third floor called the "Pullman" for its padded, reclining seats. This was the most "elite" and most expensive spot to watch movies. Celebrities were rumored to only watch movies in the Pullman section of the Cine Ipiranga. Moreover, like the separate entrances and stairwells in the cine-teatros of the 1920s, the Pullman section was physically isolated from the other sections. In modernist design, this was accomplished through a private elevator rather than a stairwell. One moviegoer remembered that this section had "very comfortable seats, almost better than first class in an airplane," and that "we went up in a private elevator." At one point, she rode the elevator with the governor and first lady of São Paulo state.[73] The Pullman section was not just the most "elite" section, but the best section for dating and kissing because, from the second floor in the back of the cinema, moviegoers remained hidden.[74] "The Pullman was a great place to be hidden, romancing [*namorando*]. It was the chic place and the place to date [*namorar*]."[75] Balconies in general were associated with darkness and romance. When I asked in one of my group interviews whether one interviewee had ever sat in the balcony, "Maria" playfully responded, "Oh no, I'm pure!" as she and others giggled, demonstrating the pervasiveness of the balcony's reputation.[76] In the Cine Ipiranga, the sides of the balcony were nicknamed *namoradeiras* or "flirts" because of the popularity of these areas for dating. Romance and dating in the cinema was by no means unique to Brazil. Anne Rubenstein also recalls jokes and stories of men and women going to the back of the cinema for kisses and romance in 1930s Mexico.[77]

The middle-classness that sanctioned and sanitized these flirtations did not apply uniformly to all moviegoers, particularly in cinemas outside of Cinelândia. In an oral history, a moviegoer named "José" recalled that he would go to the Cine Colonial, a run-down cinema in Santa Terezinha, a small neighborhood on the northern edge of the city. The manager of the cinema would allow José to watch films prohibited for children, so José went to this cinema often. At night, his parents asked that he not go alone, but go accompanied by their domestic servant. He remembers one night that the manager asked him how the "*fodas*" (screwing) was going with the servant.[78] Still in his early adolescence, José said he was both scandalized and not quite sure what the manager meant. Although it was a tongue-in-cheek joke, the manager's comment was still reflective of a long history of patriarchy and classism that presumed the sexual availability of female domestic servants—particularly Black women. The manager referred to the servant as "moça," which can refer alternatively to a young woman or to a woman of any age in a position of service. In this case, the manager's joke pointed out the stereotypically sexual relationship between a young man and the domestic workers his family employed.[79] Thus, while many of the women I interviewed giggled as they recalled memories of dating at the movies, and even poked fun at the idea of sexual "purity" and its place in the movie theater, for other women, particularly those in positions of servitude, going to the movies was still a suggestive threat to her sexual respectability. Rather than ask how the *namorando* (romancing) was going, the manager made a much more explicit accusation of about *fodas* (screwing). In the run-down Cine Colonial outside of the Centro, the "darkness of the cinema" was not tempered by modernist architecture, the wearing of lace gloves and hats, a dutiful usher, or the rigorous policing of middle-class behavior.

From Cinelândia to the Boca do Lixo

In 1944 the Cine Marabá opened to great fanfare as yet another luxurious movie theater in the São Paulo Centro. With a combination of art deco and orientalist styles, the facade of the Marabá created a glamorous appearance on Avenida Ipiranga. Yet in his 1983 novel, *A Grande Arte*, popular crime novelist Rubem Fonseca imagines a shocking and violent use of the same cinema:

> [Fuentes] crossed the street and entered the [Cinema] Marabá. . . . The film ended and the doors to the cinema opened. The lobby was emptying, and in the end, one couple and two men remained. . . . Fuentes entered the bathroom. [He] stood at a sink and watched the door to the bathroom through a mirror. . . . The door hadn't even closed when Fuentes grabbed the man in the gray suit by the lapels of his jacket, and pulled

him backward, hitting his head against the wall. . . . Fuentes left the stall, leaving the man's body to fall forward with his feet stuck in the toilet, his head resting against the closed door.[80]

Reflecting on the 1940s, film scholar Máximo Barro remembered how one of his cousins always wanted to watch films in a particular movie theater in the Centro because it had the best bathrooms, and she could never have such a nice bathroom in her own home. According to Barro, fancy bathrooms and marble columns in the cinemas of Cinelândia had no practical function, but were symbols of aspirational, escapist luxury.[81] And yet by the 1980s, in Rubem Fonseca's imagination, the bathrooms of a Cinelândia movie theater are where a corpse ends up stuck in a toilet and someone can literally get away with murder. Significantly, in the novel, the hitman, Fuentes, is a Bolivian immigrant, touching on demographic changes and the ethnic "othering" of sectors of the urban population. The contrast between Barro's memory of the 1940s movie theaters and Fonseca's characterization of them in the 1980s is a poignant encapsulation of the perceptions, narratives, and images describing perceived changes between the mid- and late-century city.

While the city center had been "chic" and respectable, with proper guardrails (aspirational dress and chaperones), it became an outright "decadent" place associated with crime, sexual deviance, and otherness in the late twentieth century. Part of this narrative rests on anxieties reacting to real, complex shifts in the Brazilian film industry, sexual mores, and political context. However, rumors, urban legends, and tongue-in-cheek stories about moviegoing reveal a persistent emphasis on how the city's perceived decadence was deeply tied to anxieties regarding changing norms of gender and sex. According to these stories, the city was in shambles, and so was the moral status of Brazilian society. However, just as stories of the respectable moviegoing in the 1940s glossed over darker corners, stories of the late twentieth century also exaggerated its decadence, even to comic and dramatic effect.

In this section, I focus on examples from oral history and literature that reveal extreme perspectives on the decadence of the Centro's movie theaters. Some of these perspectives relay urban legends and fanciful imaginings rather than observations of everyday occurrences. However, these examples reveal wider anxieties about late twentieth-century São Paulo city, and how they were channeled into sometimes shocking stories about sex and violence. Two oral history interviews conducted by film historian Inimá Simões, with filmmakers/film critics Rubem Biáfora and Jairo Ferreira, provide a longitudinal perspective on moviegoing from the mid- to late century. Both men extensively addressed "unseemly" stories in the late twentieth century that would have mortified the self-identified mid-century "middle-class" moviegoers that Heloísa Buarque de Almeida and I had interviewed. I do not claim that Biáfora, Ferreira, or other contemporary commentators represent all moviegoers' opinions of the time period, but they do reflect how apprehensions about sex, gender, and the transformation of Brazilian society were channeled into the movie theaters of the São Paulo Centro.

The 1960s through the 1980s was a turbulent time in Brazilian politics, with corresponding shifts in the Brazilian film industry. Like other Latin American nations such as Chile and Argentina, Brazil lurched to the right under an oppressive military dictatorship during this time period. After the optimism and temporary economic boom under Juscelino Kubitschek (president from 1956 to 1961), the immediately succeeding presidents were faced with economic uncertainty, unpopular austerity measures, and fractured political coalitions. Conspiring in a coup of the federal government in 1964, the military replaced then-president João with a general as a "temporary" president. Far-right-wing forces within the military ascended in power, and by 1968, the "temporary" solution became an oppressive dictatorship that stifled free speech and democracy. Although Brazilian state terror did not reach the extremes seen in Argentina or Chile, the Brazilian dictatorship tortured and murdered political dissidents and violently repressed civil rights. The dictatorship allowed for some increased political "opening up" or *abertura* in the mid-1970s, but stayed in power until 1985. Political progress and redemocratization, however, were somewhat overshadowed by Brazil's spiraling economy. The dictatorship had borrowed heavily to keep the Brazilian economy afloat during the 1970s oil crisis, leading to a cycle of international debt, austerity measures, rampant inflation, and economic recession into the 1980s and 1990s.[82]

In this time period, movements for women's and sexual liberation reverberated in Brazil and around the world. Women's participation in higher education increased so that by 1970, 41 percent of graduating university students were women.[83] Birth control pills became available in 1962, opening up practices and conversations about sexual liberation—though historians have shown that the outrage surrounding sexual liberation was more substantial than any change in premarital sexual practices.[84] Men and women experimented with gender-bending fashions and countercultural music and trends. In some ways, conservative criticism directed against hippie clothing and women's liberation in Latin America echoed the 1920s ambivalence about modern girls (the pleasure-seeking melindrosa) and new women (the bookish pioneers of female education and politics). Eric Zolov, for example, has shown how commentators in 1960s Mexico worried that long-haired men and liberated, braless women resulted in the deleterious reversal of gender roles—similar to comics about the short-haired melindrosa and effeminate almofadinha in 1920s Brazilian magazines.[85] Yet the countercultural movement in Brazil was set against a background in which the voices of right-wing moral panic grew louder throughout the 1960s. Benjamin Cowan has analyzed how the military dictatorship, as part of general efforts to dictate social values, conflated perceived sexual and cultural perversions with political subversion. By the late 1960s, far-right voices coalesced in a "cultural war" in which "police could construct pornography, blue jeans, and especially the gender and sexual unconventionality of young, middle-class women as component parts of a much larger, deviant whole."[86] In anticommunist military journals, right-wing officers feared that women would "lose their way" in unchaperoned spaces like universities, succumbing to smoking, drinking, and Marxist seducers, all affronts to proper Brazilian society.[87] Such fears echoed earlier conservative critics of women's sexual liberation while adding panic about communist subversion. As Cowan demonstrates, the dictatorship also targeted male homosexuality and sodomy as sexually and morally deviant practices that threatened to damage Brazilian society. While the criminalization of homosexuality in Brazil was not a new policy, surveillance and outrage reached new levels of intensity.[88] The dictatorship also assigned greater threat not to homosexual practices per se, but to the increasing visibility of homosexuality and the gay rights movement—outrage that, as this chapter explores, seeped into paulistanos' memories of moviegoing.

Amid these turbulent political and social changes, the Brazilian film industry struggled with various peaks and valleys, as the domestic film industry both expanded and faced challenges to growth. The ill-fated mid-century film studio Companhia Cinematográfica Vera Cruz, Brazil's answer to Hollywood, shuttered its doors in 1954. In contrast to the polished Hollywood style of this studio, a new crop of Brazilian filmmakers, influenced by Italian neorealism and the French New Wave as well as their own postcolonial ideologies, experimented with spare aesthetics and raw portraits of Brazilian society.[89] This group of Cinema Novo ("New Cinema") filmmakers met great international acclaim, but somewhat like their early twentieth-century predecessors, they had limited widespread popularity in Brazil. By the 1970s the Brazilian film industry was an uneven landscape full of contradictions. Despite its political repression and mechanisms of media censorship that forced prominent Brazilian artists into exile, the military dictatorship directly financed artistically and culturally significant films. As part of a campaign to increase domestic film production, the dictatorship developed Embrafilme, a national producer and distributor of domestic cinema.[90] In addition, even as the military dictatorship sought to censor cinema and promote sexual morality, the most prominent film genre of the decade was the *pornochanchada*, or Brazilian sex comedy. These were somewhat akin to Hollywood "B movies," but they made up for low production quality with the promise of sexual titillation and fun. The reputation of pornochanchadas among film critics and historians has been mixed, with some pointing out the inherent conservativeness of films that, while irreverent and lewd, nevertheless defaulted to heteronormative and macho depictions of sanitized sexuality.[91] However, other perspectives have analyzed strains of pornochanchadas that intentionally rejected moral and aesthetic standards and have found the genre to be more complex and even subtly subversive.[92]

In São Paulo, the production of pornochanchadas was centered in the "Boca do Lixo," or "Mouth of Garbage," an area near the historic Centro that was so nicknamed for its association with prostitution.[93] Similar to the "red light district" of 1970s Times Square in New York, this centrally located neighborhood in São Paulo became a famous hub for sex work and pornography. The area was also the home for a vibrant independent film scene, with filmmakers gathering at the local Soberano Bar to discuss their latest projects. Unlike the films financed by Embrafilme, the films of the Boca do Lixo were largely independently (and precariously) produced, with the gross of one film financing the next, so that filmmakers worked on tight deadlines and shoestring budgets.[94] In addition to pornochachadas, the Boca do Lixo filmmakers produced other popular genres and subgenres like police, horror, and action films, demonstrating the group's success and widening popularity.[95] However, by the 1980s, competition from imported pornographic films forced the Boca do Lixo filmmakers to similarly turn to the production of hardcore pornography. Global economic shifts, spiking oil prices, and government divestment resulted in rampant inflation and economic crisis in Brazil, from which the film industry could not remain untouched. Film production plummeted, and while Brazilian filmmakers like Carlos Diegues and Suzana Amaral continued to direct commercially successful and internationally renowned films, 85 percent of Brazilian film production in the 1980s was dedicated to hardcore pornography.⁹⁶ Attendant with the decreasing popularity of films and the increasing importance of television, moviegoing also entered a period of crisis. From 1955 to 1970, the moviegoing public in the city of São Paulo had decreased by 65 percent. In 1975 Brazil had 3,276 movie theaters and 275,382 attendees, which plummeted to 1,553 movie theaters and 89,939 attendees by 1984.⁹⁷

The Centro neighborhood of São Paulo, including the site of Cinelândia and its monumental cinemas, reflected these changes of political and economic strife, and of the greater visibility (if not acceptability) of gendered and sexual liberation. As Heitor Frúgoli summarizes, beginning in the 1960s, the Centro "was increasingly identified as a space of the popular classes," a trend that was visible, for example, in a diversity of "street cultures" and their use of public spaces.⁹⁸ The Centro and its immediately surrounding neighborhoods continued to be locales of commerce, leisure, and high-density living, but the economic crisis of the 1980s ushered in social disparity and homelessness, which contributed to perceptions of the decay of the historic center. Describing the 1990s, Teresa Caldeira has famously called São Paulo a "city of walls." According to Caldeira, middle- and upper-class paulistanos moved from the city center into neighborhoods to the south and west, ensconcing themselves in heavily guarded high-rises and gated neighborhoods.⁹⁹ Despite transformations, the Centro remained a vibrant area throughout the late twentieth century, but it was no longer the hub of elite (or aspirationally elite) leisure. Instead, the emergence of high-end shopping malls—including multiplex movie theaters—in the 1990s visibly demonstrated how elite leisure and retail commerce had effectively spread out across the expanding city. The ethnic composition of the city also transformed with the internal migration of northeastern Brazilians; while the population of the city increased threefold from 1950 to the 1970s, its population of northeasterners increased tenfold.¹⁰⁰ Subject to historic patterns of regionalist discrimination, these northeasterners were subject to prejudice and negative stereotyping, with racialized connotations of their undesirable "northern blood."¹⁰¹ While Barbara Weinstein and Sarah Sarzyinski have shown how negative depictions of the northeast served as a foil to the perceived modernity of São Paulo state and the nation, some of the sources in this chapter seized on these stereotypes as a marker for the city's transformation over time.¹⁰²

The changes within the Brazilian film industry and São Paulo city were emphasized in the shifting use of the city's movie theaters. The "Cinelândia" movie theaters were no longer the luxurious, escapist monuments of the mid-century. Instead, as Inimá Simões describes, "The spectators of the old cinema palaces where paulistana elegance convened, stayed away. Upon losing their status . . . there was nothing left but for the cinemas to adapt to new circumstances, splitting themselves into minuscule rooms, divided into specializations for erotic or martial arts films."[103] Some of these cinemas like the Cine Art-Palácio functioned as porn theaters continuously from the 1970s through the 2010s, while some like Cine Dom José are still porn theaters today. Other theaters were torn down, left empty, or converted to parking lots. The famed Cine Metro, which advertised the newest air-conditioning technologies in the mid-century, became a megachurch. The Cine Marabá, which Rubem Fonseca had imagined as the scene of a grisly murder, continued to function and is today a multiplex that shows the latest blockbuster films. The area of the Boca do Lixo in the 1970s and the area of Cinelândia in the 1940s were close together, even overlapping for several blocks. This created a juxtaposition of time and space in narratives and memories of moviegoing.

The comingling of what the Centro once was in the mid-century versus what it was in the late twentieth century set up a rather illustrative contrast. The same cinemas that had gathered "paulistana elegance" were now, in the memories of moviegoers, dens of sexual perversity and crime. Stories of the 1970s–1990s ranged from humorous jokes about masturbation, to rumors of murder and violence, to ethnographic observations of sexual activity and sex work. In many of these stories, specific areas within cinemas, in particular balconies and bathrooms, take on charged significance as spaces that encapsulated the deterioration of the city. If the conservative, right-wing voices within the military dictatorship feared that imagined sexual libertines would destroy "proper" Brazilian society, moviegoers' memories of São Paulo cinemas deemed this damage as already done, evident in the hypervisibility of sex and violence in the city's decaying movie theaters.

In an oral history interview from 1982, São Paulo film critic and filmmaker Jairo Ferreira recounted rumors and urban legends of illicit (or even criminally violent) behavior in the darkest areas of the cinema. Ferreira himself was an experimental filmmaker of "cinema marginal," an aesthetically subversive strain of films emerging from within the "Boca do Lixo."[104] In his long-ranging interview with film historian Inimá Simões, Ferreira details stories of illicit sex and violence with a mixture of criticism, humor, and tongue-in-cheek exaggeration bordering on the absurd. Some of these rumors specifically involved elements that once marked 1940s and 1950s cinemas as elite, like balconies and ushers. Ferreira's recounting of 1980s rumors includes the story of a man masturbating in the balcony; when his semen falls on a moviegoer below, the moviegoer yells, "*porra* [an expletive meaning 'damn' but also 'semen'], it really is porra!" Another rumor involves a female usher who performs oral sex on male moviegoers, and yet another about a woman who, while performing oral sex on a man, bites him and nearly (or actually) kills him. Ferreira referred to all of these stories as "folklore," and each is a narrative that characterizes the decadence of cinemas through forms of perceived sexual deviance.[105]

Jairo Ferreira pointed specifically to the balcony of the Cine Ipiranga as spatially and socially deviant. The Cine Ipiranga was the same cinema with the luxurious Pullman section, which moviegoers had described as being "better than first class in an airplane" in the 1950s and reserved for exclusive society. Instead, by the 1980s, Ferreira referred to this same section as "a den of *marginais*." The term "marginais," which directly translates to "marginals," can be interpreted as "criminals," but signifies more broadly anyone considered without social or moral status. Anthropologist Daniel Linger, in his study of everyday violence in the city of São Luis, writes that "marginal," along with words like *maconheiro* (pothead), *ladrão* (thief), and *palhaço* (clown), are in "a category designating social refuse. . . . These are types who simply do not count in the scheme of things." Accusing someone of being a "marginal" is a "symbolic nullification," labeling the person a nonentity.[106] Anthropologist Don Kulick, on the other hand, posits that to label someone "marginal" is to condemn them as particularly dangerous, untrustworthy, and in the case of negative *travesti* stereotypes, both sexually and morally transgressive.[107] According to Ferreira, during a showing of the Brazilian film *Os Trombadinhas* (The Little Pickpockets), there were *trombadinhas* running around the balcony, eventually creating such a reputation for misbehavior that they had to keep the balcony closed and locked.[108] The stairs leading up to the balcony also became a place of sexual and criminal violence. Whereas heading up to the Pullman section by elevator was an act of distinction in the 1940s and 1950s, Ferreira claimed that in the 1980s, heading up to the higher floors was an act of potential danger, where one would worry about being either stabbed or sexually assaulted on the stairwell—all part of the social ritual of going to the movie theater.

Ferreira associated stairwells not only with crime and violence, but also with sexual perversion, with being homosexual or nonheteronormative. In addition to the Pullman section transforming from the cinema's elite space to a place of crime, the Cine Ipiranga's side balconies, called *asas* or "wings,"

Figure 5.4. Side balconies in the Cine Ipiranga in 1943 when it was inaugurated. "Cine Ipiranga e Hotel Excelsior," *Acrópole*, February 1943, periodicos, Faculdade de Arquitetura e Urbanismo da Universidade de São Paulo (FAU USP).

also transformed through practice. Ferreira recounted that the side balconies in the 1940s were a place for the "elite," where moviegoers could literally feel as if they were floating in the air above the crowd. In the mid-century, these side balconies were even called *namoradeiras* or "sweethearts" because of the popularity of these areas for dating. By the 1980s, however, Ferreira claimed that these side balconies had become the most "deteriorated" spot, supposedly for their association with homosexuality.[109]

In his long-ranging interview with Simões, film critic Rubem Biáfora echoed similar contrasts between the mid- and late century. Biáfora had a decades-long career as a prominent film critic, and with his production of several films in the 1960s and 1970s, was part of a São Paulo–based nucleus of filmmakers who stood apart from the more commercial Boca do Lixo.[110] And while Biáfora exhibited much less irreverence than Jairo Ferreira in his film productions as well as in his oral history interview, the two filmmakers did know and collaborate with each other, with Biáfora furnishing one of the sole positive reviews of the 1970 film *The Pornographer*, on which Ferreira was a cowriter and assistant director.[111] Unlike Ferreira's somewhat comic focus on sexual deviance and sex acts, Biáfora's specter of change was a general mistrust of youth and counterculture. In this sense, Biáfora's interview reflected the conservative moral panic of the time period that read blue jeans and birth control as symbols of greater social decadence. Commenting specifically on the situation in São Paulo, Biáfora also conflated urban decline with the loss of gendered propriety and regionalist perceptions of northeastern Brazilians. In the early and mid-century, São Paulo elites depicted the northeast as a region that represented tradition, backwardness, and a mixed-race, nonwhite population, a foil to São Paulo's auto-constructed image of prosperity, modernity, and whiteness.[112] When northeastern migrants, mainly from Bahia but also Pernambuco, Ceará, and other states, came to São Paulo from the 1950s through 1970s, they met hostile stereotypes. To be called *baiano*, no matter where one might have really been from, was to be deemed racially nonwhite, violent, and unskilled.[113]

Describing the changing city center, Biáfora explained how the hub of upscale cinemas shifted south from the Centro, near the intersection of Avenida São João and Ipiranga, to the Paulista neighborhood, near Rua Augusta and Avenida Paulista—streets that continue to be bustling landmarks of business, art, and nightlife today—though in cyclical fashion, of a less genteel reputation than in years past. Although Avenida Paulista would be by today's standards very centrally located, Biáfora perceived this southward shift in the 1980s as a kind of forced flight into a more peripheral location. He also alluded to the presence of northeastern migrants and the "baianization" of the Centro for this shift, asserting that the area around Avenida São João became a "casbah," where one might fear getting mugged or assaulted.[114] In the taped recording of the interview, the interviewer, Inimá Simões, did not respond to

Figure 5.5. Facade of a former cinema in downtown São Paulo. Other cinemas of the Centro became parking lots, churches, or porn theaters, or continued to operate as cinemas. Author's photo, 2016.

this comment and quickly changed the subject. To Biáfora, the area that had once excluded moviegoers for not wearing ties had become a place of crime that alienated the respectable, white middle class.

Biáfora extended this criticism to gender norms and the habits of young women. For example, he described the way in which women dressed elegantly to go to the movies in the 1940s and 1950s, watching Hollywood movies with stars like Gene Tierney to imitate her manners, from how she opened doors to how she answered phones.[115] Biáfora compared the women of the 1940s to the "pot-smoking girls" who idolized and mimicked the bohemian styles and unruly, curly hair of singer Maria Bethania.[116] While Gene Tierney was a North American and a Hollywood movie star, Maria Bethania is a singer originally from the northeast of Brazil, and sister of the musician Caetano Veloso. They were both part of the same 1970s countercultural rock movement, called *tropicália*, that fused Brazilian rhythms with experiments in psychedelic rock.[117] While Maria Bethania and Caetano Veloso might not have been lumped together in the same racial or class category as the northeastern migrants who worked in São Paulo's factories, to Biáfora, the countercultural musicians were a similar symbol of São Paulo's cultural decadence. Complaining that women in São Paulo looked and behaved like 1970s hippies, à la Maria Bethania, instead of like 1940s Hollywood star Gene Tierney, shows how Biáfora measured social change through shifting gender norms. His comments demonstrate a general wariness of countercultural youth culture, tinged with colonialist undertones that contrasted the North American whiteness of Hollywood with nonconformist Brazilian music.

While Ferreira's tales of sex and violence in old movie theaters are, by his own admission, "folklore," Néstor Perlongher and other ethnographers have studied the rituals and practices associated with sexual activity in São Paulo's old movie theaters. These ethnographies have revealed that there was great variation in who frequented the Centro's movie theaters and for what purposes. In his 1987 ethnography of *michês*, or male sex workers who utilize markers of masculinity to cater to clients seeking homosex, Perlongher finds that some of the old cinemas of Cinelândia were the locales for new practices of public sex and sex work.[118] Perlongher remarks on the contrast between the formerly opulent cinemas versus their use in the 1980s. For example, he describes the Palácio do Cinema as "an old building, decrepit, vestige of an era in which the Avenida Rio Branco maintained a certain chic aura" that in the 1980s was used as a "cinema de *pegação*," or gathering place for public sexual activity. One informant mixed rumor with observation, commenting that at the Palácio do Cinema, "One killed a guy, I don't know where, one guy robbed another or something like that."[119] Other cinemas, however, like the Ártico or the cinema Lira, fostered "romantic" encounters in which clients and sex workers only met in the cinema as part of a more traditionally defined date before engaging in sex in a different location.

Another ethnography of movie theaters in the 1990s points out that, far from a monolithic zone of so-called illicit activity, the Centro's movie theaters presented a wide spectrum of social practices. While stereotypes of the Centro's movie theaters focused on the exhibition of pornography, a 1996 ethnography found twelve "traditional" cinemas that featured mainstream, nonerotic films and twenty-two cinemas that exhibited pornographic films. In addition, heterosexual and homosexual encounters and sex work existed alongside more "respectable" forms of dating and romance. For example, the Cine Metrópole, inside the Galeria Metrópole (a "galería" is a type of open-air shopping mall), featured mainstream nonerotic films. Depending on the time of day, the audience might include families and children who sat in the middle and on the sides of the theater or heterosexual couples sitting toward the back. During some sessions, the last rows of the theater might sit empty, with the last row a space for men seeking rapid homosexual encounters called *brincadeiras* or "games." Leaving the next seat open functioned as an invitation; taking a seat next to another man signified an acceptance of this invitation, and the space behind the last row of chairs and the wall was used for sex.[120]

The rituals of dating and romance in late twentieth-century movie theaters certainly diversified and expanded from the mid-century. While this patchwork of observations from moviegoers, filmmakers, and writers varied in perspective, they channeled their perceptions of the city's transformations through the cavernous movie theaters that were relics of a bygone age. They remembered movie theaters as places of respectable romance, but by the late twentieth century, in their minds, they had become places of disrepute. At times their stories were more "folklore" or urban legend, but these sources saw movie theaters as vessels for their memories of the city and bellwethers of how sexual norms had shifted over time.

Movie theaters were tangible, physical structures that bore witness to the dramatic shifts in politics and society from the mid- to late twentieth century. In the memories of moviegoers, the titanic movie theaters of São Paulo's historic Centro represented the city at its height and at its nadir. Whereas the idealized and chaste "romance" of the mid-century was an innocent rite of passage, the "hooking up" of the 1970s was reflective of the deterioration of family and safety. While this narrative tells a linear story of decay and decline, shades of dark and light existed across these decades. The contrast between the glamorous Cinelândia of the 1940s and that of the dilapidated 1970s and 1980s represented a dramatic extreme that captured the imaginations of paulistanos who remembered the city fondly for what it was versus what it had become. The longing for Cinelândia was a nostalgia for an idealized past that was marked by sexual respectability and conservative gender norms—a vision of "simpler" and more constrained times. As they had in the early twentieth century, movie theaters functioned as a powerful vessel for these visions of social change, norms of gender and sexuality, and their role in fashioning the urban landscape. The late twentieth century in this way mirrors the early twentieth, in focusing on gender and sexual practices as a key building block of the city's moral status.

CONCLUSION

SEDUCTIONS IN THE STREET AND GENDERED VISIONS OF URBAN LIFE

The finale of Suzana Amaral's film *The Hour of the Star* (*A Hora da Estrela*, 1985) features a dreamlike sequence in which the main protagonist imagines a Hollywood ending, but only meets with disappointment and dashed dreams. An adaptation of a novella by the famed Brazilian writer Clarice Lispector, *The Hour of the Star* centers on Macabéa, a woman from the Brazilian northeast trying to make her way in 1980s São Paulo, which by then had a population of over thirteen million, the largest city in South America. Young and romantic, Macabéa stands in contrast to her vast and industrial surroundings. She becomes enamored by men crowded against her in the subway. She smiles shyly at her boyfriend as they walk through the city, wandering through the manicured but deteriorated Parque da Luz to have their picture taken. She criss-crosses vast iron bridges over train tracks to arrive at work. However, throughout the film, her coworkers and roommates reflect the regionalist xenophobia of the time period, and they criticize her for being dirty, uncivilized, and largely out of step with city life. The film highlights this by portraying Macabéa in the act of eating in "inappropriate" situations—consuming sandwiches at work and smearing oil on her typed pages, chewing on a chicken drumstick while sitting on a chamber pot in her bedroom at night. At the end of the film, she has lost her job, her boyfriend, and has failed to find her place in the foreboding city. In the final scene, which could ambiguously be either

Macabéa's dream or her reality, she is wearing a frilly blue dress reminiscent of a nostalgic and bygone era, a shift from her typical drab clothing. When she sees a white man in a suit coming out of an expensive car, she runs to this specter of romantic fulfillment and social ascension. Shot in slow motion, the scene gestures to Macabéa's dreams of a Hollywood-style ending that would ensconce her firmly in love, respectability, and prosperity. But instead, Macabéa is hit by a car, and the final shot is of her lying in the street.

Shocking and sad, the finale of *The Hour of the Star* provides pointed commentary on Macabéa's dreams and wishes for her life in the city. While she seeks love and protection, she finds only disappointment and violence. The fateful and violent end of *The Hour of the Star* recalls the scamp-like figures in *Fragments of Life*, the 1931 film discussed in chapter 2. The darkly comic film followed the petty crimes and subterfuges of two men who eschewed the roles accorded to their gender, choosing each other's company and life on the streets instead of acting as paternal father, prosperous husband, or dutiful son in a patriarchal home. At the end of the film, the main character dies in prison, despite his vow of redemption. As that film characterized São Paulo as a city whose rapid growth "consumes its own citizens," so does *The Hour of the Star* see Macabéa as a victim of a vast and impregnable city. The films are separated by more than fifty years, and while *The Hour of the Star* hints at a nostalgic perspective of São Paulo through the eyes of the naive Macabéa, *Fragments of Life* looks to the murky future of São Paulo through the perspective of the doomed scamp. Yet both can be seen as odd bookends for the hopes, dreams, and disappointments associated with urban life and the ways in which it is entangled with gender, romance, and propriety.

Contrast these to the story of the powerfully seductive, moviegoing woman in the city streets of Maria Eugenia's Celso's short story "Photogenica"—a popularized term for possessing an aesthetic appearance apt for the silver screen. Celso, born to an elite family of rural Minas Gerais, was a poet, author, and early suffragist. Her short story provides humorous commentary on a moviegoing woman with dreams of becoming a "vamp," or exotic, modern seductress of Hollywood films. The story begins when the anonymous narrator, whose gender is ambiguous, stops in the middle of the street, "stunned from the elegance" of a woman's "irresistible smile" and "indescribable" clothes. The stunning woman describes how she goes to the movies as a serious and true disciple of cinema, called to Hollywood stardom as a "vocation, truly a vocation." As an exhibition of her prowess, she purposefully seduces a man passing by: "She gave a smile so alluring towards an unsuspecting passer-by that the bewildered man began to walk haphazardly, only stopping confused upon reaching the edge of the sidewalk a few meters away." In response, she remarks, "See how that fool is eating me with his eyes. . . . He little suspects that it's a future Nita Naldi that he dares to 'cook.'" Although Celso pokes fun at the vamp-like woman who thinks of cinema as a "vocation," she also highlights that the behaviors, attitudes, and aesthetics of cinema created new gender dynamics in which women took on the role of seducer. In the story, the man is the unsuspecting victim whose solo ramble in a city street puts him in danger. Celso's story is a farce, and by the numerous accounts of bolinas who sexually harassed women in movie theaters, the figure of the vamp did not dramatically reverse the gender dynamics of public sexual aggression. However, Celso's story presents a vision of modern life in which these dynamics are possible, an imagined city in which women, through the social habits and images associated with cinema, challenge the traditional order.

Are women the consumed or the consuming in these imaginings of the city? Is the city a vast industrial monster that cannibalizes its own citizens when they are not modern, industrious, and heteronormative? Or is the city a playground of spectacles that feeds the hunger of the vamps, movie-struck girls, melindrosas, and dandies who seek pleasure in its spaces of consumption and leisure? Alternatively, is the city a place of potential, a cosmopolitan node among other global metropoles that, with some regulation, might realize the dream of order, progress, and modernity in Brazil? *In the Darkness of the Cinema* finds that the city has represented this full spectrum of hope and fear—the dark and the light and many shades between—in both real and symbolic ways. A salient theme throughout these contrasting visions was the role that women, gender, and sexuality played in forming the modern city. Whether individuals, especially women, could walk the fine line between appearing modern while upholding certain traditions of gender relations was key to defining what urban life might portend in Brazil.

In the early twentieth century, the darkness of the cinema sparked the imagination of many Brazilians, from politicians and municipal officials to artists, intellectuals, filmmakers, and moviegoers. Artists and intellectuals depicted the movie theater as a place where family relationships would break down, where men went to cheat on their wives, or where daughters were sexually assaulted by strangers. They also depicted the city as intertwined with the fate of the melindrosa and other modern girls whose habits ranged from innocent to dangerous. Filmmakers used the medium of cinema to imagine how Brazilian men, women, and family relations might evolve in urban environments while maintaining patriarchal and heteronormative hierarchies. Film intellectuals and state legislators in São Paulo incorporated medical discourse to regulate the built spaces of movie theaters and define establishments and sections that were "appropriate for senhoras." Moviegoers used the movie theater and moviegoing habits to assert their own and others' status in São Paulo, navigating the intersections of gender, class, and race to find their place in a dynamic society. The themes that emerged in the 1920s persisted into the late twentieth century. By the 1980s, in a period of economic dissipation, moviegoers in São Paulo looked to mid-century moviegoing as a symbol of the city's promise, of a time and space that represented the full potential of urban life, gendered propriety, and middle-class respectability. They reflected the desires of the 1920s for what moviegoing and urbanization might mean for Brazil, but from the perspective of nostalgic longing for what the city might have been, rather than what it had become.

The time period of much of this book is concurrent with prodigious shifts in urbanization and urban reform in Brazil. Massive demographic change in the post-abolition period encouraged immigration to rural Brazil. Economic shifts resulted in populations moving from rural to urban areas. The Old Republic embarked on the top-down reorganizing of cities according to Haussmanian ideals of aesthetic and social order. With the adoption of eugenics, urban reformers strove for cities that would engineer a superior Brazilian population and contain poor people and people of color. Geographers and urban historians have extensively documented the visible wounds that such methods of control inflicted on the landscape of Brazilian cities, as well as the popular resistance and community building that existed in tandem with them.

By focusing on gender and sexual morality, this book adds a narrative thread to Brazil's complex picture of urbanization. I argue that gender, too, was a fundamental frame of reference for the building of Brazilian cities, both physically and symbolically. While historians have examined the role of gender ideology in constructions of urban Brazil, and in women's labor, sex work, motherhood, and honor, *In the Darkness of the Cinema* focuses on an arena that brought forth new images of women's sexuality—seductive, frivolous, and both desirable and desiring. In so doing, the book sheds light on understudied aspects of femininity and new feminine identities, as well as how these women negotiated their place in Brazil's urban hierarchies. Where women sat in movie theaters, how they circulated through the city from home to work to cinema, whom they met in the streets—these were key questions for the meanings of urbanization. The fate of Brazilian cities, according to filmmakers, moviegoers, and commentators, could be determined by these quotidian interactions. Although ephemeral, these urban behaviors were deemed to have such importance because of the deeply rooted societal fixation on women's sexual morality, a fixation that permeated the realms of artistic, cinematic, architectural, and cultural production. This preoccupation persisted into the late twentieth century, when elderly paulistanos deplored the decadence of the city, as evidenced and measured by the collapse of gender and sexual norms.

The novelty of women's participation in public life was less shocking by the mid-century. During the Vargas years, or the political era associated with the authoritarian president Getúlio Vargas (1930–1954), the federal government advanced an image of a strong Brazilian nation that included women as productive citizens. Women were workers who were essential to industrial and economic growth, and they were mothers who were key to the scientific raising of children and moral buttress of family life—with a patriarchal state as the true head of household. Monumental shifts in gender relations occurred in political participation and gender roles in this time period, including women's right to vote in 1932, which became compulsory (though still limited) for men and women by 1945. While women were included in visions of the idealized mid-century Brazilian nation, historians like Susan Besse have shown how they were still contained in the spheres and roles accorded to their gender.

In the Darkness of the Cinema explores a window of time preceding the Vargas era, one in which commentators, both men and women, began to reconcile the idea of women as consuming and desiring individuals, visibly and socially active in public spaces. The objective of this book has not been to elucidate direct connections between women's leisure and consumption and the organized political movements for women's civic rights in the twentieth century. Rather, it has been to emphasize the history of women's participation in film and leisure culture as inherently valuable to the formation of modern Brazil. Though separate from the seats of federal power and popular political movements that propelled change before and during the Vargas era, artists and cultural producers imagined and depicted a new Brazilian society that included women and what they perceived as modern gender roles. The arena in which these roles were at play was not the traditional realm of organized politics, but the social spaces of the cinema and other sites of leisure. They debated and vacillated on what these shifts meant for their cities, and struggled with the image of women as desiring subjects, which was contradictory to traditional standards of femininity. Yet women's presence in the city was also a foregone conclusion—there was no putting Pandora back in the box. Rather than a vision of the modern city in which women were cloistered in private spaces, instead, a panoply of voices sought to rationalize women's presence in public, even as they also voiced their anxieties about it.

While more casual and disjointed than state-sponsored attempts at urban reform, the spread of movie theaters and moviegoing was swept up and entangled with these other processes. Movie theaters, sometimes clustered in multiples on a block in the city center, or standing as a monumental hub in a suburb, changed the landscape of Brazilian cities. Cinema as a medium allowed for new visions of urban life. As a space of sociability, it fostered new rituals of dating and romance, and was a source for the gossip that brewed in a multicultural, urban population. Within cinema—this arena that sparked so much fascination and intrigue—the question of women's place was paramount. The breadth of this discussion did not just reach across the vast realm of film culture, including film intellectuals, filmmakers, exhibitors, and moviegoers, but also extended into tangential sectors such as the growing sector of public health officials, literary circles, modernist artists, and cartoonists.

By analyzing a vast panoply of sources across multiple sectors of the Brazilian population, *In the Darkness of the Cinema* offers a rumination, a historical walking tour, on images of urban space from a gendered perspective. There were many ways to be modern, and these identities existed along a spectrum of dark and light. Commentators did not reach any consensus as to whether modern, urban life held more promise or threat, but many agreed that women and sexual morality were an essential litmus test to define it. Their anxieties and hopes had effects for both the imagined and lived city—what it was supposed to become and what it was remembered to be. The meanings of private and public, rural and urban, as well as racial, gendered, and class schisms, came to the fore in debates over women's relationship to cinema. Through the movie theater, we see how understandings of sexual respectability were central, not just to women's social status, but to the hopes and dreams for urbanization in Brazil.

NOTES

Introduction: A Night Out at the Movies

1. The following section narrates "one night" at a movie theater, but culls from various sources about moviegoing in order to reconstruct the likely actions that could occur in one night.

2. Emprezas Cinematográficas Reunidas, "Cine Republica—Duas Guardas de Ferro," April 1, 1924, Petition to Municipal Government, Arquivo Histórico de São Paulo (hereafter abbreviated as AHSP), Cinemas 1, processo 0.053.673-24.

3. Simões, *Salas de cinema em São Paulo*, 21.

4. Adhemar Gonzaga, "Impressões de New York," *Cinearte*, August 24, 1927.

5. On the transformation of samba from popular music with Afro-Brazilian roots to a "national rhythm" of Brazil, see the classic text Vianna, *Mystery of Samba*. Also on the role of music in nation-building, see McCann, *Hello, Hello Brazil*; and on the interplay of samba and samba musicians in social and racial hierarchies of Brazil, see Hertzman, *Making Samba*.

6. J. Canuto, "Tudo o que eu disse . . . ," song lyrics in Cinema República program "O Vaqueiro," June 29, 1926, Cinemateca Brasileira São Paulo.

7. "O Perfume da Aristocracia," Ambra, advertisement, Cine-Teatro República program, n.d., Cinemateca Brasileira São Paulo, D1981/28.

8. Gabus Mendes, "O círculo do matrimonio—o que se exibe em São Paulo," *Para Todos*, May 16, 1925, p. 12.

9. Mendes, "O círculo do matrimonio," 12.

10. J. Canuto, "Peixe-Frito," in Cine República program, "Noiva da Tempestade," September 4, 1926, Cinemateca Brasileira, D1481-33. This is the author's translation, though the English translation does not do justice to the clever rhyming of the "ão" sounds in the song.

11. "O Cinema ás Claras e ás Escuras" in *Vida Doméstica*, July 1925, p. 16.

12. On the idea of "category drift" and the ways in which people shifted in legal and social status in Brazil, see Beattie, *Punishment in Paradise*.

13. On shifting definitions of working and middle-class peoples in the early twentieth century, with particular attention to the city of São Paulo, see Saes, *Classe média e sistema político*; Peixoto-Mehrtens, *Urban Space and National Identity*; Weinstein, *Color of Modernity*.

14. Lesser, *Immigration, Ethnicity*, 62.

15. Andrews, *Blacks & Whites in São Paulo*, 21.

16. On an example of a neighborhood that reflects various ethnic communities, see the description of Bom Retiro in the introduction of Lesser, *Negotiating National Identity*. Also on Black Brazilians making space in São Paulo, see Butler, *Freedoms Given, Freedoms Won*; Andrews, *Blacks and Whites in São Paulo*.

17. On early movements for women's rights, see Hahner, *Emancipating the Female Sex*.

18. For an analysis of the republican era in the state of São Paulo, see Woodard, *A Place in Politics*. Bethell, *Brazil*.

19. As two examples of republican efforts for urban reform in Rio de Janeiro, among a larger historiography to be explored in chapter 3, see Chazkel, *Laws of Chance*. Meade, *"Civilizing" Rio*; Benchimol, *Pereira Passos*.

20. Maluf and Mott, "Recônditos do mundo feminino."

21. See, for example, the Afro-Brazilian female street vendors in Rio de Janeiro in Acerbi, *Street Occupations*, 28–30.

22. On the global phenomenon of the "modern girl," see Weinbaum et al., *Modern Girl Around the World*. Specifically for the "chica moderna" and the cultural significance of white-collar women in Mexico City, see Hershfield, *Imagining La Chica Moderna*. In Brazil, the flapper was called the "melindrosa," a figure analyzed in Conde, *Consuming Visions*, and Beatriz Resende, "A volta de Mademoiselle Cinema" in Costallat, *Mademoiselle Cinema*.

23. On sound and femininity, see Ehrick, *Radio and the Gendered Soundscape*; Ma, *Sounding the Modern Woman*.

24. Graham, *House and Street*.

25. Besse, *Restructuring Patriarchy*, Kindle ed., chap. 6, location 3021 of 7612.

26. Besse, *Restructuring Patriarchy*, Kindle ed., chap. 6, location 2760 of 7612.

27. Siblings, for example, can identify as different races based on their skin tone and appearance. For the dynamics of colorism and affective relationships within contemporary Brazilian families, see Hordge-Freeman, *Color of Love*.

28. On the concept of "deflowering" and the importance of virginity to demonstrate sexual chastity, see Abreu Esteves, *Meninas perdidas*.

29. On masculinity and honor, see Beattie, *Tribute of Blood*. Braga-Pinto, "Journalists, Capoeiras."

30. Caulfield, *In Defense of Honor*.

31. Caulfield, *In Defense of Honor*, 73.

32. Matta, *Casa e a rua*.

33. Graham, *House and Street*; Dias, *Power and Everyday Life*. The concept of public as masculine and private as feminine is not a concept unique to Brazil, and histories of working women in Latin America have questioned the validity of such divisions from the colonial era to the twentieth century. For example, see Porter, "'And That It Is Custom Makes It Law.'"

34. See the analysis of crônicas, and how modern technologies at the turn of the century influenced this literary style in Süssekind, *Cinematograph of Words*.

35. Rabinovitz, *For the Love of Pleasure*.

36. Souza, *Imagens do passado*, 45.

37. For a concise and helpful analysis of "public space" versus "public sphere" see Chattopadhyay, *Representing Calcutta*. For a thorough analysis of Habermas's definition of the "public sphere" and the treatment of it in Latin American historiography, see Piccato, "Public Sphere in Latin America."

38. See Vaughan, *Portrait of a Young Painter*, 12–13, and notes 22–29. Also see Aiala Levy's definition of "public" that rejects the more Habermasian definition in Levy, "Forging an Urban Public."

39. Peiss, *Cheap Amusements*. Also see Enstad, *Ladies of Labor*; Sewell, *Women and the Everyday City*.

40. Chalhoub, *Trabalho, lar e botequim*; Rago, *Do cabaré ao lar*.

41. On the intersections of gender and space, and how space can be constructed as gendered through social practice, see Massey, *Space, Place, and Gender*.

42. Lefebvre, *Production of Space*. Historian Jessica Ellen Sewell neatly delineates between the "imagined landscape" (how people imagine and understand a shared landscape), the "experienced landscape" (how they physically interact and experience it), and the "built landscape" (its physical and environmental spaces). The distinctions are loosely inspired by Henri Lefebvre's definitions of different types of spaces and processes for making meaning, but they are very accessible to an undergraduate audience. See Sewell, *Women and the Everyday City*, xiv–xvii.

43. On collaborative projects with female designers and architects that sought to create feminine aesthetics in urban Berlin, see Stratigakos, *A Women's Berlin*.

44. Sluis, *Deco Body, Deco City*.

45. Conde, *Consuming Visions*.

46. Rago, *Prazeres da noite*. Though not explicitly about gender, Nicolau Sevcenko's work is in this vein of exploring artistic expression, leisure, and the construction of São Paulo in the 1920s. Sevcenko, *Orfeu extático na metrópole*.

47. See, for example, Guy, *Sex and Danger in Buenos Aires*; Bliss, *Compromised Positions*; Caulfield, "Birth of Mangue."

48. Hansen, *Babel and Babylon*. Less theoretical than Hansen's work, there is also focus on film history as social history in the field of "new film history," Richard Maltby's calls for film historians to make film history "matter more" and to embed cinema into social and cultural history, often through audience studies and reception studies. See "Introduction" in Maltby, *Going to the Movies*, 3. For issues related to identity and moviegoing, especially in relation to race, class, gender, and space in the US, see Stewart, *Migrating to the Movies*; Klenotic, "Class Markers in the Mass Movie Audience"; Fuller-Seeley, *Hollywood in the Neighborhood*. Film historians in Latin America have been documenting the histories of exhibition for decades and also more recently (Souza, Gonzaga, Schvarzman, Mizala, Rubenstein). Also see the collection Kriger and Poppe, *Salas, negocios y públicos de cine*, which includes a questioning of the "newness" of new film history from the perspective of Latin America.

49. See, for example, British women's interpretation of the Hollywood film *Gone with the Wind* in Stacey, *Star Gazing*.

50. Vaughan, *Portrait of a Young Painter*.

51. On men performing different roles of masculinity in movie theaters, see Anne Rubenstein, "Theaters of Masculinity," in Macías-González and Rubenstein, *Masculinity and Sexuality in Modern Mexico*.

52. See the discussion on the variability of the "first" Brazilian film in Souza, "Os primórios do cinema no Brasil," 29. On the various filmmakers credited with the invention of motion pictures, see Roberta Pearson, "Early Cinema," in Nowell-Smith, *Oxford History of World Cinema*, 13.

53. Araújo, *Bela época do cinema brasileiro*.

54. Thompson, *Exporting Entertainment*.

55. Johnson, *Film Industry in Brazil*, 34. For data on Hollywood's market share around the world, as well as how Hollywood studios adapted films to cater to foreign audiences, see Vasey, *World According to Hollywood*.

56. Souza, "Os primórios do cinema no Brasil," 44.

57. On early forms of exhibition in Porto Alegre and Rio Grande do Sul, see Trusz, *Entre lanternas mágicas e cinematógrafos*. Also Alice Dubina Trusz, "A produção cinematográfica no Rio Grande do Sul," and Glênio Póvoas, "O cinema no Rio Grande do Sul," in Ramos and Schvarzman, *Nova história do cinema brasileiro I*.

58. Guerreiro to Nil, "Modest but Sincere Admirer," July 2, 1932.

59. Souza, *Imagens do passado*.

60. On this range of movie theaters in Rio de Janeiro, see Gonzaga, *Palácios e poeiras*. On the early exhibition circuit in São Paulo, see Barro, *A primeira sessão de cinema*; Galvão, *Crônica do cinema paulistano*.

61. On theaters in São Paulo in a slightly earlier time period, see Levy, "Forging an Urban Public."

62. Averages in 1927 for factory workers in textile, flour, glass, and shoe factories, as well as breweries, are found in Wolfe, *Working Women, Working Men*, 47, table 2.2, and the cost of "half-price" tickets is listed in cinema advertisements on Wednesday, November 9, 1927, in *Estado de S. Paulo*, pp. 18–19. In the 1920s the cost of living and foodstuffs increased dramatically, and wages did not keep pace. In addition, George Reid Andrews details the wage and career differences between Black and white workers. Andrews, *Blacks & Whites in São Paulo*. Molly Ball also details the variations of wages according to ethnicity, and across different factories and sectors, in *Navigating Life and Work in Old Republic São Paulo*. Because of this variation and volatility, 1927 cannot serve as truly representative of the dynamics of purchasing power in this decade. However, I've chosen 1927 as a snapshot of approximate wages and ticket prices because it follows the establishment of several major movie "palaces" and an uptick in movie theaters overall in São Paulo. That year also affords the opportunity to compare the price of a ticket to the price of a meal at the Women's Restaurant, which in the same year, fixed prices at 2$000 for a full lunch and $600 for an "affordable soup"—roughly within the same range as full-price and balcony tickets—considering these prices to be an accessible daily lunch fee for women working as shopgirls. On the women's restaurant, see Suk, "'Only the Fragile Sex Admitted.'"

63. Men earned consistently more than women, one and a half times as much to twice as much, and could be a source for paying for leisure and entertainment. At the same time that women and girls were subject to these structures of dependency, families counted on women and girls to contribute their meager salaries to the household income. Ball, *Navigating Life and Work*, 109. On dating for movie tickets, see, for example, Pepe's offer of buying a movie ticket for Octavia on "girls' night" in Galvão, *Industrial Park*, 17. On dating and informal sex work as a way to pay for leisure and consumption in New York, see Peiss, *Cheap Amusements*.

64. Cinema advertisements, November 9, 1927, *Estado de S. Paulo*, 18–19.

65. Besse, *Restructuring Patriarchy*, Kindle ed., chap. 1, location 586 of 7612.

66. On early film intellectuals and magazines, see Xavier, *Sétima arte, um culto moderno*. Lucas, "Cinearte."

67. See definition of *críticos* as intellectuals whose approach was more akin to literary intellectuals than to film "reviewers" in Schvarzman, "Ir ao cinema em São Paulo nos anos 20," 156. For a similar discussion in the US context, Schvarzman references Koszarski, *An Evening's Entertainment*.

68. For more extended discussion of modernism in Rio de Janeiro versus São Paulo, see Denis, *Modernity in Black and White*; Conde and Shaw, "Towards an Alternative 1922."

69. See article on the debut of sound film in São Paulo in *Cinearte*, April 4, 1929, p. 3.

70. On the US, see Singer, *Melodrama and Modernity*. For a study of early, pre-Soviet Russian cinema, see Tsivian, *Early Cinema in Russia*. For a brief introduction to the theme of modernity in Latin American cinemas, see López, "Early Cinema and Modernity in Latin America."

71. Ana M. López, "'A Train of Shadows': Early Cinema and Modernity in Latin America," in Schelling, *Through the Kaleidoscope*.

72. Serna, *Making Cinelandia*.
73. Süssekind, *Cinematograph of Words*; Wells, *Media Laboratories*.
74. Canclini and Rosaldo, *Hybrid Cultures*.
75. Mizala, *Modernity at the Movies*.
76. See this theory explained in Saliba, *Cinema contra cinema*.
77. Simis, *Estado e cinema no Brasil*, 26.
78. Campelo, "Jonathas Serrano."
79. Quoted in Morettin, "Cinema educativo," 15.
80. Robert Stam refers to the whitening of Brazilian cinema as the "structuring absence" of Afro-Brazilians. Stam, *Tropical Multiculturalism*, 63–65.
81. Stamp, *Movie-Struck Girls*; Hallett, *Go West, Young Women!*
82. Serna, *Making Cinelandia*; Purcell, ¡De película! On US cultural imperialism in later decades, see Tota, *O imperialismo sedutor*.
83. One recent sociological examination of colorism and anti-Blackness in contemporary Brazil and Latin America is Telles, *Pigmentocracies*.
84. Throughout the book, I primarily use the terms Black and Afro-Brazilian as an approximation for the term *negro* in Brazil. Socially and colloquially throughout the twentieth century, Brazilians have used a variety of terms to describe people of different races and phenotypes. In the national census, *preto* or the color "black" refers to dark-skinned Black individuals, while *pardo* refers to mixed-race brown or light-skinned Black individuals. See Nobles, *Shades of Citizenship*. But these official terms are only two of many colloquially used terms to describe people with different skin tones, hair textures, and varying degrees of identification with Blackness. And while colorism runs deep, so that lighter-skinned Black Brazilians find greater educational and economic advantages in contemporary Brazilian society than darker-skinned individuals (see Telles, *Pigmentocracies*), scholars have explored how the variety of these terms can obscure the shared experiences of racism and fracture identification with Blackness within the Black community. Carneiro, *Racismo, sexismo*. Also see Adelia Romo's explanation for using the term "Black" to refer to *preto* and *pardo* populations in Bahia in Romo, *Brazil's Living Museum*, 162n8.
85. Skidmore, *Black into White*.
86. Stepan, *The Hour of Eugenics*; Dávila, *Diploma of Whiteness*.
87. On the reception of jazz and the Charleston in the Black press, see Seigel, *Uneven Encounters*. Gomes and Domingues, *Da nitidez e invisibilidade*. Jason Borge also underscores the combination of attraction and fear that Latin American intellectuals felt for jazz music. Borge, *Tropical Riffs*.
88. Xavier, *Sétima arte, um culto moderno*, 186.
89. Studlar, *This Mad Masquerade*; Bernstein and Studlar, *Visions of the East*.
90. On the spectacle and condemnation of mixed-race coupling, see Courtney, *Hollywood Fantasies of Miscegenation*.
91. "Apresentação," *Cinearte*, in *Álbum de 1928*, special issue, January 1928.
92. See note 48 for references on "new film history." See the chapters on early cinema, which touch on both production and exhibition, in Ramos and Schvarzman, *Nova história do cinema brasileiro I*.

Chapter 1. Melindrosas and Movie-Struck Girls in Brazilian Print Culture

1. "Civilização e cinemas," *Gazeta de Notícias*, no. 210 (July 29, 1913): 1. My thanks to Rielle Navitski for sharing this material with me.

2. "Civilização e cinemas," 1.
3. "Civilização e cinemas," 1.
4. "Civilização e cinemas," 1.
5. Ilka Stern Cohen, "Diversificação e Segmentação dos Impressos," in Martins and Luca, *História da imprensa no Brasil*, 107.
6. Various scholars have produced in-depth analyses of the São Paulo Black press, including Andrews, *Blacks & Whites in São Paulo*; Butler, *Freedoms Given, Freedoms Won*; Alberto, *Terms of Inclusion*.
7. For a brief survey of female archetypes in workers' publications, see Martins and Matos, "Meio anjo—meio demônio."
8. Glaucia, *Os direitos das mulheres*, 50.
9. Mme. X, "A origem da melindrosa," in *Para Todos*, no. 139, August 13, 1921.
10. Rago, *Do cabaré ao lar*, 117.
11. Denis, *Modernity in Black and White*; Conde, *Consuming Visions*.
12. Resende, "Melindrosa e almofadinha," 221.
13. Besse, *Restructuring Patriarchy*, Kindle ed., chap. 5, location 2480 of 7612, table 7. Data from Brazil, Diretoria Geral de Estatística, *Recenseamento . . . 1920*, vol. 4, part 4, xxii–xiii.
14. Owensby, *Intimate Ironies*, 58.
15. Besse, *Restructuring Patriarchy*, Kindle ed., chap. 1, location 656 of 7612.
16. Weinbaum et al., *Modern Girl Around the World*.
17. Weinbaum et al., *Modern Girl Around the World*, 9.
18. Weinbaum et al., *Modern Girl Around the World*, 8.
19. Conde, "Negotiating Visions of Modernity," and a revision of this article appears as "Consuming Visions: Female Stars, the Melindrosa and Desires for a Brazilian Film Industry," in Bergfelder, Shaw, and Vieira, *Stars and Stardom in Brazilian Cinema*. While Conde refers to the melindrosa as the "new woman" across her work on the topic, I prefer the translation of "modern girl," in keeping with the distinctions between consumption-oriented "modern girl" versus the more diffuse "new woman" outlined by Weinbaum et al.
20. Rago, *Do cabaré ao lar*, 75. See also Suann Caulfield's analysis of "modern daughters" and implications of public leisure habits on perceptions of gendered honor in *In Defense of Honor*, 127–28.
21. Besse, *Restructuring Patriarchy*, Kindle ed., chap. 1, location 602 of 7612.
22. Rago, *Prazeres da noite*, 75.
23. Larissa Pinheiro finds oft-repeated themes of gender role inversion and the social effects of the melindrosa's androgyny and sexuality (i.e., the emasculation of male breadwinners and the commercialization of romantic relationships). Pinheiro, "Melindrosas e almofadinhas de J. Carlos."
24. Maluf and Mott, "Recônditos do Mundo Feminino."
25. Weinbaum et al., *Modern Girl Around the World*, Kindle ed., chap. 1, subheading "Visual Economies," location 362 of 7471.
26. These debates were certainly not limited to Latin America, as seen in the chapters on the modern girl in South Africa, Okinoawa, India, etc., in Weinbaum et al., *Modern Girl Around the World*. See in particular Lynn Thomas's chapter, "The Modern Girl and Racial Respectability in 1930s South Africa."
27. Hershfield, *Imagining La Chica Moderna*.
28. Sluis, "Bataclanismo!"
29. Tossounian, *La Joven Moderna in Interwar Argentina*, 43. On the modern girl in Argentina, also see Ehrick, *Radio and the Gendered Soundscape*, chap. 1.

30. Beatriz Resende, "A volta de Mademoiselle Cinema," in Costallat, *Mademoiselle Cinema*, 18.
31. On eugenics in Latin America, see Stepan, *Hour of Eugenics*.
32. On public health initiatives to improve maternal health in the state of Bahia, see Otovo, *Progressive Mothers, Better Babies*. Also see Besse, *Restructuring Patriarchy*, chapter 4.
33. Caulfield, "Getting into Trouble."
34. Medeiros, "Melindrosas e almofadinhas," 105. Also on the construction of masculinity and gender in this time period, in the context of cultures and social practices related to homosexuality, see Green, *Beyond Carnival*.
35. Resende, "Melindrosa e almofadinha," 229.
36. Resende, "Melindrosa e almofadinha," 17, 20. Tania Regina Luca and Ana Luiza Martins also associate J. Carlos with the melindrosa. Luca and Martins, *Imprensa e cidade*, 47.
37. Rago, *Prazeres da noite*, 48. For the "classic" interpretation of Afro-Brazilian women and sexuality, see Gilberto Freyre's treatise on Brazilian society, which argues that Afro-Brazilian enslaved women, as wet nurses and sexual partners for their masters, were foundational to a mixed-race Brazilian culture. Freyre, *Masters and the Slaves*. Though it feeds the myth of racial democracy, it belies histories of violence and oppression that were also part of this structure.
38. Needell, *Tropical Belle Epoque*.
39. On social hierarchies of prostitution, considering factors of race and national origin, see Caulfield, "Birth of Mangue."
40. Rago, *Prazeres da noite*, 50.
41. Mme. X, "A origem da melindrosa," in *Para Todos*, no. 139, August 13, 1921.
42. Conde, *Consuming Visions*, Kindle ed., chap. 4, location 3236 of 4597.
43. João Escreve, "Uma Mlle. Cinema," *Para Todos*, no. 320, January 31, 1925, RC *Para Todos*, Cinemateca Brasileira São Paulo.
44. "La Garçonne," *O Clarim da Alvorada*, November 15, 1925, p. 1.
45. "Salão Brasil," advertisement, *O Progresso*, August 19, 1928, p. 4.
46. "A Beleza da Mulher," advertisement, *A Rua*, February 24, 1916, p. 4.
47. Sluis, *Deco Body, Deco City*.
48. Da Silva, "Teatro de revista," 23.
49. Barros, *Corações de chocolat*.
50. Seigel, *Uneven Encounters*, 110.
51. Enciclopédia Itaú Cultural de Arte e Cultura Brasileira, "Belmonte," http://enciclopedia.itaucultural.org.br/pessoa10131/belmonte, last updated November 5, 2018.
52. Stamp, *Movie-Struck Girls*.
53. Souza, *Imagens do Passado*, 57.
54. Besse, *Restructuring Patriarchy*, Kindle ed., chap. 1, location 552 of 7612, quoting Malheiros, "Abril"; "Os sátyros na penumbra," RF 10:110 (July 1923); "Julho," RF 12:134 (July 1925).
55. For analysis of one writer's memories of the Colmeia group, see Paulillo, *Tradição e modernidade*, 72–80.
56. Lellis Vieira, "Os noivinhos," *Correio Paulistano*, December 12, 1921, microfilm, Centro Cultural São Paulo (hereafter abbreviated as CCSP).
57. Vieira, "Os noivinhos."
58. Vieira, "Os noivinhos."
59. On the Pathé-Baby in Rio de Janeiro and amateur filmmaking, see Foster and Leão, "A presença da 'Pathé-Baby.'" On amateur filmmaking in Brazil, see Foster, "Cinema amador brasileiro."

60. Gonzaga, *Palácios e poeiras*, 132.

61. Advertisement, "Pathé-Baby," *Cinearte* 3, no. 147 (1928), reprinted in Foster and Leão, "A presença da 'Pathé-Baby,'" 345.

62. On women's participation in sports in early twentieth-century Rio de Janeiro, see Melo, "Mulheres em movimento."

63. Translated and quoted by Wolfe, *Working Women, Working Men*, 29, 216n103. The lyrics are from a popular street song that writer Antônio de Alcântara do Machado recorded and published as "Liras Paulistanas." Lira 1, *Antonio de Alcântara Machado: Obras*, vol. 1, 298–99.

64. I discuss Galvão's views on cinema more fully in chapter 4.

65. Patrícia Galvão, "Garotas Modernas," in Andrade and Galvão, *O homem do povo*, 4.

66. Patrícia Galvão, "Garotas Modernas," in Andrade and Galvão, *O homem do povo*, 4.

67. Allen and Gomery, *Film History*.

68. Teixeira Furlani and Galvão Ferraz, *Viva Pagu*, 39. On the racial and gender implications of the Fox Film beauty contest in Brazil, see Suk, "Beauty in Black and White?" For a collection of Pagú's work, see Teixeira Furlani, *Os cadernos de Pagu*.

69. "Alguem Que Pague o Cinema, o Chá, o Automovel . . . ," *Para Todos*, December 27, 1924, RC *Para Todos*, Cinemateca Brasileira São Paulo.

Chapter 2. Region and Race, Gender and Urbanization in Brazilian Silent Cinema

Epigraph: "O que se exhibe no Rio, o que se exhibe em São Paulo." *Para Todos*, May 23, 1925, RC *Para Todos*, Cinemateca Brasileira São Paulo.

1. Ismail Xavier has detailed this perspective of the magazine and how it espoused a nationalist rhetoric and sought to use cinema as a vehicle for eugenic ideals. Xavier, *Sétima arte, um culto moderno*, 176–204.

2. For a short list of similar films, see Morettin, "Dimensões históricas do documentário brasileiro." The term Gonzaga used to describe such films was "exploração," which can be translated as either exploration or exploitation. It's possible that Gonzaga intended this double meaning. However, I translate this term as "exploration," because films on the "discovery" of Brazilian regions were their own distinct genre, and I want to differentiate these films from the subgenre of early twentieth-century "exploitation films" in the US and Europe, which were more open about using the guise of educational ethnography to display graphic images of nudity and sex. On US exploitation films, see Eric Schaefer, *Bold! Daring! Shocking!* Exploitation films in Brazil were called "scientific films," discussed briefly in chapter 3.

3. Adhemar Gonzaga, *Cinearte* 8, no. 310 (February 3, 1932): 7. Also cited in Schvarzman, *Humberto Mauro*, 33.

4. Besse, *Restructuring Patriarchy*, Kindle ed., chap. 1, location 434 of 7612.

5. See Navitski's analysis of regional films in Navitski, *Public Spectacles of Violence*, 208–10.

6. Lucas, "Cinearte," 63.

7. Lucas, "Cinearte," 68.

8. Braga, Coelho, and David, "Mulheres em revista," 6.

9. Salles Gomes, *Humberto Mauro*, 303.

10. On the appearance of racism and the influence of eugenic thought in early Brazilian film intellectual circles, particularly in the film magazine *Cinearte*, see Salles Gomes, *Humberto Mauro*, 310. Xavier, *Sétima arte, um culto moderno*, 186; Bicalho, "Art of Seduction," 24–25; Schvarzman, *Humberto Mauro*, chap. 1, 34–35 of 399.

11. Salles Gomes, *Humberto Mauro*, 304–5.

12. Salles Gomes, *Humberto Mauro*, 295–354; Xavier, *Sétima arte, um culto moderno*, 167–97.
13. Lucas, "Cinearte."
14. Salles Gomes, *Humberto Mauro*.
15. Autran, "A noção de 'ciclo regional.'"
16. Filho, *A utopia provinciana*.
17. Araújo, "O cinema em Pernambuco," 33, 71–76.
18. On nation-building via music, radio, and telegraphs, see McCann, *Hello, Hello Brazil*; Diacon, *Stringing Together a Nation*. Conde makes this link explicit in her examination of the Rondon Commission's use of photography and film in Conde, *Foundational Films*, part 3, "The Rondon Commission." On the interaction between musicians across Latin America for the development of a Latin American identity, see Palomino, *Invention of Latin American Music*.
19. Conde, *Foundational Films*.
20. On "classic" interpretations of Brazilian national cinema and its relationship to Hollywood imperialism, see Salles Gomes, *Cinema*; Xavier, *Allegories of Underdevelopment*; Bernadet, *Historiografia clássica*. See chap. 1 of Conde, *Foundational Films*, for an overview of this historiography through the lens of Brazilian cinema as a tool of nation-building in capitalist context.
21. One classic tome is Euclides da Cunha's turn-of-the-century account of the War of Canudos. Cunha, *Os sertões*.
22. On *Santa* and the virgin/whore dichotomy in Mexican national cinema, see Hershfield, *Mexican Cinema/Mexican Woman*, 13–14. On intellectual and public health debates on prostitution in Mexico, see Bliss, *Compromised Positions*.
23. Bicalho, "Art of Seduction," 21–33.
24. Araújo, "O cinema em Pernambuco," 33, 71–76.
25. See Blake, *Vigorous Core of Our Nationality*; Albuquerque, *A invenção do nordeste*. For northeastern regional identity in a global context, see Campbell, *Region Out of Place*.
26. Freyre, *Masters and the Slaves*. On intellectual debates on the public representation of regional identity through museums in the state of Bahia, see Romo, *Brazil's Living Museum*.
27. Weinstein, *Color of Modernity*.
28. da Cunha Filho, *Utópia Provinciana*.
29. On the representation of jangadeiros in a global film context, see Campbell, "Four Fishermen," 173–212.
30. See Figueirôa, *Cinema pernambucano*, 17; Holanda, *Documentário nordestino*, 97.
31. Weinbaum et al., *Modern Girl Around the World*, Kindle ed., location 270 of 7471.
32. Mulvey, "Visual Pleasure and Narrative Cinema," 6–18.
33. On the contrast between urban and rural spaces in Pernambucan fiction and documentary films, with the former's adulation of urban spaces, see Araújo, "Tensões, idealizações e ambiguidades."
34. On natural films and the showcasing of modernity in Latin America, and the symbolic meanings of trains and modes of transportation, see Ana M. López, "'A Train of Shadows': Early Cinema and Modernity in Latin America," in Schelling, *Through the Kaleidoscope*, 153–54. On natural films and the representation of urban modernity specific to Rio de Janeiro, see "Cinematic Vistas of Rio de Janeiro's Worldly Modernity," chapter 2 of Conde, *Foundational Films*.
35. da Cunha Filho, *Utópia Provinciana*, 34–35.
36. Holanda, *Documentário nordestino*, 96.
37. For further analysis of the character of Gerôncio and negative racial stereotyping, see Autran, "O personagem Negro no cinema silencioso brasileiro."

38. Stam, *Tropical Multiculturalism*.
39. Mario Mendonça ["M.M."], "A Filha do Advogado," *Cinearte*, no. 37 (November 10, 1926): 4.
40. Mendonça, "A Filha do Advogado," 4.
41. Mendonça, "A Filha do Advogado," 4.
42. Pedro Lima, "A Filha do Advogado," *A Selecta* 13, no. 16 (April 20, 1927).
43. Sheila Schvarzman points out that the film presents the perspectives of both filmmakers, so that while Gonzaga sought to portray fantasy and glamour, Mauro's camerawork and aesthetics, in a more documentary style, were constantly undercutting Mauro's vision. Schvarzman, *Humberto Mauro*, chap. 1, p. 69 of 399.
44. The Delegation of Customs and Games—Cabinet of Investigations, Theater and Film Censorship. Schvarzman, *Humberto Mauro*, chap. 1, p. 70 of 399, referring to Adhemar Gonzaga, *50 anos de Cinédia* (Record, 1987), 37.
45. Mulvey, "Visual Pleasure and Narrative Cinema," 6–18.
46. Shelley Stamp points out that, contrary to the moralizers' wishes, female moviegoers in the US enjoyed the films about sexual seduction that were supposed to frighten them. Stamp, *Movie-Struck Girls*.
47. Early feminist film theorists, writing from the framework of semiotics and psychoanalysis, addressed these representations in classical Hollywood cinema. See Mulvey, "Visual Pleasure and Narrative Cinema," 6–18; Silverman, *Acoustic Mirror*; Doane, *Desire to Desire*. Also see Bean and Negra, *Feminist Reader in Early Cinema*, for feminist film analyses in global context.
48. Schvarzman, *Humberto Mauro*, chap. 1, 69 of 399.
49. On bicycles in turn-of-the-century Mexico, see William Beezley, *Judas at the Jockey Club*.
50. Schvarzman, *Humberto Mauro*, chap. 1, 48 of 399.
51. On the representation of bucolic nature in Humberto Mauro's film *Brasa Dormida*, see Schvarzman, *Humberto Mauro*, chap. 1, 47 of 399.
52. "*Lábios sem Beijos*—A Tela em Revista," *Cinearte*, no. 253 (December 5, 1930): 28.
53. "*Lábios sem Beijos*," *Cinearte*, no. 253 (December 5, 1930): 28.
54. Filmografia Brasileira—Cinemateca Brasileira, "Lábios sem beijos."
55. Ângela Maria de Castro Gomes, "Essa gente do Rio," 62–77.
56. Sevcenko, *Orfeu extático na metrópole*.
57. See Eleni Kefala's analysis of the Argentine film "Perdón Viejita" for a reading of a similarly bleak outlook on the modern city. Kefala, *Buenos Aires Across the Arts*, chapter 3, "Melotopian City."
58. Gilberto Rossi, "Rossi Actualidades," D516-5, Cinemateca Brasileira São Paulo, 1926.
59. Rossi, "Rossi Actualidades."
60. For an analysis of the city spaces that were depicted in the film, see Machado. "Para uma análise interpretativa," 23–40.
61. On masculinity and honor, and masculinity and dueling culture, see Beattie, *Tribute of Blood*; Braga-Pinto, "Journalists, Capoeiras," 581–614.
62. On constructions of masculinity in relation to these two figures, see Hertzman, "Making Music and Masculinity," 591–625.
63. Filmografia Brasileira, "Fragmentos da Vida."
64. Octavio Gabus Mendes, "De São Paulo," *Cinearte* 4, no. 198 (December 11, 1929): 31–32.
65. Mendes, "De São Paulo," 31–32.
66. On the intersections of eugenics, health, and appearance, see Borges, "'Puffy, Ugly, Slothful,'" 235–56.

67. *Cinearte* 5, no. 201 (January 1, 1930): 10, 33.
68. *Cinearte* 5, no. 201 (January 1, 1930): 10, 33.
69. *Cinearte* 5, no. 204 (January 22, 1930): 4–5.
70. Octavio Gabus Mendes, "De São Paulo," *Cinearte* 4, no. 198 (December 11, 1929): 31–32.

Chapter 3. Making Cinemas Safe for "Senhoras" in 1920s Rio de Janeiro and São Paulo

1. *Cinearte*, April 24, 1929, p. 3.
2. Souza, *Imagens do passado*.
3. On neo-Lamarckian eugenics in Latin America, see Stepan, *Hour of Eugenics*.
4. On the sanitation movement in Brazil, see Gilberto Hochman, *A era do saneamento: As bases da política de saúde pública no Brasil*, vol. 113 (Editora Hucitec, 1998), which has been translated into English: Hochman, *Sanitation of Brazil*. On education in Brazil as a tool of "whitening," see Dávila, *Diploma of Whiteness*. On the pathologization and criminalization of male homosexuality in early twentieth-century Brazil, see chapter 3 of Green, *Beyond Carnival*.
5. On urban reform and resistance in the name of hygiene in Rio de Janeiro, see Meade, *"Civilizing" Rio*. Also on law and regulation in Rio de Janeiro, see Leu, *Defiant Geographies*; Chazkel, *Laws of Chance*; Fischer, *A Poverty of Rights*.
6. On large-scale projects of urban reform and their relationship to modernity in São Paulo, see Peixoto-Mehrtens, *Urban Space and National Identity*. Also on the intertwining of eugenics and architecture in Latin America, see López-Durán, *Eugenics in the Garden*.
7. Souza, *Imagens do passado*, 143. Also see, on the process of legitimization in São Paulo, Levy, "'Art, Luxury, Elegance.'"
8. Gonzaga, *Palácios e poeiras*, 86. Photo from Arquivo Funarte, circa 1910.
9. Slide, *Nitrate Won't Wait*, 2–3.
10. Penteado, *Belènzinho*, 172.
11. Penteado, *Belènzinho*, 172. Anselmo Duarte, one of Brazilian cinema's most famous actors and directors, revealed that this practice continued into the 1920s in the countryside of São Paulo. Growing up in the town of Salto, his first job in the film industry was to use this makeshift "syringe" to douse the screen at his local movie theater. Anselmo Duarte, interview by Roberval Lima, in Lima, "Ninguem segura esse Russo louco."
12. See municipal petition 0.061.558-24 "Cine Brasil (Theatro)—jogo de box," June 10, 1924, Cinema 16, 2009-0.085.967-5, Arquivo Municipal de São Paulo.
13. *O Estado de S. Paulo*, September 2, 1926, p. 16.
14. *O Estado de S. Paulo*, September 16, 1926, p. 17.
15. Schvarzman, "Ir ao cinema em São Paulo nos anos 20," 163.
16. "Kursaal Bife," *O Estado de S. Paulo*, October 30, 1927, clipping in "Cine Kursaal Bife—cinema sem licença," Cinemas caixa 26, Cinemas 52, processo 2009-0-226.983-2, AHSP.
17. For example, the Cine República, inaugurated in 1921, seated 1,800 spectators. The Cine Central, inaugurated in 1924, seated 1,945 spectators. The Oberdan, inaugurated as a cinema in 1929, also seated close to 2,000 spectators. In addition to these, José Inácio de Melo Souza lists thirteen other large cinemas in neighborhoods outside of the Centro. The Cine Odeon, inaugurated in 1930, had two screening rooms, which, combined, seated 4,530 spectators total. Souza, "Cine República," "Cine Central," "Cine Oberdan," "Grandes Salas de Bairro," in Souza, *Salas de cinema em São Paulo*.
18. Steward, "Moral Economies and Commercial Imperatives."

19. "Cine Kursaal Bife—cinema sem licença," processo 2009-0-226.983-2, Cine caixa 26, Cinemas 52, AHSP.

20. Hochman, *Sanitation of Brazil*, 41–42.

21. See, for example, the state's targeting of factories and workers' living spaces in Rago, *Do cabaré ao lar*, 56–60.

22. Hochman, *Sanitation of Brazil*.

23. This journal ran from 1893 to 1949 with a national and international circulation that not only extended to the medical schools of São Paulo, but was even available in Paris as a French edition.

24. Cunha, Cunha, and Pizarro, "Inspecção hygienica," *Medico-Cirurgica do Brazil* 24, no. 5 (May 1916): 125–26, Cinemateca Brasileira São Paulo.

25. Cunha, Cunha, and Pizarro, "Inspecção hygienica," 103.

26. On the rise of moviegoing among elite cariocas, see Souza, *Imagens do passado*.

27. Cunha, Cunha, and Pizarro, "Inspecção hygienica," 104–5.

28. Apart from the language related directly to hygiene, Aiala Levy has found that movie theater owners in São Paulo used terms like "artistic and elegant" to legitimize moviegoing and broaden its appeal, but also to reinforce racial and cultural hierarchies that valued global and local notions of Europeanness and whiteness. Levy, "'Art, Luxury, Elegance,'" 30.

29. "O Operador," "A Hygiene e os Cochicholos da Avenida," *Para Todos*, September 5, 1925, p. 32.

30. "O que se exhibe no Rio," *Para Todos*, August 8, 1925, p. 53.

31. *Cinearte*. April 4, 1929, p. 3.

32. Mademoiselle Moreno, "Chronica: Varia."

33. Salles Gomes, *Humberto Mauro*, 305.

34. Moraes, "Valencian Tycoon in Brazil."

35. *Para Todos*, "O Cinema Theatro Capitólio." Alice Gonzaga has also found female "usherettes" at the Rialto Cinema in Rio de Janeiro. Gonzaga, *Palácios e poeiras*, 133.

36. Weinstein, *Color of Modernity*, 174–75.

37. The strategic use of female figures in movie theater employment was not unique to the Cine Capitólio in 1925. Ina Rae Hark has pointed out the gendered roles of theater managers and female employees in the US. A 1938 manual for theater management was quite direct in capitalizing on an usherette's feminine appeal. It advised theater managers in the US to utilize female beauty to improve the overall appearance of their theaters: "In showhouses where the carpets, draperies, and furnishings are worn and some of the luster of the theater has faded, beautiful young usherettes, attractively costumed, help to keep the public's glances off the shabby spots." Ricketson, *The Management of Motion Picture Theaters* (McGraw-Hill, 1938), 126, quoted in Hark, "'Theater Man.'"

38. Rolnik, "City and the Law," 88–90, 244. Also see the book Rolnik, *A cidade e a lei*.

39. Caldeira, *City of Walls*, 218.

40. Peixoto-Mehrtens, *Urban Space and National Identity*, 83.

41. Peixoto-Mehrtens, *Urban Space and National Identity*, 90.

42. This section relies heavily on municipal processes that were curated by historian José Inácio de Melo Souza. With Ricardo Mendes and the Historical Archive of São Paulo, Souza's project curated a breadth of municipal records related to cinema from 1895 to 1929. The collection resulted in a series of exhibits and an online, searchable database, as well as his book *Salas de cinema e história urbana de São Paulo (1895–1930)*. The latter provides a compendium of

cinematographic spaces in the city as well as a broader contextualization of movie theaters in the development of the city. The online database is *Salas de cinema em São Paulo: 1895–1929*, available at http://cinema.acervo.site/opac/php/index.php through his personal website https://joseinaciodemelosouza.com.br/ along with two other databases on Brazilian theses on cinema and foreign films exhibited in Brazil. The *Salas de cinema* database is also available at http://www.arquiamigos.org.br/bases/expo.htm.

43. "Grandes Salas de Bairro," in the exposition for Arquivo Histórico de São Paulo, *Salas de cinema em São Paulo, 1895–1929*. Used with permission.

44. See Souza, *Salas de cinema*, for a detailed examination of many examples. For archival documents, see, for example, José Marino, "Cine Sant-Anna" January 23, 1924, Cinemas caixa 13, Cinemas 21, processo 2009-0.094.532-6, AHSP. See, for example, "Reforma do Cine Olimpia," February 27, 1922, Cinemas caixa 7, processo 2008.0294.484-4, AHSP; "Dez mezes de reforma Cine Apollo-Odeon," April 9, 1924, Cinemas caixa 14, Cinemas 24, processo 2009-0.115.846-8, AHSP; "Cine Esperia, Oberdan, São Luiz," October 4, 1930, Cinemas caixa 25, Cinemas 51, processo 2010-0.066.136-5, AHSP.

45. Souza, *Salas de cinema*, 16.

46. "Cine Carlos Gomes—Inquerito sobre uma representação dirigida á Camara Municipal com referencia ao Theatro Carlos Gomes," August 8, 1923, Cinemas caixa 15, Cinemas 26, processo 2009-0.149.091-8, número da capa 0.028.007-23, AHSP.

47. "Cine Cambucy," February 9, 1925, and May 5, 1925, Cinemas caixa 13, Cinemas 18, processo 2009-0.077.686-9, número da capa 0.005.778-25, AHSP.

48. Ferreira Procopio, "Cine Apollo (Teatro 24 de Maio)—prorogação de prazo para reforma, para baile," December 18, 1931, Cinema 17, numero da capa 0.055.198-31, Arquivo Histórico São Paulo.

49. *Jornal do Comércio*, July 22, 1928, Cine caixa 22, Cinemas 45 2009-0.335.700-0, número de capa 0.044.867-28, AHSP.

50. São Paulo Municipal Act 1235, article 121.

51. São Paulo Municipal Act 1235, article 121.

52. São Paulo Municipal Act 1235, May 11, 1918, article 120.

53. Chalhoub, *Trabalho, lar e botequim*.

54. Garfield, *Guaraná*, 128.

55. See Besse, *Restructuring Patriarchy*, chapter 6. Also on the status of women who worked in commercial retail, see the analysis of Mappin Department Store workers in Ball, *Navigating Life and Work*. Also on the "in-between" status of shopgirls, see Suk, "'Only the Fragile Sex Admitted.'"

56. Wolfe, *Working Women, Working Men*, 47. See also my discussion of wages versus ticket prices in my introductory chapter on p. 25 and in note 61.

57. Souza, *Salas de cinema*, 360.

58. McCleary, *Staging Buenos Aires*.

59. Anne Rubenstein, "Theaters of Masculinity: Moviegoing and Male Roles in Mexico Before 1960," in Macías-González and Rubenstein, *Masculinity and Sexuality in Modern Mexico*.

60. Michel de Certeau, *The Practice of Everyday Life* (Berkeley: University of California Press, 1984).

61. Nascimento, "A tragédia do Cine Oberdan."

Chapter 4. Class, Race, and Desire at the Movies

1. Mary Kay Vaughan finds a similar opportunity for exploring individual and collective experiences in Pepe Zuñiga's memories of moviegoing in *Portrait of a Young Painter*.
2. Andrews, *Blacks & Whites in São Paulo*, 21.
3. On working men and women and working-class politics in this time period in São Paulo, see French, *Brazilian Workers' ABC*; Weinstein, *For Social Peace in Brazil*; Wolfe, *Working Women, Working Men*.
4. Rolnik, *A cidade e a lei*, 19, table 1.
5. Alberto, *Terms of Inclusion*, 28.
6. *Cinearte* 4, no. 165 (April 24, 1929).
7. On Serrador and other prominent immigrant film exhibitors see Moraes, "Valencian Tycoon in Brazil"; Souza, *Imagens do passado*.
8. Pedro Lima, "Cinema brasileiro," *Cinearte*, no. 134 (September 19, 1928): 6.
9. Lima, "Cinema brasileiro," 6.
10. Lima, "Cinema brasileiro," 6.
11. "Annuario estatistico de São Paulo (Brazil), 1920," São Paulo (Estado), Departamento de Estatística, 1923, vol. 1, pt. 1, p. 295.
12. Souza, *Salas de cinema*, table 3, 253–61.
13. Schvarzman, "Ir ao cinema em São Paulo nos anos 20," 164. Schvarzman's count came before Souza's project on film exhibition with AHSP, but still provides a general sense of distribution between Centro vs. Brás; see a more complete tabulation of cinemas in Souza, *Salas de cinema*, table 3, 253–61.
14. "Cinema," *Salas de cinema em São Paulo, 1895–1929*.
15. For Rio de Janeiro, see this discussion in chapter 3, as well as the development of Rio de Janeiro's Cinelândia in Souza, *Imagens do passado*. Mizala, *Modernity at the Movies*. Also on Buenos Aires, see Karush, *Culture of Class*.
16. Mizala, *Modernity at the Movies*, 60.
17. *Cinearte*, April 4, 1929, p. 3.
18. G. M., "O que se exhibe no Rio, o que se exhibe em São Paulo," *Para Todos*, no. 342 (July 4, 1925), RC *Para Todos*, Cinemateca Brasileira São Paulo.
19. G. M., "O que se exhibe no Rio," 342.
20. G. M., "O que se exhibe no Rio," 342.
21. Schvarzman, "Ir ao cinema em São Paulo nos anos 20," 171–72.
22. Ribeiro Couto, "Cinema de arrabalde," *Klaxon: Mensário de Arte Moderna*, October 15, 1922, p. 4, reprinted in facsimile edition, Cultura, Ciência e Tecnologia do Estado de São Paulo, 1976.
23. On intersections of modernist literature and early cinema and technology, see Sarah Ann Wells, *Media Laboratories*. Süssekind, *Cinematograph of Words*.
24. On an analysis of wage inequality in São Paulo in this time period, see Ball, *Navigating Life and Work*.
25. See an analysis of sexual exploitation and the depictions of bodies in Kanost, "Body Politics," 90–102.
26. Galvão, *Industrial Park*, 78. For consistency, my quotes are from Elizabeth Jackson and K. David Jackson's English translation of the novel.
27. Galvão, *Industrial Park*, 78.
28. On early Soviet cinema and propaganda, see Taylor, *Politics of the Soviet Cinema*.

29. Galvão, *Industrial Park*, 100.
30. Galvão, *Industrial Park*, 99.
31. Ribeiro Couto, "Cinema de arrabalde."
32. Gonzaga, *Palácios e poeiras*.
33. Sevcenko, *Orfeu extático na metrópole*.
34. Galvão, *Crônica do cinema paulistano*, 37–38.
35. Galvão, *Crônica do cinema paulistano*, 37–38.
36. Levy, "'Art, Luxury, Elegance,'" 25–53.
37. See, for example, "Cine-Teatro República," February 18, 1922, advertisement, *Folha da Noite*, February 18, 1922, p. 16.
38. *O Estado de S. Paulo*, December 29, 1921, p. 4.
39. "Os Tres Mosqueteiros," Cine-Teatro República program, February 18, 1922.
40. On the complicated meanings of the term "middle class" in different contexts, see López and Weinstein, *Making of the Middle Class*; Heiman, Freeman, and Liechty, *Global Middle Classes*.
41. "as archibancadas, os camarotes e as frisas foram construidos de tal maneira que de qualquer dessas localidades não se poderá devassar as outras que fiquem em plano inferior." *O Estado de S. Paulo*, December 29, 1921, p. 4.
42. *O Estado de S. Paulo*, December 29, 1921, p. 4.
43. Dean, *Industrialization of São Paulo*.
44. "explora o publico Paulistano," "abusa vergonhosamente"; Joaquim Franco de Mello, letter addressed to mayor of São Paulo (Firmiano Morais Pinto) in "Cine Republica—Reclamação Sob Cinema," May 28, 1923, Cine caixa 1, Cinemas 1, processo 2007-0.323.120-7, número da capa 0.075.243-22.
45. Joaquim Franco de Mello, letter to mayor, May 28, 1923.
46. Dean, *Industrialization of São Paulo*.
47. Font, *Coffee, Contention and Change*, 169.
48. Graham, *House and Street*.
49. Adhemar Gonzaga, "Impressões de New York," *Cinearte*, August 24, 1927.
50. "Mariana," interview by Heloísa Buarque de Almeida, transcript, São Paulo, August 1992.
51. Gabus Mendes, "O círculo do matrimonio—o que se exibe em São Paulo," *Para Todos*, May 16, 1925, p. 12.
52. Yolanda Penteado, *Tudo em cor rosa*, 53–54, quoted in Souza, "O cinema em São Paulo," in section 1, "Os primórdios, o cinema mudo e o início do cinema sonoro," Kindle ed., 277 of 946.
53. "Julia," interview by author, October 8, 2011.
54. Johnson, "That Guilty Third Tier," 575–84. Outside the US in Australia, another discussion of various class distinctions in the theater can be found in Sowerwine and Wolf, "Echoes of Paris," 81–98.
55. Doherty, "Race Houses, Jim Crow Roosts, and Lily White Palaces," in Maltby, *Going to the Movies*.
56. Caddoo, *Envisioning Freedom*.
57. Stewart, *Migrating to the Movies*.
58. See Rolnik, *A cidade e a lei*; Leu, *Defiant Geographies*; Britt, "Spatial Projects of Forgetting," 561–92; Siqueira, "O Largo da Banana." See Siqueira, note 39, for additional sources on formation and displacement of Black communities in São Paulo, especially in relation to music.
59. On contemporary Brazilians' perspectives of anti-Black racist discrimination, see Telles, *Pigmentocracies*.

60. "Laura," interview by author, São Paulo, July 7, 2012.
61. Butler, *Freedoms Given, Freedoms Won*.
62. Alberto, *Terms of Inclusion*, 34–37.
63. Horacio Cunha, *O Progresso*, January 13, 1929, p. 3; also discussed in Butler, *Freedoms Given, Freedoms Won*, 108.
64. Guerrero, *Framing Blackness*; Bogle, *Toms, Coons, Mulattoes*.
65. Foster, Lockhart, and Lockhart, *Culture and Customs of Argentina*, 135. On the related genre of zarzuelas in late nineteenth-century Argentina, see McCleary, "Mass, Popular, and Elite Culture?" On representations of ethnicity and national identity in Argentine visual culture, see Adamovsky, "La cultura visual."
66. Aristeu de Moraes, "Os pretos e o theatro moderno," *O Progresso*, no. 3 (August 19, 1928): 2.
67. Alberto, *Terms of Inclusion*, 56–63.
68. Alberto, *Terms of Inclusion*, 105–6.
69. L. Asobrac, "Casamento," *O Clarim da Alvorada*, February 20, 1927, p. 3.
70. Horacio da Cunha, "Os pretos e o jardim publica," *O Clarim da Alvorada*, January 15, 1927, no. 28, p. 3.
71. Butler, *Freedoms Given, Freedoms Won*, 93.
72. *A Rua*, February 24, 1916, p. 3.
73. *A Liberdade*, September 28, 1919, p. 4.
74. *A Liberdade*, September 28, 1919, p. 4.
75. *A Rua*, February 24, 1916, p. 2. Also cited in Butler, *Freedoms Given, Freedoms Won*, 93.
76. Aidoo, *Slavery Unseen*.
77. On the construction of the term "Syrian-Lebanese," see Lesser, *Negotiating National Identity*.
78. Penteado, *Belènzinho*, 171–76.
79. Kishimoto, "A experiencia do cinema japonês."
80. Decca, *A vida fora das fábricas*.
81. "Ana," interview by Heloísa Buarque de Almeida, São Paulo, n.d., likely 1993.
82. On Jewish filmmakers and the use of racial masquerade in asserting national identity, see Rogin, *Blackface, White Noise*.
83. "A Rosa da Irlanda," advertisement, *O Estado de S. Paulo*, June 7, 1929, p. 17.
84. Translation by Ariel Svarch from Yiddish. *A Rosa da Irlanda*, *O Estado de S. Paulo*, advertisement, June 8, 1929, p. 25. Similar advertisements promoted Yiddish-language films in London, England. Toffell, "'Come See, and Hear, the Mother Tongue!'"
85. An analysis of the transnational interpretation of films like *Abie's Irish Rose*, which glamorized the "melting pot" theory and the assimilation of US immigrants, would be a fascinating study, especially within the context of Brazilian national myths of nationhood and racial mixing. But this is the beyond the scope of the present study.
86. "Varieté," Cine República program, n.d., Cinemateca Brasileira São Paulo, 1481-31.
87. Miguel Pendás, "Varieté," *San Francisco Silent Film Festival*, https://silentfilm.org/variete/, accessed November 5, 2023.
88. On ethnic otherness of famous Hollywood actresses and the "vamp" persona, see Negra, *Off-White Hollywood*.
89. "O Condemnado," pamphlet advertisement for film, "Cine Apollo-Odeon, Ainda Funcionando," January 30, 1923, Cinema 14, Arquivo Histórico São Paulo.
90. Besse, *Restructuring Patriarchy*, Kindle ed., chap. 1, location 656 of 7612.

91. This issue represents a sample from the many editions of *A Cigarra* that are digitally available through the Acervo da Fundação Biblioteca Nacional–Brasil, BN Digital Collection. In comparison to at least one issue a year (from varying months) from 1925 to 1930, the personal ads in this issue broadly conform to the format and content seen in other issues. My thanks to José Inácio de Melo Souza for encouraging me to further explore these personal ads.

92. "Capital," *A Cigarra*, no. 344, first fortnight of March 1929, p. 6, Acervo da Fundação Biblioteca Nacional–Brasil.

93. "A quem desejar," *A Cigarra*, no. 344, first fortnight of March 1929, p. 9, Acervo da Fundação Biblioteca Nacional–Brasil.

94. "B. do Rei," *A Cigarra*, no. 344, first fortnight of March 1929, p. 7, Acervo da Fundação Biblioteca Nacional–Brasil.

95. "Penha P-9270," *A Cigarra*, no. 345, second fortnight of March 1929, p. 6, Acervo da Fundação Biblioteca Nacional–Brasil.

96. "Á Procura do Amor," *A Cigarra*, second fortnight of March 1929, p. 6, Acervo da Fundação Biblioteca Nacional–Brasil.

97. In 1926 the same magazine sponsored a beauty contest separately for "blondes" ("loiras") and "brunettes" ("morenas"). In this latter category, "morenas" meant women with dark hair, and they could be of Middle Eastern and European descent, but none had dark skin or identified as Black. Goulart, "A ilusão da imagem," 94–95. While Black people were excluded from beauty contests in white publications, the Black press held their own beauty contests, which solicited votes for women within the Black community.

Chapter 5. Dreams and Memories of a Respectable City

1. Rita Lee and Roberto de Carvalho, "Flagra," EMI Records Brasil Ltda., 1982. My thanks to Roney Cytrynowicz and Monica Cytrynowicz for first introducing me to this song.

2. On cultural production under Vargas, see Williams, *Culture Wars in Brazil*. On populism and Vargas, see Hentschke, *Vargas and Brazil*; Levine, *Father of the Poor?*

3. See chapter 1 on radio and the Estado Novo in McCann, *Hello, Hello Brazil*.

4. On the meanings of developmentalism and the challenges of unified support, see Ioris, *Transforming Brazil*.

5. Shaw and Dennison, *Brazilian National Cinema*, 31–59.

6. Roberts, "Lady in the Tutti-Frutti Hat"; Bishop-Sanchez, *Creating Carmen Miranda*.

7. Stam, *Tropical Multiculturalism*, 135.

8. On the importance of cinema and mass media to the formation of class politics before the rise of Peronism in Argentina, see Karush, *Culture of Class*.

9. On female spectatorship and women's reception of golden-age Hollywood cinema and female stars with a focus on the reception of Hollywood in the United Kingdom, see Stacey, *Star Gazing*.

10. Berg, *Classical Mexican Cinema*.

11. Johnson, *Film Industry in Brazil*, 41–43.

12. For a summary of these theories as they were debated in the 1920s and early 1930s, especially as they related to the campaign to bring "educational cinema" to schools, see Morettin, "Cinema educativo." Also see Saliba, *Cinema contra cinema*.

13. For an analysis of film production under Vargas and the interplay of cinema, history, and politics through a focus on two historical films, see Morettin, *Humberto Mauro*.

14. A similar model of indirect control of popular media can be seen in the Estado Novo's

relationship with Radio Nacional, which proved to be more effective and popular than other state-controlled stations. See McCann, *Hello, Hello Brazil*, chapter 1. On the legacy of Adhemar de Barros, his political style, and his relation to populism, see French, "Workers and the Rise of Adhemarista Populism."

15. Archangelo, "Um bandeirante nas telas."

16. See their personal letters to each other about moviegoing. Adhemar de Barros to Leonor Mendes de Barros, "Muita saude e felicidades," December 6, 1932; Leonor Mendes de Barros to Adhemar de Barros, "Não vou ao cinema hoje," n.d., AP630, Arquivo Público do Estado de São Paulo.

17. Cowan, *Securing Sex*, chap. 1, under "Moral Crisis, Anticommunism, and the Early Right," Kindle location 599 of 7662.

18. Acta do 4 reunião, May 1, 1941, "Actas da Associação do Restaurante Feminino," 5, Archive of the Ligas das Senhoras Católicas.

19. In Uruguay, one charitable women's organization took the exceptional step of actually producing their own films as cautionary tales against promiscuous sex and single motherhood. See Ehrick, "Beneficent Cinema."

20. Morettin, "Cinema educativo," 15.

21. For a brief description of the JUC (Juventude Universitária Católica or Catholic Youth University) and liberation theology, see Langland, *Speaking of Flowers*, 70–71.

22. "Oração pelo cinema," Boletim Nacional das Adjuntas da JECF, vol. 1, issue 3, 1957, Centro de Documentação e Informação Científica, Pontifícia Universidade Católica de São Paulo (hereafter abbreviated as CEDIC PUC) FJECB R6 D41.

23. "Acompanhando o programa," Boletim Nacional das Adjuntas da JECF, vol. 1, issue 3, 1957, pp. 10–11, CEDIC PUC FJECB R6 D41.

24. "Sugestões para o seu jornal mural," Boletim Nacional das Adjuntas da JECF, no. 42, 1957, pp. 6–11, CEDIC PUC FJECB R7 D02.

25. "Acompanhando o Programa," Boletim Nacional das Adjuntas da JECF, vol. 1, issue 3, 1957, pp. 10–11, CEDIC PUC FJECB R6 D41.

26. See this concept in Besse, *Restructuring Patriarchy*, and Cowan, *Securing Sex*, chapter 1.

27. Besse, *Restructuring Patriarchy*. See chapters 4 and 6 on motherhood and women's work.

28. Simili, *Mulher e política*.

29. On women's charitable organizations as simultaneously progressive see Mott, Byington, and Alves, *O gesto que salva*. On women's participation in right-wing politics, see Deutsch, *Las Derechas*.

30. Otovo, *Progressive Mothers, Better Babies*.

31. Owensby, *Intimate Ironies*. For an analysis on the formation of the middle class and its role in politics, see Saes, *Classe média e sistema político*.

32. On constructions of the middle class around the world, see Heiman, Freeman, and Liechty, *Global Middle Classes*; López and Weinstein, *Making of the Middle Class*.

33. Weinstein, *Color of Modernity*, 112–13.

34. Weinstein, *Color of Modernity*, 112–13. For Rio de Janeiro and federal education policy see Dávila, *Diploma of Whiteness*.

35. On multinational companies and the development of consumer culture in the mid-twentieth century, see Woodard, *Brazil's Revolution in Commerce*.

36. For an examination of the role of consumption on middle-class identity in the 1990s, see O'Dougherty, *Consumption Intensified*.

37. Weinstein, "'They Don't Even Look Like Women Workers.'"
38. See Seth Garfield's description of this in Garfield, *Guaraná*, 138. The racial stereotyping in advertisements continues into the late twentieth century. See Dial, "Race and Ethnic Stereotyping in Brazilian Advertising," https://www.academia.edu/968144/Racial_and_Ethnic_Stereotypes_in_Brazilian_Advertising.
39. Gonzaga, *Palácios e poeiras*, 86. Photo from Arquivo Funarte, circa 1910.
40. "centenas de 'habitués' desapontados"; *O Correio Paulistano*, July 1, 1948, p. 12, microfilm, CCSP.
41. "a subita e radical decisão dos dirigentes das empresas cinematograficas." *O Correio Paulistano*, July 1, 1948, p. 12, microfilm, CCSP.
42. "povo prejudicado . . ."; "Num país como é o Brasil, onde não existe quase nehum divertimento para o povo, fica o seu Estado mais industrial, por capricho de determinados servidores publicos, privado de seu principal passa tempo, que é, sem duvida, o cinema. Não ha palavras para explicações"; "Fechados todos os Cinemas de São Paulo," *Folha Carioca*, June 30, 1948, reprinted in *Correio Paulistano*, July 2, 1948, p. 11, microfilm, CCSP.
43. Gama, *Nos bares da vida*.
44. Anelli, "Arquitetura de cinemas."
45. Simões, *Salas de cinema em São Paulo*, 35.
46. Simões, *Salas de cinema em São Paulo*, 37.
47. Simões, *Salas de cinema em São Paulo*, 42.
48. Simões, *Salas de cinema em São Paulo*, 89.
49. Simões, *Salas de cinema em São Paulo*, 69.
50. "Inaugural Program," Cine Metro São Paulo, n.d. (likely 1938, date of inauguration), Cinemateca Brasileira São Paulo D1466/1.
51. Simões, *Salas de cinema em São Paulo*, 91.
52. Barbara Weinstein posits that uniforms and dressing up could be a means for asserting respectability in public for female supporters of the São Paulo revolution. Weinstein, *Color of Modernity*, 174–75.
53. *Jornal do Comércio*, July 22, 1928, Cine caixa 22, Cinemas 45, 2009-0.335.700-0, número de capa 0.044.867-28, AHSP.
54. Waldemar Paiva, "Gangsters na Cinelândia," "Cinema" column, *O Mundo*, October 13, 1954, newspaper clipping, Cinemateca Brasileira São Paulo.
55. I have anonymized the names of these interviewees, as they were unpublished interviews by people outside of the film industry.
56. Cassette tapes and transcripts of interviews conducted by Inimá Simões for *Salas de cinema em São Paulo* are available in the Multimedia Archive of the Centro Cultural de São Paulo. I listened to the tapes while reading the transcripts. There are five interviews available; in addition to the interview with Máximo Barro, a professor of film studies, other interviews are with film critic Rubem Biáfora, film exhibitor Dante Ancona Lopez, cinema manager and then-president of the Union of Cinema Employees Maria Lourenço Torres, and filmmaker Jairo Ferreira.
57. The Cinemateca Brasileira, which is the largest film archive in Brazil, hosts a program called "Cinema for the Elderly," or "Cine Maior Idade." Sponsored by the São Paulo state government, the program brings members of elderly associations, with the attempt to include clubs from various social levels and areas of São Paulo, to the Cinemateca to watch films. With permission from the organizers, I participated in four of these sessions, which provided a more

diverse sample population, speaking to groups of participants over coffee and cookies. I also held two interviews with the students of the Oficina do Cérebro, a private school for elderly people (more or less white and upper-middle class, reflecting the population of Higienópolis, the neighborhood where it was located) to exercise their memories. I asked similar questions as I did in the individual interviews, but these interviews were much briefer, and it was difficult to record facts about who these people were, when they were born, or their social background. Given the hurried nature of the interviews, I took notes rather than audio recordings. Most of the women were in their 60s or 70s and told me stories about moviegoing in the 1940s, 1950s, and 1960s, but some had memories of the 1920s and 1930s or were otherwise familiar with the structure of cine-teatros, some of which remained in use for decades. The Cine Oberdan, discussed in the next section, for example, was a cine-teatro that maintained private boxes and galleries at least until 1939.

58. Almeida, "Cinema em São Paulo," 74.

59. "Lina," interview by Heloísa Buarque de Almeida, transcript. São Paulo, March 22, 1991.

60. Simões, *Salas de cinema em São Paulo*, 47, quoting from interview with Aldo Lúcio, interview by Inimá Simões, 1982, p. 4.

61. Máximo Barro, interview by Inimá Simões, transcript, July 2, 1982, p. 4, Arquivo Multimeios, CCSP.

62. Máximo Barro, interview by Inimá Simões.

63. Máximo Barro, interview by Inimá Simões.

64. Jairo Ferreira, interview by Inimá Simões, transcript, March 23, 1982, Arquivo Multimeios, CCSP.

65. Simões, *Salas de cinema em São Paulo*, 102n11.

66. Group interview by author, Oficina do Cérebro, São Paulo, July 18, 2011.

67. Rubem Biáfora, interview by Inimá Simões, transcript and cassette tape, São Paulo, March 31, 1982, Arquivo Multimeios, CCSP.

68. Almeida, *Carolina, sua vida vai ser Linda*.

69. Máximo Barro, interview by Inimá Simões.

70. Group interview by author, Cinemateca Brasileira, São Paulo, July 24, 2012.

71. Almeida, "Cinema em São Paulo—Hábitos e representações do público (anos 40–50 e 90)," 71.

72. Almeida, "Cinema em São Paulo," 75.

73. Almeida, "Cinema em São Paulo," 54, quoting from Maria Leopoldina, interview by Heloísa Buarque de Almeida.

74. Almeida, "Cinema em São Paulo," 54, quoting from Maria Leopoldina, interview by Heloísa Buarque de Almeida.

75. Almeida, "Cinema em São Paulo," 54, quoting from "Rui e Marisa," interview by Heloísa Buarque de Almeida. Also I translate *namorar* as both "romancing" and "dating," because the term could signify both the social act of "going on a date," and also a more nebulous concept involving physical intimacy (holding hands, kissing, "making out").

76. Group interview by author, Oficina do Cérebro, São Paulo, July 18, 2012.

77. Anne Rubenstein, "Theaters of Masculinity," in Macías-González and Rubenstein, *Masculinity and Sexuality in Modern Mexico*.

78. "José," interview by Heloísa Buarque de Almeida, transcript, São Paulo, n.d., likely 1993, 4.

79. Brazilian anthropologist Gilberto Freyre fetishized this relationship in his work on the sociocultural impact of African slaves in Brazil, describing the young master's contact with Afro-descendant female house slaves as his first sexual relationship. Historians have detailed how domestic servant workers in Rio de Janeiro and São Paulo had to negotiate sexual advances and power relationships with their masters. The early twentieth-century Black press, consisting of Black community leaders in São Paulo, cautioned women to avoid domestic service because of the risk of "loss of honor" and pregnancy. Freyre, *Masters and the Slaves*; Graham, *House and Street*; Dias, *Power and Everyday Life*; Andrews, *Blacks & Whites in São Paulo*, 513.

80. Fonseca, *A Grande Arte*, 145–47.

81. Máximo Barro, interview by Inimá Simões.

82. For a readable introduction to the dictatorships in Brazil, Argentina, and Chile, see Dávila, *Dictatorship in South America*.

83. Langland, *Speaking of Flowers*, 134.

84. Cowan, *Securing Sex*, chap. 2, Kindle location 1205 of 7662, see note 11.

85. See the comic entitled "Which One is the Woman? Which One is the Man?," in Zolov, *Refried Elvis*, 106, figure 6. Also see chapter 5, "A Fraternity of Long-Haired Boys," in Manzano, *Age of Youth in Argentina*, on the intersections of long hair, youth culture, counterculturalism, and gender norms among 1960s Argentine male youth.

86. Cowan, *Securing Sex*, chap. 5, Kindle location 3052 of 7662.

87. Cowan, *Securing Sex*, chap. 5, Kindle location 3286–3306 of 7662.

88. Green, *Beyond Carnival*. See Green on the criminalization of homosexuality according to eugenic ideology.

89. Johnson, *Film Industry in Brazil*, 90–92.

90. For a summary of the contradictions of the military dictatorship's approach to cinema via the state-sponsored film producer and distributor Embrafilme, see Johnson, *Film Industry in Brazil*, 155–70. One of Johnson's points was that the dictatorship was not a monolith, which allowed Embrafilme to finance films that served certain purposes (increasing domestic film production and Brazilian cultural capital internationally) even as they were contradictory to others (overall censorship of the arts).

91. See, for example, film critic Jean Claude Bernadet's take on the pornochanchada in "A pornô-moral," *Movimento*, July 7, 1975. A short summary of the historiography of the pornochanchada is in Shaw and Dennison, *Brazilian National Cinema*, 161.

92. See Cowan, *Securing Sex*, chap. 7, Kindle location 4477–96 of 7662, for an analysis of the pornochanchada "Vereda Tropical" and its critique of both masculinity and the dictatorship's moral double standards. On the uses and effects of parody in Brazilian cinema and pornochanchadas, see João Luiz Vieira, "From *High Noon to Jaws*: Carnival and Parody in Brazilian Cinema," in Johnson and Stam, *Brazilian Cinema*.

93. Renata Bortoleto et al., *Contos de bordel*; Pinchiaro and Casarin, *Glamour e boca do lixo*.

94. Silveira and Carvalho, "Embrafilme x Boca do Lixo," 85–88.

95. Alessandro Gamo and Luís Alberto Rocha Melo, "Boca de Cinema de São Paulo," in Ortiz et al., *Nova história do cinema brasileiro II*.

96. Johnson, *Film Industry in Brazil*, 172.

97. Johnson, *Film Industry in Brazil*, 172, table 26.

98. Frúgoli, *Centralidade em São Paulo*, 38. On popular street cultures, see Frúgoli, *São Paulo: Espaços públicos*.

99. Caldeira, *City of Walls*.

100. Fontes, *Migration and the Making of Industrial São Paulo*, 20.

101. Fontes, *Migration and the Making of Industrial São Paulo*, 37. On northeastern immigration to São Paulo and the social struggles they faced, also see Fontes, *Um nordeste em São Paulo*.

102. Weinstein, *Color of Modernity*; Sarzynski, *Revolution in the Terra do Sol*.

103. Simões, *Salas de cinema em São Paulo*, 107.

104. Though Ferreira was not as famous as his counterparts during his lifetime, retrospective studies of his films and film criticism have given him posthumous praise for his experimental style. Coelho, *O cinema e a crítica de Jairo Ferreira*; Coelho, *Mostra Jairo Ferreira*. On cinema and its relation to counterculture, see Dunn, *Contracultura*.

105. In the book *Salas de cinema em São Paulo*, for which Ferreira's interview was conducted, Inimá Simões briefly discusses the appearance of porn theaters in the Centro. However, in a book published by the São Paulo municipal government, he otherwise avoids the topic of sexual acts within the cinemas, and excludes Ferreira's stories and rumors from the book.

106. Daniel Touro Linger, *Dangerous Encounters: Meanings of Violence in a Brazilian City* (Stanford University Press, 1995), 239.

107. Kulick, *Travesti*, 10. *Travesti* might be loosely translated as "transfeminine," but that does not capture the class and moral associations of this term or its transformation from an originally pejorative usage. On the nuances of travesti identity and the impact of this purported "untranslatability" within normative biomedical transsexual care in Brazil, see Jarrín, "Untranslatable Subjects," 357–75.

108. Ferreira, "Entrevista com Jairo Ferreira," 18.

109. Ferreira, "Entrevista com Jairo Ferreira," 13.

110. Leme, "Nacional e cosmopolita."

111. Ferreira and Walton, "Striptease of Language."

112. Weinstein, *Color of Modernity*.

113. Fontes, *Migration and the Making of Industrial São Paulo*, 37–39. On the propagation of negative stereotypes of the rural northeast in cinema and media, and the role these stereotypes had in Brazil's embrace of military authoritarianism, see Sarzynski, *Revolution in the Terra do Sol*.

114. Rubem Biáfora, interview by Inimá Simões, 11, Arquivo Multimeios, CCSP.

115. The historiography on the presence of Hollywood in Brazil in the mid- and late twentieth century is too extensive to adequately present here, but a classic text is Tota, *O imperialismo sedutor*.

116. Rubem Biáfora, interview by Inimá Simões, 10, Arquivo Multimeios, CCSP.

117. On tropicalism and counterculture, see Dunn, *Brutality Garden*.

118. Perlongher, *O negócio do michê*. Anne Rubenstein finds a similar transformation of old movie theaters in Mexico City. See her analysis of the Cine Teresa in Rubenstein, "A Sentimental and Sexual Education."

119. Perlongher, *O negócio do michê*, 169.

120. Ripó Neto, "Práticas homossexuais masculinas nos cinemas do centro de São Paulo," 40.

BIBLIOGRAPHY

Archives, Collections, and Libraries
Arquivo do Estado de São Paulo (São Paulo)
Arquivo Histórico de São Paulo (São Paulo)
Arquivo Multimeios, Centro Cultural São Paulo (São Paulo)
Biblioteca Nacional (Rio de Janeiro)
Biblioteca Sergio Millet, Centro Cultural São Paulo (São Paulo)
Centro de Documentação e Informação Científica, Pontifícia Universidade Católica de São Paulo (São Paulo)
Cinemateca Brasileira de São Paulo (São Paulo)
Faculdade de Arquitetura e Urbanismo, Universidade São Paulo (São Paulo)
Ligas das Senhoras Católicas, Private Collection (São Paulo)

Newspapers and Periodicals
Acrópole
A Careta
A Cigarra
Cinearte
O Clarim da Alvorada
Correio Paulistano
O Estado de S. Paulo
Folha de São Paulo
O Homem do Povo
A Liberdade
Para Todos
Revista Feminina
A Rua
Selecta
Vida Doméstica

Databases
Banco de Conteúdos Culturais. Cinemateca Brasileira. http://bcc.cinemateca.org.br.
Base Filmografia Brasileira. Cinematecas Brasileira. https://bases.cinemateca.org.br/cgi-bin/wxis.exe/iah/?IsisScript=iah/iah.xis&base=FILMOGRAFIA&lang=p.
Salas de cinema em São Paulo 1895–1929: Inventário dos espaços de sociabilidade cinematográfica na cidade de São Paulo: 1895-1929. Arquivo Histórico de São Paulo. Accessible at http://fotoplus.info/bases/cine.htm and José Inácio de Melo Souza's collection of databases at http://cinema.acervo.site/opac/php/index.php.

Interviews by Author
All interviewees anonymized to protect privacy.
"Julia." São Paulo, March 24, 2012.
"Laura and Lucia." São Paulo, July 16, 2012.
Group Interviews at the Cine Maior Idade Program, Cinemateca Brasileira. São Paulo, April 12, 2012, July 3, 2012, July 17, 2012, and July 24, 2012.
Group Interviews at the Oficina do Cérebro, São Paulo, July 11, 2012, and July 18, 2012.

Unpublished Interviews
All interviewees anonymized to protect privacy, except for famous individuals.
"Ana." interview by Heloisa Buarque de Almeida. Transcript. São Paulo, n.d., likely 1993.
Barro, Máximo. Interview by Inimá Simões. Transcript. July 2, 1982, p. 4. Arquivo Multimeios, CCSP.
Biáfora, Rubem. Interview by Inimá Simões. Transcript and cassette tape. São Paulo, March 31, 1982. Arquivo Multimeios, CCSP.
Ferreira, Jairo. Interview by Inimá Simões. Transcript. March 23, 1982. Arquivo Multimeios, CCSP.
"Jose." Interview by Heloisa Buarque de Almeida. Transcript. São Paulo, n.d., likely 1993.
"Lina." Interview by Heloisa Buarque de Almeida. Transcript. São Paulo, March 22, 1991.
"Mariana." Interview by Heloisa Buarque de Almeida. Transcript. São Paulo, August 1992.

Films
A Filha do Advogado. Directed by J. Soares 1926, Recife, Brazil. Restored by the Cinemateca Brasileira. Available from the Cinemateca Pernambucana Jota Soares.
Fragmentos da Vida. Directed by José Medina. Rossi Film, 1929. Restored by the Cinemateca Brasileira.
A Hora da Estrela. Directed by Suzana Amaral. Embrafilme, 1985.
Lábios sem Beijos. Directed by Humberto Mauro. Cinédia, 1930. Restored by the Cinemateca Brasileira.

Published Interviews and Memoirs
Almeida, Luara. *Carolina, sua vida vai ser Linda.* Graphic biography of great-grandmother Carolina Seixas. Independently published, 2015.
Duarte, Anselmo. "Ninguem segura esse Russo louco: Anselmo Duarte continua sendo nosso único Palma de Ouro." Interview by Sandro Fortunato, Roberval Lima, Anahi de Castro, n.d. Originally published in Memória Viva: Historia rima com a memória, 2004. Republished in *Travessias* 1, no. 1 (2007): 1–10.
Ferreira, Jairo. Translated by Michael Walton. "The Striptease of Language." *Framework: The Journal of Cinema and Media*, no. 28 (1985): 104–7.
Penteado, Jacob. *Belènzinho, 1910: Retrato de uma época.* 2nd ed. Carrenho Editorial, Narrativa Um, 2003.

Fictional Novels
Fonseca, Rubem. *A Grande Arte.* 12th ed. Companhia das Letras, 1990.
Galvão, Patrícia. *Industrial Park: A Proletarian Novel.* Translated by Elizabeth Jackson and K. David Jackson. University of Nebraska Press, 1993. Originally published in Brazil as *Parque Industrial: Romance Proletário* (1933).

Galvão (Pagú), Patrícia. *Parque Industrial: Romance proletário*. Mercado Aberto, EDUFSCar, 1994. Originally published in 1933.

Secondary Sources

Abreu Esteves, Martha de. *Meninas perdidas: Os populares e o cotidiano do amor no Rio de Janeiro da Belle Époque*. Paz e Terra, 1989.

Acerbi, Patricia. *Street Occupations: Urban Vending in Rio de Janeiro, 1850–1925*. 1st ed. University of Texas Press, 2017.

Adamovsky, Ezequiel. "La cultura visual del criollismo: etnicidad, 'color' y nación en las representaciones visuales del criollo en Argentina, c. 1910–1955." *Corpus: Archivos virtuales de la alteridad americana* 6, no. 2 (December 20, 2016). https://doi.org/10.4000/corpusarchivos.1738.

Aidoo, Lamonte. *Slavery Unseen: Sex, Power, and Violence in Brazilian History*. Duke University Press, 2018.

Alberto, Paulina L. *Terms of Inclusion: Black Intellectuals in Twentieth-Century Brazil*. University of North Carolina Press, 2011.

Albuquerque, Durval Muniz, Jr. *A invenção do nordeste e outras artes*. Editora Massangana, 1999.

Allen, Robert Clyde, and Douglas Gomery. *Film History: Theory and Practice*. Knopf, 1985.

Almeida, Heloisa Buarque de. "Cinema em São Paulo—hábitos e tepresentações do público (Anos 40–50 e 90)." Master's thesis, Universidade de São Paulo, 1995.

Andrade, Oswald de, and Patrícia Galvão. *O homem do povo: Coleção completa e fac-similar do jornal criado e dirigido por Oswald de Andrade e Patrícia Galvão (Pagu): Março/abril 1931*. Imprensa Oficial do Estado de São Paulo, Editora Globo, Museu Lasar Segall, 2009.

Andrews, George. *Blacks & Whites in São Paulo, Brazil, 1888–1988*. University of Wisconsin Press, 1991.

Anelli, Renato Luiz Sobral. "Arquitetura de cinemas na cidade de São Paulo." Master's thesis, Universidade de Campinas, 1990.

Araújo, Luciana Correa de. "O cinema em Pernambuco nos anos 1920." In *I jornada brasileira de cinema silencioso (catálogo)*, 33, 71–76. Cinemateca Brasileira São Paulo, 2007. http://www.academia.edu/30800224/O_cinema_em_Pernambuco_nos_anos_1920.

Araújo, Luciana Correa de. "Tensões, idealizações e ambiguidades: As relações entre campo e cidade no cinema em Pernambuco nos anos 1920." *Imagofagia*, no. 8, 2013.

Araújo, Vicente de Paula. *Bela época do cinema brasileiro*. 2nd ed. Debates, 116. Perspectiva, 1985.

Archangelo, Rodrigo. "Um bandeirante nas telas de São Paulo: O discurso adhemarista em cinejornais, 1947–1956." Master's thesis, Universidade de São Paulo, 2007. https://www.teses.usp.br/teses/disponiveis/8/8138/tde-03032008-140811/.

Autran, Arthur. "A noção de 'ciclo regional' na historiografia do cinema brasileiro." *Revista Alceu* 10, no. 20 (2010). http://revistaalceu.com.puc-rio.br/media/Alceu20_Autran.pdf.

Autran, Arthur. "O personagem Negro no cinema silencioso brasileiro: Estudo de caso sobre A Filha do Advogado." *Sessões do Imaginário* 6, no. 7 (December 2001): 5–9.

Ball, Molly C. *Navigating Life and Work in Old Republic São Paulo*. 1st ed. University of Florida Press, 2020.

Barro, Máximo. *A primeira sessão de cinema em São Paulo*. Tanz do Brasil, 1996.

Barros, Orlando de. *Corações de chocolat: A história da Companhia Negra de Revistas (1926–1927)*. Livre Expressão, 2005.

Bean, Jennifer M., and Diane Negra, eds. *A Feminist Reader in Early Cinema*. Duke University Press, 2002.

Beattie, Peter. *The Tribute of Blood: Army, Honor, Race, and Nation in Brazil, 1864–1945*. Duke University Press, 2001.

Beattie, Peter M. *Punishment in Paradise: Race, Slavery, Human Rights, and a Nineteenth-Century Brazilian Penal Colony*. Duke University Press, 2015.

Beezley, William. *Judas at the Jockey Club and Other Episodes of Porfirian Mexico*. 2nd ed. University of Nebraska Press, 2004.

Benchimol, Jaime L. *Pereira Passos, um Haussmann tropical: A renovação urbana da cidade do Rio de Janeiro no início do século XX*. Prefeitura da Cidade do Rio de Janeiro, 1990.

Berg, Charles Ramírez. *The Classical Mexican Cinema: The Poetics of the Exceptional Golden Age Films*. University of Texas Press, 2015.

Bergfelder, Tim, Lisa Shaw, and João Luiz Vieira. *Stars and Stardom in Brazilian Cinema*. 1st ed. Berghahn Books, 2016.

Bernadet, Jean Claude. *Historiografia clássica do cinema brasileiro: Metodologia e pedagogia*. Annablume, 1995

Bernstein, Matthew, and Gaylyn Studlar. *Visions of the East: Orientalism in Film*. I. B. Tauris, 1997.

Besse, Susan K. *Restructuring Patriarchy: The Modernization of Gender Inequality in Brazil, 1914–1940*. Kindle ed. University of North Carolina Press, 1996.

Bethell, Leslie. *Brazil: Empire and Republic, 1822–1930*. Cambridge University Press, 1989.

Bicalho, Maria Fernanda Baptista. "The Art of Seduction: Representation of Women in Brazilian Silent Cinema." *Luso-Brazilian Review* 30, no. 1, "Changing Images of the Brazilian Woman: Studies of Female Sexuality in Literature, Mass Media, and Criminal Trials, 1884–1992" (Summer 1993): 21–33.

Bishop-Sanchez, Kathryn. *Creating Carmen Miranda: Race, Camp, and Transnational Stardom*. Vanderbilt University Press, 2016.

Blake, Stanley E. *The Vigorous Core of Our Nationality*. University of Pittsburgh Press, 2011.

Bliss, Katherine Elaine. *Compromised Positions: Prostitution, Public Health, and Gender Politics in Revolutionary Mexico City*. Pennsylvania State University Press, 2001.

Bogle, Donald. *Toms, Coons, Mulattoes, Mammies, and Bucks: An Interpretive History of Blacks in American Films*. 4th ed. New York: Continuum, 2001.

Borge, Jason. *Latin American Writers and the Rise of Hollywood Cinema*. Routledge, 2008.

Borge, Jason. *Tropical Riffs: Latin America and the Politics of Jazz*. Duke University Press, 2018.

Borges, Dain. "'Puffy, Ugly, Slothful and Inert': Degeneration in Brazilian Social Thought, 1880–1940." *Journal of Latin American Studies* 25, no. 2 (1993): 235–56.

Bortoleto, Renata, Ana Laura Diniz, and Michele Izawa. *Contos de bordel: A prostituição feminina na Boca do Lixo de São Paulo*. Carrenho Editorial, 2003.

Braga, Regina Stela, Andréa Coelho, and Flávia David. "Mulheres em revista: O jornalismo feminino no Brasil," n.d., http://www.rio.rj.gov.br/dlstatic/10112/4204434/4101415/memoria4.pdf.

Braga-Pinto, César. "Journalists, Capoeiras, and the Duel in Nineteenth-Century Rio de Janeiro." *Hispanic American Historical Review* 94, no. 4 (November 1, 2014): 581–614. https://doi.org/10.1215/00182168-2802642.

Britt, Andrew G. "Spatial Projects of Forgetting: Razing the Remedies Church and Museum to the Enslaved in São Paulo's 'Black Zone,' 1930s–1940s." *Journal of Latin American Studies* 54, no. 4 (November 2022): 561–92. https://doi.org/10.1017/S0022216X22000669.

Butler, Kim D. *Freedoms Given, Freedoms Won: Afro-Brazilians in Post-Abolition, São Paulo and Salvador*. Rutgers University Press, 1998.

Caddoo, Cara. *Envisioning Freedom: Cinema and the Building of Modern Black Life*. Harvard University Press, 2014.

Caldeira, Teresa. *City of Walls: Crime, Segregation, and Citizenship in São Paulo*. University of California Press, 2000.

Campbell, Courtney J. "Four Fishermen, Orson Welles, and the Making of the Brazilian Northeast." *Past & Present* 234, no. 1 (February 1, 2017): 173–212. https://doi.org/10.1093/pastj/gtw052.

Campbell, Courtney J. *Region Out of Place: The Brazilian Northeast and the World, 1924–1968*. University of Pittsburgh Press, 2022.

Campelo, Taís. "Jonathas Serrano, narrativas sobre cinema." *Especiaria: Cadernos de ciências humanas* 10, no. 17 (2016). http://periodicos.uesc.br/index.php/especiaria/article/view/799.

Canclini, Néstor García, and Renato Rosaldo. *Hybrid Cultures: Strategies for Entering and Leaving Modernity*. Translated by Christopher L. Chiappari and Silvia L. López. Expanded ed. University of Minnesota Press, 2005.

Carneiro, Sueli. *Racismo, sexismo e desigualdade no Brasil*. Selo Negro, 2015.

Caulfield, Sueann. "The Birth of Mangue: Race, Nation, and the Politics of Prostitution in Rio de Janeiro, 1850–1942." In *Sex and Sexuality in Latin America*, edited by Daniel Balderston and Donna Guy, 86–100. NYU Press, 1997.

Caulfield, Sueann. *In Defense of Honor: Sexual Morality, Modernity, and Nation in Early-Twentieth Century Brazil*. Duke University Press, 2000.

Caulfield, Sueann. "Getting into Trouble: Dishonest Women, Modern Girls, and Women-Men in the Conceptual Language of 'Vida Policial,' 1925–1927." *Signs* 19, no. 1 (October 1, 1993): 146–76. https://doi.org/10.2307/3174748.

Chalhoub, Sidney. *Trabalho, lar e botequim: O cotidiano dos trabalhadores no Rio de Janeiro da belle époque*. 2nd ed. Unicamp, 2005.

Chattopadhyay, Swati. *Representing Calcutta: Modernity, Nationalism, and the Colonial Uncanny*. Routledge, 2006.

Chazkel, Amy. *Laws of Chance: Brazil's Clandestine Lottery and the Making of Urban Public Life*. Duke University Press, 2011.

Coelho, Renato, ed. *Mostra Jairo Ferreira: Cinema de invenção*. Centro Cultural, 2012.

Coelho, Renato. *O cinema e a crítica de Jairo Ferreira*. São Paulo: Alameda, 2015.

Conde, Maite. *Consuming Visions: Cinema, Writing, and Modernity in Rio de Janeiro*. University of Virginia Press, 2011.

Conde, Maite. *Foundational Films: Early Cinema and Modernity in Brazil*. California Scholarship Online. University of California Press, 2018. https://doi.org/10.1525/9780520964884.

Conde, Maite. "Negotiating Visions of Modernity: Female Stars, the Melindrosa and Desires for a Brazilian Film Industry." *Studies in Spanish & Latin-American Cinemas* 10, no. 1 (2013): 23–43.

Conde, Maite, and Lisa Shaw. "Towards an Alternative 1922: Popular Culture and Rio de Janeiro's Vernacular Modernisms." *Revista brasileira de história* 42 (August 1, 2022): 97–123. https://doi.org/10.1590/1806-93472022v42n90-07.

Costallat, Benjamin. *Mademoiselle Cinema: Novela de costumes do momento que passa*. Casa da Palavra, 1999.

Courtney, Susan. *Hollywood Fantasies of Miscegenation: Spectacular Narratives of Gender and Race, 1903–1967*. Princeton University Press, 2005.

Cowan, Benjamin A. *Securing Sex: Morality and Repression in the Making of Cold War Brazil*. Kindle ed. University of North Carolina Press, 2016.

Cunha, Alberto da, Domingos Cunha, and João de Almeida Pizarro. "Inspecção hygienica dos cinematographos: Os cinematographicos e a saude publica." *Medico-cirurgica do Brazil* 24, no. 5 (May 1916).

Cunha, Euclides da. *Os sertoes*. Translated by Samuel Putnam. University of Chicago Press, 1944.

Cunha Filho, Paulo Carneiro da. *A utopia provinciana: Recife, cinema, melancolia*. Ed. Universitária da UFPE, 2010.

Da Silva, Renata Cardoso. "Teatro de revista e representação social do feminino no início do século XX." *dObra[s]—revista da Associação Brasileira de Estudos de Pesquisas em Moda* 9, no. 19 (June 9, 2016): 23. https://doi.org/10.26563/dobras.v9i19.450.

Dávila, Jerry. *Dictatorship in South America*. John Wiley & Sons, 2013.

Dávila, Jerry. *Diploma of Whiteness: Race and Social Policy in Brazil, 1917–1945*. Duke University Press, 2003.

Dean, Warren. *The Industrialization of São Paulo, 1880–1945*. Published for the Institute of Latin American Studies by the University of Texas Press, 1969.

Decca, Maria Auxiliadora Guzzo. *A vida fora das fábricas: Cotidiano operário em São Paulo (1920–1934)*. Vol. 3. Paz e Terra, 1987.

de Certeau, Michel. *The Practice of Everyday Life*. University of California Press, 1984.

Denis, Rafael Cardoso. *Modernity in Black and White: Art and Image, Race and Identity in Brazil, 1890–1945*. Cambridge University Press, 2021.

Deutsch, Sandra McGee. *Las Derechas: The Extreme Right in Argentina, Brazil, and Chile, 1890–1939*. Stanford University Press, 1999.

Diacon, Todd A. *Stringing Together a Nation: Candido Mariano da Silva Rondon and the Construction of a Modern Brazil, 1906–1930*. Duke University Press, 2004.

Dias, Maria Odila Leite da Silva. *Power and Everyday Life: The Lives of Working Women in Nineteenth-Century Brazil*. Rutgers University Press, 1995.

Doane, Mary Anne. *The Desire to Desire: The Woman's Film of the 1940s*. 2nd ed. Indiana University Press, 1987.

Dunn, Christopher. *Brutality Garden: Tropicália and the Emergence of a Brazilian Counterculture*. University of North Carolina Press, 2001.

Dunn, Christopher. *Contracultura*. Illustrated ed. University of North Carolina Press, 2016.

Ehrick, Christine. "Beneficent Cinema: State Formation, Elite Reproduction, and Silent Film in Uruguay, 1910s–1920s." *The Americas* 63, no. 2 (2006): 205–24.

Ehrick, Christine. *Radio and the Gendered Soundscape: Women and Broadcasting in Argentina and Uruguay, 1930–1950*. 1st ed. Cambridge University Press, 2015.

Enstad, Nan. *Ladies of Labor, Girls of Adventure: Working Women, Popular Culture, and Labor Politics at the Turn of the Twentieth Century*. Columbia University Press, 1999.

Figueirôa, Alexandre. *Cinema pernambucano: uma história em ciclos*. Recife: Prefeitura da Cidade do Recife, Secretaria de Cultura, Turismo e Esportes, Fundação de Cultura Cidade do Recife, 2000.

Filmografia Brasileira—Cinemateca Brasileira. "Lábios sem Beijos." Accessed October 21, 2017. http://bases.cinemateca.gov.br/cgi-bin/wxis.exe/iah/.

Fischer, Brodwyn. *A Poverty of Rights: Citizenship and Inequality in Twentieth-Century Rio de Janeiro*. Stanford University Press, 2010.

Fonseca, Rubem. *A Grande Arte*. 12th ed. São Paulo: Companhia das Letras, 1990.

Font, Mauricio A. *Coffee, Contention and Change in the Making of Modern Brazil*. Blackwell Publishers, 1990.

Fontes, Paulo. *Migration and the Making of Industrial São Paulo*. Duke University Press Books, 2016.

Fontes, Paulo. *Um nordeste em São Paulo: Trabalhadores migrantes em São Miguel Paulista*. Editora FGV, 2008.

Foster, David William, Melissa Fitch Lockhart, and Darrell B. Lockhart. *Culture and Customs of Argentina*. Greenwood Publishing Group, 1998.

Foster, Lila, and Roberto Souza Leão. "A presença da 'Pathé-Baby' no Rio de Janeiro e a coleção Paschoal Nardone no acervo do AGCRJ." *Revista do Arquivo Geral do Rio de Janeiro*, no. 9 (2015): 341–53.

Foster, Lila Silva. "Cinema amador brasileiro: História, discursos e práticas (1926–1959)." Dissertation, Universidade de São Paulo, 2016. https://doi.org/10.11606/T.27.2017.tde-10032017-164617.

French, John. *The Brazilian Workers' ABC: Class Conflict and Alliances in Modern São Paulo*. University of North Carolina Press, 1992.

French, John D. "Workers and the Rise of Adhemarista Populism in São Paulo, Brazil 1945–47." *Hispanic American Historical Review* 68, no. 1 (February 1, 1988): 1–43. https://doi.org/10.1215/00182168-68.1.1.

Freyre, Gilberto. *The Masters and the Slaves*. University of California Press, 1986.

Frúgoli, Heitor, Jr. *Centralidade em São Paulo: Trajetórias, conflitos e negociações na metrópole*. Edusp, 2006.

Frúgoli, Heitor, Jr. *São Paulo: Espaços públicos e interação social*. Marco Zero; SESC, 1995.

Fuller-Seeley, Kathryn. *Hollywood in the Neighborhood: Historical Case Studies of Local Moviegoing*. University of California Press, 2008.

Galvão, Maria Rita. *Crônica do cinema paulistano*. Ática, 1975.

Gama, Lúcia Helena. *Nos bares da vida: Produção cultural e sociabilidade em São Paulo, 1940–1950*. Editora Senac São Paulo, 1998.

Garfield, Seth. *Guaraná: How Brazil Embraced the World's Most Caffeine-Rich Plant*. University of North Carolina Press, 2022.

Glaucia, Fraccaro. *Os direitos das mulheres: Feminismo e trabalho no Brasil (1917–1937)*. Editora FGV, 2018.

Gomes, Ângela Maria de Castro. "Essa gente do Rio . . . os intelectuais cariocas e o modernismo." *Revista estudos históricos* 6, no. 11 (July 1, 1993): 62–77.

Gomes, Flávio dos Santos, and Petrônio Domingues. *Da nitidez e invisibilidade: Legados do pós-emancipação no Brasil*, 2013.

Gonzaga, Alice. *Palácios e poeiras: 100 anos de cinema no Rio de Janeiro*. GR Record, 1996.

Goulart, Isabella Regina Oliveira. "A ilusão da imagem: O sonho do estrelismo brasileiro em Hollywood." Master's thesis, Universidade de São Paulo, 2013. http://www.teses.usp.br/teses/disponiveis/27/27161/tde-06052014-104345/.

Graham, Sandra Lauderdale. *House and Street: The Domestic World of Servants and Masters in Nineteenth-Century Rio de Janeiro*. University of Texas Press, 1992.

Green, James. *Beyond Carnival: Male Homosexuality in Twentieth-Century Brazil*. University of Chicago Press, 2002.

Guerreiro, Antonio Luis. Letter to Eva Nil. "Modest but Sincere Admirer," July 2, 1932. EN 32.07.02. Cinemateca Brasileira São Paulo.

Guerrero, Ed. *Framing Blackness: The African American Image in Film*. 1st ed. Temple University Press, 1993.

Guy, Donna. *Sex and Danger in Buenos Aires: Prostitution, Family, and Nation in Argentina*. University of Nebraska Press, 1991.

Hahner, June Edith. *Emancipating the Female Sex: The Struggle for Women's Rights in Brazil, 1850–1940*. Duke University Press, 1990.

Hallett, Hilary A. *Go West, Young Women! The Rise of Early Hollywood*. University of California Press, 2013.

Hansen, Miriam. *Babel and Babylon*. Harvard University Press, 1991.

Hark, Ina Rae. "The 'Theater Man' and 'The Girl in the Box Office': Gender in the Discourse of Motion Picture Theatre Management." *Film History* 6, no. 2 (July 1, 1994): 178–87. https://www.jstor.org/stable/3814964.

Heiman, Rachel, Carla Freeman, and Mark Liechty, eds. *The Global Middle Classes: Theorizing Through Ethnography*. SAR Press, 2012.

Hentschke, Jens R., ed. *Vargas and Brazil: New Perspectives*. Palgrave Macmillan, 2007.

Hershfield, Joanne. *Imagining La Chica Moderna: Women, Nation, and Visual Culture in Mexico, 1917–1936*. Duke University Press, 2008.

Hershfield, Joanne. *Mexican Cinema/Mexican Woman, 1940–1950*. University of Arizona Press, 1996.

Hertzman, Marc A. "Making Music and Masculinity in Vagrancy's Shadow: Race, Wealth, and Malandragem in Post-Abolition Rio de Janeiro." *Hispanic American Historical Review* 90, no. 4 (November 1, 2010): 591–625. https://doi.org/10.1215/00182168-2010-043.

Hertzman, Marc A. *Making Samba: A New History of Race and Music in Brazil*. Duke University Press Books, 2013.

Hochman, Gilberto. *The Sanitation of Brazil: Nation, State, and Public Health, 1889–1930*. Translated by Diane Grosklaus Whitty. Reprint ed. University of Illinois Press, 2016.

Holanda, Karla. *Documentário nordestino: Mapeamento, história e análise*. Annablume Editora, 2008.

Hordge-Freeman, Elizabeth. *The Color of Love: Racial Features, Stigma, and Socialization in Black Brazilian Families*. University of Texas Press, 2015.

Ioris, Rafael R. *Transforming Brazil: A History of National Development in the Postwar Era*. Routledge, 2014. https://doi.org/10.4324/9781315772974.

Jarrín, Carmen Alvaro. "Untranslatable Subjects: Travesti Access to Public Health Care in Brazil." *TSQ: Transgender Studies Quarterly* 3, no. 3–4 (2016): 357–75. https://doi.org/10.1215/23289252-3545095.

Johnson, Claudia D. "That Guilty Third Tier: Prostitution in Nineteenth-Century American Theaters." *American Quarterly* 27, no. 5 (December 1, 1975): 575–84. https://doi.org/10.2307/2712442.

Johnson, Randal. *The Film Industry in Brazil: Culture and the State*. University of Pittsburgh Press, 1987.

Johnson, Randal, and Robert Stam, eds. *Brazilian Cinema*. 3rd ed. Columbia University Press, 1995.

Kanost, Laura M. "Body Politics in Patrícia Galvão's 'Parque Industrial.'" *Luso-Brazilian Review* 43, no. 2 (2006): 90–102.

Karush, Matthew B. *Culture of Class: Radio and Cinema in the Making of a Divided Argentina, 1920–1946*. Duke University Press, 2012.

Kefala, Eleni. *Buenos Aires Across the Arts: Five and One Theses on Modernity, 1921–1939*. 1st ed. University of Pittsburgh Press, 2022.

Kishimoto, Alexandre. "A experiencia do cinema japonês no bairro da Liberdade." Universidade de São Paulo, 2009.

Klenotic, Jeffrey F. "Class Markers in the Mass Movie Audience: A Case Study in the Cultural Geography of Moviegoing, 1926–1932." *The Communication Review* 2, no. 4 (1998): 461–95. https://doi.org/10.1080/10714429809368568.

Koszarski, Richard. *An Evening's Entertainment: The Age of the Silent Feature Picture, 1915–1928.* University of California Press, 1994.

Kriger, Clara, and Nicolás Poppe, eds. *Salas, negocios y públicos de cine en Latinoamérica.* Prometo Editorial, 2023.

Kulick, Don. *Travesti: Sex, Gender, and Culture Among Brazilian Transgendered Prostitutes.* University of Chicago Press, 1998.

Langland, Victoria. *Speaking of Flowers: Student Movements and the Making and Remembering of 1968 in Military Brazil.* Duke University Press Books, 2013.

Lefebvre, Henri. *The Production of Space.* Wiley, 1992.

Leme, Caroline Gomes. "Nacional e cosmopolita, arcaico e moderno: O Brasil pelas lentes dos cineastas 'paulistas do entre-lugar.'" *Sociologias plurais*, no. 1 (June 1, 2012). https://doi.org/10.5380/sclplr.v0i1.64791.

Lesser, Jeffrey. *Immigration, Ethnicity, and National Identity in Brazil, 1808 to the Present.* Cambridge University Press, 2013.

Lesser, Jeffrey. *Negotiating National Identity: Immigrants, Minorities, and the Struggle for Ethnicity in Brazil.* Duke University Press, 1999.

Leu, Lorraine. *Defiant Geographies: Race and Urban Space in 1920s Rio de Janeiro.* 1st ed. University of Pittsburgh Press, 2020.

Levine, Robert M. *Father of the Poor? Vargas and His Era.* Cambridge University Press, 1998.

Levy, Aiala. "'Art, Luxury, Elegance': Crafting an Aesthetic of Aspiration in São Paulo's Early Cinemas." *Journal of Global South Studies* 38, no. 1 (2021): 25–53. https://doi.org/10.1353/gss.2021.0003.

Levy, Aiala Teresa. "Forging an Urban Public: Theaters, Audiences, and the City in São Paulo, Brazil, 1854–1924." PhD dissertation, University of Chicago, 2016. https://doi.org/10.6082/M19K485J.

Linger, Daniel Touro. *Dangerous Encounters: Meanings of Violence in a Brazilian City.* Stanford University Press, 1995.

López, A. Ricardo, and Barbara Weinstein. *The Making of the Middle Class: Toward a Transnational History.* Duke University Press, 2012.

López, Ana M. "Early Cinema and Modernity in Latin America." *Cinema Journal* 40, no. 1 (2000): 48–78.

López-Durán, Fabiola. *Eugenics in the Garden: Transatlantic Architecture and the Crafting of Modernity.* Austin: University of Texas Press, 2018.

Luca, Tania Regina de, and Ana Luiza Martins. *Imprensa e cidade.* SciELO—Editora UNESP, 2006.

Lucas, Taís Campelo. "Cinearte: O cinema brasileiro em revista (1926–1942)." Master's thesis, Universidade Federal Fluminense, 2005. https://www.historia.uff.br/stricto/teses/Dissert-2005_LUCAS_Tais_Campelo-S.pdf.

Ma, Jean. *Sounding the Modern Woman: The Songstress in Chinese Cinema.* Duke University Press Books, 2015.

Machado, Rubens. "Para uma análise interpretativa de Fragmentos da vida (São Paulo, 1929) de José Medina." *Narrativas audiovisuais nos países lusófonos: encontros, fronteiras e territórios comuns.* Editora Fi, 2022.

Macías-González, Víctor M., and Anne Rubenstein, eds. *Masculinity and Sexuality in Modern Mexico.* University of New Mexico Press, 2012.

Maltby, Richard, ed. *Going to the Movies: Hollywood and the Social Experience of Cinema.* University of Exeter Press, 2007.

Maluf, Marina, and Maria Lúcia Mott. "Recônditos do mundo feminino." In *História da vida privada no Brasil,* vol. 3, *República: Da belle époque à era do rádio,* edited by Nicolau Sevcenko and Fernando A. Novais, 367–421. Companhia das Letras, 1998.

Manzano, Valeria. *The Age of Youth in Argentina: Culture, Politics, and Sexuality from Perón to Videla.* University of North Carolina Press, 2014.

Martins, Ana Luiza, and Tania Regina de Luca. *História da imprensa no Brasil.* Editora Contexto, 2010.

Martins, Ângela Maria Roberti, and Maria Izilda Santos de Matos. "Meio anjo—meio demônio: Representações do feminino na imprensa operária." *Projeto história: Revista do programa de Estudos Pós-Graduados de História* 35 (2007). https://revistas.pucsp.br/index.php/revph/article/view/2211.

Massey, Doreen B. *Space, Place, and Gender.* University of Minnesota Press, 1994.

Matta, Roberto da. *Casa e a rua.* Rocco, 1997.

McCann, Bryan. *Hello, Hello Brazil: Popular Music in the Making of Modern Brazil.* Duke University Press, 2004.

McCleary, Kristen. "Mass, Popular, and Elite Culture? The Spanish Zarzuela in Buenos Aires, 1890–1900." *Studies in Latin American Popular Culture* 21 (2002): 1–27.

McCleary, Kristen L. *Staging Buenos Aires: Theater, Society, and Politics in Argentina, 1860–1920.* University of Pittsburgh Press, 2024.

Meade, Teresa. *"Civilizing" Rio: Reform and Resistance in a Brazilian City, 1889–1930.* Pennsylvania State University Press, 1997.

Medeiros, Hugo Augusto Vasconcelos. "Melindrosas e almofadinhas: Relações de gênero no Recife dos anos 1920." *Revista tempo e argumento* 2, no. 2 (December 9, 2010): 93–120.

Melo, Victor Andrade de. "Mulheres em movimento: a presença feminina nos primórdios do esporte na cidade do Rio de Janeiro (até 1910)." *Revista brasileira de história* 27 (December 2007): 127–52. https://doi.org/10.1590/S0102-01882007000200008.

Mizala, Camila Gatica. *Modernity at the Movies: Cinema-Going in Buenos Aires and Santiago, 1915–1945.* University of Pittsburgh Press, 2023.

Moraes, Julio Lucchesi. "A Valencian Tycoon in Brazil: The Economic Trajectory of Francisco Serrador Carbonell (1887–1921)." *Filmhistoria Online,* no. 2 (2012).

Morettin, Eduardo Victorio. "Cinema educativo: Uma abordagem histórica." *Comunicação & educação* 2, no. 4 (2008).

Morettin, Eduardo Victorio. "Dimensões históricas do documentário brasileiro no período silencioso." *Revista brasileira de história* 25, no. 49 (January 2005): 125–52. https://doi.org/10.1590/S0102-01882005000100007.

Morettin, Eduardo. *Humberto Mauro, Cinema, Historia.* Alameda, 2013.

Mott, Maria Lúcia, Maria Elisa Botelho Byington, and Olga Sofia Fabergé Alves. *O gesto que salva: Pérola Byington e a cruzada pró-infância.* Grifo Projetos Históricos, 2005.

Mulvey, Laura. "Visual Pleasure and Narrative Cinema." *Screen* 16, no. 3 (October 1, 1975): 6–18. https://doi.org/10.1093/screen/16.3.6.

Nascimento, Douglas. "A tragédia do Cine Oberdan." *São Paulo Antiga* (blog), January 13, 2011. http://www.saopauloantiga.com.br/a-tragedia-do-cine-oberdan/.

Navitski, Rielle. *Public Spectacles of Violence: Sensational Cinema and Journalism in Early Twentieth-Century Mexico and Brazil*. Duke University Press Books, 2017.

Navitski, Rielle, and Nicolas Poppe, eds. *Cosmopolitan Film Cultures in Latin America, 1896–1960*. Indian University Press, 2017.

Needell, Jeffrey D. *A Tropical Belle Epoque: Elite Culture and Society in Turn-of-the-Century Rio de Janeiro*. 1st ed. Cambridge University Press, 1987.

Negra, Diane. *Off-White Hollywood: American Culture and Ethnic Female Stardom*. Routledge, 2001.

Nobles, Melissa. *Shades of Citizenship: Race and the Census in Modern Politics*. 1st ed. Stanford University Press, 2000.

Nowell-Smith, Geoffrey. *The Oxford History of World Cinema*. Oxford University Press, 1997.

O'Dougherty, Maureen. *Consumption Intensified: The Politics of Middle-Class Daily Life in Brazil*. Duke University Press, 2002.

Ortiz, José Mario, Arthur Autran, Guiomar Ramos, Lucas Murari, Tunico Amancio, Alessandro Gamo, Luís Alberto Rocha Melo, et al. *Nova história do cinema brasileiro II*. Vol. 2. 1st ed. Edições Sesc, 2018.

Otovo, Okezi T. *Progressive Mothers, Better Babies: Race, Public Health, and the State in Brazil, 1850–1945*. Reprint ed. University of Texas Press, 2016.

Owensby, Brian. *Intimate Ironies: Modernity and the Making of Middle-Class Lives in Brazil*. Stanford University Press, 2001.

Palomino, Pablo. *The Invention of Latin American Music: A Transnational History*. Oxford University Press, 2020.

Paulillo, Maria Célia Rua de Almeida. *Tradição e modernidade: Afonso Schmidt e a literatura paulista, 1906–1928*. Annablume, 2002.

Peiss, Kathy. *Cheap Amusements: Working Women and Leisure in Turn-of-the-Century New York*. Temple University Press, 1986.

Peixoto-Mehrtens, Cristina. *Urban Space and National Identity in Early Twentieth Century São Paulo, Brazil: Crafting Modernity*. Palgrave Macmillan, 2010.

Perlongher, Néstor. *O negócio do michê: A prostituição viril em São Paulo*. Editora Brasiliense, 1987.

Piccato, Pablo. "Public Sphere in Latin America: A Map of the Historiography." *Social History* 35, no. 2 (May 2010): 165–92. https://doi.org/10.1080/03071021003795055.

Pinchiaro, Gustavo, Luciano Costa, Ricardo Casarin, and Renan Rodrigues. *Glamour e boca do lixo: Histórias da prostituição no centro de São Paulo*. Editora Multifoco, 2010.

Pinheiro, Larissa Brum Leite Gusmão. "Melindrosas e almofadinhas de J. Carlos: Questões de gênero na Revista Para Todos . . . (1922–1931)." Master's thesis, Universidade Federal do Paraná, 2015.

Porter, Susie S. "'And That It Is Custom Makes It Law': Class Conflict and Gender Ideology in the Public Sphere, Mexico City, 1880–1910." *Social Science History* 24, no. 1 (2000): 111–48.

Purcell, Fernando. *¡De película!: Hollywood y su impacto en Chile, 1910–1950*. Taurus, 2012.

Rabinovitz, Lauren. *For the Love of Pleasure: Women, Movies, and Culture in Turn-of-the-Century Chicago*. Rutgers University Press, 1998.

Rago, Margareth. *Do cabaré ao lar: A utopia da cidade disciplinar, Brasil 1890–1930*. 4th ed. Editora Paz e Terra, 2014.

Rago, Margareth. *Prazeres da noite: Prostituição e códigos da sexualidade feminina em São Paulo (1890–1930)*. 2nd ed. Paz e Terra, 2008.

Ramos, Fernão Pessoa, and Sheila Schvarzman, eds. *Nova história do cinema brasileiro I*. Vol. 1. Edição ampliada, Kindle ed. Edições Sesc, 2018.

Resende, Beatriz. "Melindrosa e almofadinha, cock-tail e arranha-céu: a literatura e os vertiginosos anos 20." In *Entre Europa e Africa: A invenção do carioca*, edited by Antônio Herculano Lopes, 217–30. Fundação Casa Rui Barbosa, Topbooks, 2000.

Ripó Neto, Francisco Romero. "Práticas homossexuais masculinas nos cinemas do centro de São Paulo." Undergraduate thesis, Fundação Escola de Sociologia e Política de São Paulo, 1996. Cinemateca Brasileira São Paulo.

Roberts, Shari. "'The Lady in the Tutti-Frutti Hat': Carmen Miranda, a Spectacle of Ethnicity." *Cinema Journal* 32, no. 3 (1993): 3–23. https://doi.org/10.2307/1225876.

Rogin, Michael. *Blackface, White Noise: Jewish Immigrants in the Hollywood Melting Pot*. University of California Press, 1998.

Rolnik, Raquel. *A cidade e a lei: Legislação, política urbana e territórios na cidade de São Paulo*. Studio Nobel, 1997.

Rolnik, Raquel. "The City and the Law: Legislation, Urban Policy and Territories in the City of São Paulo (1886–1936)." New York University, Graduate School of Arts and Sciences, 1995.

Romo, Anadelia A. *Brazil's Living Museum: Race, Reform, and Tradition in Bahia*. University of North Carolina Press, 2010.

Rubenstein, Anne. "A Sentimental and Sexual Education." *Mexican Studies/Estudios Mexicanos* 36, no. 1–2 (August 12, 2020): 216–42. https://doi.org/10.1525/msem.2020.36.1-2.216.

Rubenstein, Anne. "Theaters of Masculinity." In Macías-González and Rubenstein, eds., *Masculinity and Sexuality in Modern Mexico*. University of New Mexico Press, 2012.

Saes, Décio. *Classe média e sistema político no Brasil*. TA Queiroz, 1985.

Saliba, Maria. *Cinema contra cinema: O cinema educativo de Canuto Mendes, 1922–1931*. Annablume, 2003.

Salles Gomes, Paulo Emilio. *Cinema: Trajetória no Subdesenvolvimento*. 2nd ed. Paz e Terra, 1996.

Salles Gomes, Paulo Emílio. *Humberto Mauro, Cataguases, Cinearte*. 1st ed. Perspectiva, 1974.

Sarzynski, Sarah. *Revolution in the Terra do Sol: The Cold War in Brazil*. 1st ed. Stanford University Press, 2018.

Schaefer, Eric. *Bold! Daring! Shocking! True: A History of Exploitation Films, 1919–1959*. Duke University Press Books, 1999.

Schelling, Vivian. *Through the Kaleidoscope: The Experience of Modernity in Latin America*. Verso, 2000.

Schvarzman, Sheila. *Humberto Mauro e as imagens do Brasil*. Kindle ed. UNESP, 2004.

Schvarzman, Sheila. "Ir ao cinema em São Paulo nos anos 20." *Revista brasileira de história* 25, no. 49 (2005): 153–74.

Schpun, Mônica Raisa. *Beleza em jogo: Cultura física e comportamento em São Paulo nos anos 20*. Editora SENAC São Paulo, 1999.

Seigel, Micol. *Uneven Encounters: Making Race and Nation in Brazil and the United States*. Duke University Press, 2010.

Serna, Laura Isabel. *Making Cinelandia: American Films and Mexican Film Culture Before the Golden Age*. Duke University Press, 2014.

Sevcenko, Nicolau. *Orfeu extático na Metrópole: São Paulo, sociedade e cultura nos frementes anos 20*. Companhia das Letras, 1992.

Sewell, Jessica Ellen. *Women and the Everyday City: Public Space in San Francisco, 1890–1915*. University of Minnesota Press, 2011.

Shaw, Lisa, and Stephanie Dennison. *Brazilian National Cinema*. Routledge, 2007.

Silveira, Rafael Gavião da, and Francione Oliveira Carvalho. "Embrafilme x Boca do Lixo: as relações entre financiamento e liberdade no cinema brasileiro nos anos 70 e 80." *Aurora: Revista de Arte, Mídia e Política* 8, no. 24 (2015): 73–93.

Silverman, Kaja. *The Acoustic Mirror: The Female Voice in Psychoanalysis and Cinema*. Indiana University Press, 1988.

Simili, Ivana Guilherme. *Mulher e política: A trajetória da primeira-dama Darcy Vargas, 1930–1945*. Editora Unesp, 2008.

Simis, Anita. *Estado e cinema no Brasil*. Annablume, 2008.

Simões, Inimá. *Salas de cinema em São Paulo*. Secretaria Municipal de Cultura de São Paulo, 1990.

Simões, Inimá. *Roteiro da intolerância: A censura cinematográfica no Brasil*. Editora SENAC, 1998.

Singer, Ben. *Melodrama and Modernity: Early Sensational Cinema and Its Contexts*. Columbia University Press, 2001.

Siqueira, Renata Monteiro. "O Largo da Banana e a presença negra em São Paulo." *Anais do Museu Paulista: História e Cultura Material* 28 (July 15, 2020): d1e9. https://doi.org/10.1590/1982-02672020v28d1e9.

Skidmore, Thomas E. *Black into White: Race and Nationality in Brazilian Thought: With a Preface to the 1993 Edition and Bibliography*. Duke University Press, 1993.

Slide, Anthony. *Nitrate Won't Wait: A History of Film Preservation in the United States*. McFarland, 2000.

Sluis, Ageeth. "Bataclanismo! Or, How Female Deco Bodies Transformed Postrevolutionary Mexico City." *The Americas* 66, no. 4 (2010): 469–99. https://doi.org/10.1353/tam.0.0258.

Sluis, Ageeth. *Deco Body, Deco City: Female Spectacle and Modernity in Mexico City, 1900–1939*. Reprint ed. University of Nebraska Press, 2016.

Souza, Carlos Roberto de. "O cinema em São Paulo (1912–1930)." In *Nova história do cinema brasileiro I*, vol. 1, edited by Fernão Pessoa Ramos and Sheila Schvarzman, Edição ampliada, Kindle ed. Edições Sesc, 2018.

Souza, José Inácio de Melo. *Imagens do passado: São Paulo e Rio de Janeiro nos primórdios do cinema*. Senac, 2003.

Souza, José Inácio de Melo. "Os primórios do cinema no Brasil." In *Nova história do cinema brasileiro I. Vol. 1*, edited by Fernão Pessoa Ramos and Sheila Schvarzman, Edição ampliada, Kindle ed. Edições Sesc, 2018.

Souza, José Inácio de Melo. *Salas de cinema e história urbana de São Paulo (1895–1930): O cinema dos engenheiros*. 1st ed. Senac São Paulo, 2016.

Sowerwine, Charles, and Gabrielle Wolf. "Echoes of Paris in the Antipodes: French Theatre and Opera in Melbourne (1850–1914)." *Australian Journal of French Studies* 45, no. 1 (January 2008): 81–98.

Stacey, Jackie. *Star Gazing: Hollywood Cinema and Female Spectatorship*. Routledge, 1994.

Stam, Robert. *Tropical Multiculturalism: A Comparative History of Race in Brazilian Cinema and Culture*. Duke University Press, 1997.

Stamp, Shelley. *Movie-Struck Girls: Women and Motion Picture Culture After the Nickelodeon*. Princeton University Press, 2000.

Stepan, Nancy. *The Hour of Eugenics: Race, Gender, and Nation in Latin America*. Cornell University Press, 1991.

Steward, Jill R. "Moral Economies and Commercial Imperatives: Food, Diets and Spas in

Central Europe: 1800–1914." *Journal of Tourism History* 4, no. 2 (August 2012): 181–203. https://doi.org/10.1080/1755182X.2012.697487.

Stewart, Jacqueline Najuma. *Migrating to the Movies: Cinema and Black Urban Modernity*. University of California Press, 2005.

Stratigakos, Despina. *A Women's Berlin: Building the Modern City*. University of Minnesota Press, 2008.

Studlar, Gaylyn. *This Mad Masquerade: Stardom and Masculinity in the Jazz Age*. Columbia University Press, 1996.

Suk, Lena Oak. "Beauty in Black and White? Race, Beauty, and the 1926 Fox Film Photogenic Beauty Contest in Brazil." *Latin American Research Review* 54, no. 4 (October 2019): 909–26. https://doi.org/10.25222/larr.4.

Suk, Lena Oak. "'Only the Fragile Sex Admitted': The Women's Restaurant in 1920s São Paulo, Brazil." *Journal of Social History* 51, no. 3 (2018): 592–620. https://doi.org/10.1093/jsh/shw116.

Süssekind, Flora. *Cinematograph of Words: Literature, Technique, and Modernization in Brazil*. Translated by Paulo Henriques Britto. Stanford University Press, 1997.

Taylor, Richard. *The Politics of the Soviet Cinema 1917–1929*. Cambridge University Press, 2008.

Teixeira Furlani, Lúcia Maria. *Os cadernos de Pagú: manuscritos de Patrícia Galvão*. 1st ed. Nocelli, 2023.

Teixeira Furlani, Lúcia Maria, and Geraldo Galvão Ferraz. *Viva Pagu: Fotobiografia de Patrícia Galvão*. Editora Unisanta, 2010.

Telles, Edward. *Pigmentocracies: Ethnicity, Race, and Color in Latin America*. University of North Carolina Press, 2014.

Thompson, Kristin. *Exporting Entertainment: America in the World Film Market, 1907–34*. BFI Publishing, 1985.

Toffell, Gil. "'Come See, and Hear, the Mother Tongue!': Yiddish Cinema in Interwar London." *Screen* 50, no. 3 (October 1, 2009): 277–98. https://doi.org/10.1093/screen/hjp018.

Tossounian, Cecilia. *La Joven Moderna in Interwar Argentina: Gender, Nation, and Popular Culture*. 1st ed. University of Florida Press, 2019.

Tota, Antonio Pedro. *O imperialismo sedutor: A americanização do Brasil na época da Segunda Guerra*. Companhia das Letras, 2000.

Trusz, Alice Dubina. *Entre lanternas mágicas e cinematógrafos*. Terceiro nome, 2010.

Tsivian, Yuri. *Early Cinema in Russia and Its Cultural Reception*. Edited by Richard Taylor. Translated by Alan Bodger. University of Chicago Press, 1998.

Vasey, Ruth. *The World According to Hollywood, 1918–1939*. University of Wisconsin Press, 1997.

Vaughan, Mary Kay. *Portrait of a Young Painter: Pepe Zúñiga and Mexico City's Rebel Generation*. Duke University Press Books, 2014.

Vianna, Hermano. *The Mystery of Samba: Popular Music and National Identity in Brazil*. 1st ed. University of North Carolina Press, 1999.

Weinbaum, Alys Eve, Lynn M. Thomas, Priti Ramamurthy, Uta G. Poiger, Madeleine Yue Dong, and Tani E. Barlow. *The Modern Girl Around the World: Consumption, Modernity, and Globalization*. Duke University Press, 2008.

Weinstein, Barbara. *The Color of Modernity: São Paulo and the Making of Race and Nation in Brazil*. Duke University Press, 2015.

Weinstein, Barbara. *For Social Peace in Brazil: Industrialists and the Remaking of the Working Class in São Paulo, 1920–1964*. University of North Carolina Press, 1996.

Weinstein, Barbara. "'They Don't Even Look Like Women Workers': Femininity and Class in Twentieth-Century Latin America." *International Labor and Working-Class History* 69, no. 1 (2006): 161–76. https://doi.org/10.1017/S0147547906000093.

Wells, Sarah Ann. *Media Laboratories: Late Modernist Authorship in South America*. Chicago: Northwestern University Press, 2017.

Williams, Daryle. *Culture Wars in Brazil: The First Vargas Regime, 1930–1945*. Duke University Press, 2001.

Wolfe, Joel. *Working Women, Working Men: São Paulo and the Rise of Brazil's Industrial Working Class, 1900–1955*. Duke University Press, 1993.

Woodard, James P. *Brazil's Revolution in Commerce: Creating Consumer Capitalism in the American Century*. University of North Carolina Press, 2020.

Woodard, James P. *A Place in Politics: São Paulo, Brazil, from Seigneurial Republicanism to Regionalist Revolt*. Duke University Press, 2009.

Xavier, Ismail. *Allegories of Underdevelopment: Aesthetics and Politics in Modern Brazilian Cinema*. University of Minnesota Press, 1997.

Xavier, Ismail. *Sétima arte, um culto moderno: o idealismo estético e o cinema*. 2nd ed. SESC, 2017.

Zolov, Eric. *Refried Elvis: The Rise of the Mexican Counterculture*. University of California Press, 1999.

INDEX

Note: Page numbers in *italics* indicate figures

Abie's Irish Rose (film), 134–35
A Cigarra, 30, 133, 138
Acrópole, *156*, *169*
advertisements, 3, 6, 9, 85, 94; Afro-Brazilian women in, 39; elegant women in, 88, 101; exploitation films in, 85–86, *87*; fashions and hairstyles in, 38; in mid- and late twentieth century, 148–49; and moralism, 148–49; Pathé-Baby in, 43–44, *44*; in São Paulo, 107, *108*, 120, 134–35, 137; *senhoras* and, 101–2, 106
Afro-Paulista newspapers, 37–38, 129, 131, 133
A Grande Arte (Fonseca), 161–62
Aitaré of the Beach (film), 57–58, 64
A Liberdade, 28, 131–32
Almeida, Heloísa Buarque de, 124, 155–58, 163
almofadinha, 43, 149; as counterpart to *melindrosa*, 32–33; mocking fashion/grooming procedures of, 58–59, *59*
Amaral, Suzana, 165, 175–76
Andrews, George Reid, 184n63
"anthropophagy," concept, 29
architecture (of movie theaters): balconies, 104, 168–69; bathrooms, 98–106, *103*; tiered seating, 119–20. *See also* movie theaters
Argentina, 31, 38–39, 103, 113, 129, 163
A Rua, 38, 132
Avenida Rio Branco (in Rio de Janeiro), 92–95
Barros, Leonor Mendes de (Dona Leanor), 145
Barreto, Benedito Bastos (Belmonte), 39–41
Barro, Máximo, 158–59, 162
Barros, Adhemar de, 144
Barros, Dona Leonor Mendes de, 144–45
Bataclan, 38–39, 42

Behring, Mario, 53
Belmonte. *See* Barreto, Benedito Bastos
Besse, Susan, 9, 179
Bethania, Maria, 171–72
Biáfora, Rubem, 159, 162–63, 170–73
Black characters in Hollywood films, documenting, 129–30
Black communities in São Paulo, moviegoing in, 8, 24, 28, 37–38, 132, 197n97; comparison to US racial segregation, 126; early twentieth-century Black press, 201n79; identification with Blackness, 185n85; interpretations of cinema, 128–31; silence and erasures, 127–28
Black and immigrant communities, comparisons and interactions in moviegoing in, 128–31, 134–35, 137. *See also* Black communities in São Paulo, moviegoing in; immigrant communities in São Paulo, moviegoing in
Black Man Who Had a White Soul, The (film), 129
Boca do Lixo (film subgenre), 165–68
Boca do Lixo (neighborhood), 161, 165–68, 170
bolinas, 6–7, 42, 93
bourgeois woman consumer, 149–50
Brasa Dormida (film), 77
Brás (neighborhood), 102, 115–19
Brazil, 3, 27, 51, 85, 107, 141; aspirational models, 22; fatherhood and patriarchy in, 57–66; film criticism growth in, 18; geography of moviegoing in, 111–19; global changes in filmmaking in, 16–17; house-street contrast, 46–50; light-darkness dichotomy, 20–21; microhierarchies,

119–26; moralism, 143–52; movie-struck girls in, 42–46; overview, 3–7, 175–80; racial hierarchies in, 21–22, 53, 92, 181n5; relationship between film culture and modernity in, 19–20; respectable womanhood in, 93–97; rise of grander movie theaters in, 17–18; sanitation movement in, 87–93; in the twenties, 110–11; twentieth-century São Paulo, 8–13, 141–73; urban space, 22–23; women and gender norms shaping society of, 5–6. *See also* Cinelândia (Centro neighborhood of São Paulo); gender; moviegoing, culture of; São Paulo (city), moviegoing in; women, moviegoing activities of

Brazilian cinema, 56, 66, 76, 79, 82, 111, 143; *chanchadas* (musical comedies), 54, 143–44; educational cinema, 20, 25, 141, 147, 197n12; exploitation films, 85–87, 188n2; "golden age" of, 16; nationalist vision of, 54–55; *pornochanchada* (Brazilian sex comedy), 165–66; regional film cycles, 55–57; "scientific" films, 86–88, 106–7; silent cinema, 51–84. *See also* moviegoing, culture of

Brazilian Old Republic, 8–9
Brito e Cunha, José Carlos de (Belmonte), 33–35
Butler, Kim, 127, 129

Caldeira, Teresa, 166
cartoons, 33, 35, 42, 46, 50, 58, 149
Catholic Action, 145–46
Catholic Church, 18, 145–46
Caulfield, Sueann, 11, 32, 132–33
cazuelas. *See* architecture (of movie theaters): balconies
Celso, Maria Eugenia, 176–77
Centro (São Paulo neighborhood), 116–19, 134; Boca de Lixo, 161–73; Cinelândia, 152–61. *See also* São Paulo (city), moviegoing in
Certeau, Michel de, 105, 125–26
chanchadas (musical comedies), 54, 143–44
Cinearte, 18, 19, 33, 56, 86, 110–11; circulation of, 54; covering moviegoing scene in São Paulo, 113–14; emphasizing image of progress, 54–55; establishing, 53–54; and gendered respectability, 93–97; 123–24; praising *Lips Without Kisses*, 75–76; reviewing *The Lawyer's Daughter*, 64–66; specific commentary on race and eugenics in, 54–55, 127, 188n10; supporting *Fragments of Life*, 82–84

Cine Art-Palácio, 152–53, 167
Cine Capitólio, 95–97, *96*, 154
cine-clubs, 18, 134
Cine Ipiranga, *156*, 160; side balconies of, 168–70, *169*
Cinelândia (Centro neighborhood of São Paulo): advent of 3D films in, 154–55; ambivalence surrounding moviegoing in, 153–54; movie theaters of, 152–53; popularity of moviegoing in, 153; shifting use of movie theaters in, 166–67; and social status of cinemas, 155–61
cinemas. *See* movie theaters
"Cinema in the Light and the Dark" (essay), 6–7, 131–32, 141, 141
"cinema marginal" (film genre), 167
Cinema Novo, 164
Cinema Odeon (São Paulo), 88, 101, 107, 109, 137, 139, 141, 149
cinema of the outskirts, 92–93, 101, 113–15
Cine Marabá (São Paulo), 161–62, 167
Cinemateca Brasileira (São Paulo), 157, 199n57
Cine Metro (São Paulo), 149, *150*, 153–54
Cine Oberdan (São Paulo), 102–6, *103*, 134
Cine Paramount (São Paulo), 134–35, 152
Cine República, 3, 99, 135–37, 152, 154; establishment of, 119–23, *121*,
cine-teatros, 89, 119, 152
city, 175–80; Black and immigrant communities in, 126–37; finding love in, 137–40; *Fragments of Life* depicting, 76–84; geography of moviegoing in, 111–26; ideologies of hygiene in, 87–93; in *Lips Without Kisses*, 66–76; modern city, 5–6, 14–15, 25–26, 43, 53, 75, 77, 81, 84, 177, 180; moralism in, 143–52; moviegoers' experiences, 109–11; municipal regula-

tion in, 97–100; polarized perspectives, 161–72; portrayal in *The Lawyer's Daughter*, 61–66; social status, 152–61; urban reform, 87–93. *See also* Brazil; São Paulo (city), moviegoing in

Civilization and Barbarism (Belmonte), 39

Conde, Maite, 14, 30–31, 37, 55

consumer culture, growth of, 30–31, 148

Costallat, Benjamim, 37

Couto, Ribeiro, 114–15, 118–19

Cowan, Benjamin, 164

Crawford, Joan, 45–47

crônistas, 13, 41–42

cultural imperialism, women and, 45–46

Cunha, Horacio da, 130–31

Cunha Filho, Paulo Carneiro da, 55, 64

da Matta, Roberto, 11, 43

"darkness": associating cinema with, 20–21, 50, 118, 142, 158–61, 177; meaning of, 6–7

dating, oral histories of, 155–56, 184n64; certain cinemas as more romantic than others, 160; darkness of the cinema, 159–60; gendered respectability, 158–59; nostalgia, 157; personal ads, 137–40; sanctioning flirtations, 160–61; São Paulo moviegoing communities, 126–37. *See also* ethnography, conducting interviews for; oral histories; polarized perspectives

Department for Public Works (São Paulo), 98

domestic space, 13, 45

domestic sphere, 13, 30–31, 42, 46, 142

educational cinema, 20, 25, 141, 147, 197n12

elite class, cultural construction of, 120

Embrafilme, 164–65

Estado de S. Paulo, 85

"Estado Novo," establishment of, 143

ethnography, conducting interviews for, 155–56; certain cinemas as more romantic than others, 160; gendered respectability, 158–59; legitimizing formerly illicit activities, 158; nostalgia, 157; recalling darkness of the cinema, 159–60;

sanctioning flirtations, 160–61; speaking with more women than men, 157. *See also* oral histories

exhibitors (of film), 17, 89, 98, 102, 126–27, 134

exploitation films, 85–87, 188n2

exploration films, critiquing, 51, 54–55, 144

Facundo: Civilización y Barbarie (Sarmiento), 39–40

family, 5–6, 11, 24, 97, 110, 115; defining "traditional" Brazilian family, 52–53, 147–49; depiction in *Fragments of Life*, 76, 80–81, 84; depiction in *Lips Without Kisses*, 67, 73–75; depiction in *The Lawyer's Daughter*, 58, 61–64, *62*, 66, 75; gender and urban space, 13; moviegoing "modern girls" and, 31–33; movie-struck girls and, 42–45, 146; predicting downfall of, 46–50, 142, 155, 161, 173, 177–78; and rise of Brazilian film culture, 21

Female Catholic Student Youth. *See* Juventude Estudantíl Católica Feminina (JECF)

Ferreira, Jairo, 158, 162–63, 167–73

filmmakers, Brazilian, 16, 23, 25, 52–53, 164–65

fire hazards, film material and, 89

flaneur, concept, 13

Fonseca, Rubem, 161–62, 167

Fragments of Life (film), 52, 56, 111, 176; *Cineart* supporting, 82–84; comparing/contrasting with other films, 76–84; demonstrating working poor desperation/futility, 77–79, *78*; exploring urban poverty in, 76–77; last scenes of, 79–81; perspective on urban life in, 81; plot of, 76–77; visual contrast between progress and poverty in, *78*; women as minor "extras" in, 81; working-class immigrants in, 81–82

Fraissat, J., 98

French monikers, *melindrosa* adopting, 36–37

Freyre, Gilberto, 57, 201n79

Galvão, Maria Rita, 119
Galvão, Patrícia, 29, 45, 115–19
gender, 178; in Brazilian print culture, 27–28; defining roles of, 147–48; in early twentieth-century Brazil, 8–13; gender-bending, 33, 35, 163; "good" and "improper" neighborhoods, 114; influence of Frensh fashions on gender norms, 37–38; methodology, 23–26; modern girls, 28–42; movie-struck girls, 42–46; propriety and, 6–7, 11, 70, 93, 95, 100, 124, 130, 142, 148, 170, 178; and respectability, 52, 93, 140, 158; and rise of Brazilian film culture, 16–23; roles, 15–16, 20, 24–25, 27, 30–33, 41, 52, 56, 61, 74–75, 81, 142, 164, 179, 192n37; sex-segregated bathrooms, 100–106; and urban space, 13–16
gendered respectability, 52, 93, 140, 158
geography (of São Paulo moviegoing): division between center and periphery, 113–14; expanding beyond the Triangle, 112–13; fluid microhierarchies among people living in peripheral neighborhoods, 114–15; "good" and "improper" neighborhoods, 114–15; *Industrial Park* and, 115–19; map of cinemas in São Paulo, *112*; places of amusement, 111–12
Germany, eugenicists in, 88
Gillette, advertisement from, *148*, 149
girl. See *moça*
Gomes, Paulo Emílio Salles, 54–55
Gonzaga, Adhemar, 51, 53, 55–56, 152; and moralism, 143–45; reporting on "cathedrals of cinema," 123–24
Gonzaga, Alice, 101, 119
"good neighborhoods," geographical and social hierarchies within, 114

Habermas, Jürgen, 13
Hark, Ina Rae, 192n37
Helvécio (character). See *Lawyer's Daughter, The* (film)
Hershfield, Joanne, 31
Hochman, Gilberto, 91
Hollywood, 4, 15, 56, 64, 153–54; appropriating symbols of, 141; B movies, 165; conforming to style of, 61; criticizing gender roles in films of, 130; depiction of Black characters in, 126, 128–29; fearing cultural imperialism of, 50; films in "good" central neighborhoods, 114; gendered visions of urban life, 175–76; and moralism, 145–46; and movie-struck girls, 42–46, 117; and rise of Brazilian film culture, 16–23
honor: early twentieth-century Brazil and, 8–13; masculine honor, 80–82; violations of, 132–33; women and, 15, 41, 58, 63, 140
Hour of the Star, The, 175–76
house, safety of, 11. See also family; women, moviegoing activities of
hygiene (in movie theaters): "corrupted air" (*ar viciado*), 91–94, 98; defining *senhoras* in public bathrooms, 101–6, *103*; glasses and, 154–55; and gendered respectability, 93–97; municipal regulation, 97–100; overview, 85–87; public health and movie theaters, 87–93; race and eugenics, 87–88, 106, 178; sex-segregated bathrooms, 100–101; ventilation, 88, 92, 95. See also sanitation

illicit behavior, rumors and urban legends of, 166–70
illustrated magazines, audiences of, 29–30
immigrant communities in São Paulo, moviegoing in, 123, 126, 130; creating diasporic experiences, 133; diasporic and interethnic experiences, 137; "immigrant" themes in films, 134–35; mutual aid societies, 134; and social etiquette, 131; theaters for specific ethnic communities, 133–37
immigrants, 8, 16, 19, 22, 81, 98, 110; in contrast to and interactions with Black community of São Paulo, 126–40
Industrial Park (Galvão), 115–19

J. Carlos (pseudonym), 33–35, *34*, *35*, 39, 43, 53, 58; presenting divisions between house and street, 46–50, *47*, *48*, *49*

Japanese cinema, movie theaters of, 133–34
JECF. *See* Juventude Estudantíl Católica Feminina
jeitinhos, 125
Jewish Brazilians, 134–35
Jornal do Brasil, 75–76
Jornal do Comércio, 91, 99
joven moderna (modern youth), 31
Juventude Estudantíl Católica Feminina (JECF), 146

Kiss That Kills, The (film), 85–87, 106
Klaxon, 29, 115
Kubitschek, Juscelino, 143, 163
Kursaal Steaks (São Paulo), 89–90, 93, 98

ladies, title. See *senhoras*
landscape (urban), defining, 14
Lawyer's Daughter, The (film), 52, 56; city-country dichotomy in, 64–65, *65*; gendered archetypes in, 58
League of Catholic Women, 145
Lee, Rita, 141–42
Liberdade (neighborhood), 133–34
"light," associating cinema with, 20, 26, 88, 132, 138, 140, 157
Lima, Pedro, 54, 66
Lips Without Kisses (film), 52, 56, 66, 101; cosmopolitanism of, 67; depicting urban space, 70–73, *71, 72, 73*; first scenes of, 68; happing ending of, 73–75; restoration of gender norms and family in, 67; reviews of, 75–76; "romantic" encounters in, 68–70, *69*
López, Ana M., 19–20

mademoiselle, 12, 37, 94
Mademoiselle Cinema (Costallat), 37
magazines, personal ads in, 137–40. *See also* personal ads, themes of love and romance in
Maltby, Richard, 183n49
masculinity, 11, 32, 52, 80–81, 172
Matta, Roberto da, 11
Mauro, Humberto, 54, 77
Medina, José, 76, *78*, 79, *80*, 82

melindrosa (modern girl), 5, 12, *69*, 81, 97, 149, 159, 164, 177; *almofadinha* (male counterpart to), 32–33; anxieties channeled into, 27–28; appearance and habits of, 31–32; Black women in role of, 38–39; cartoons representing ambivalence of, 33–35, *34, 35*; historical context of, 28–30; influence of French fashions on, 37; in *Lips Without Kisses*, 66–76; and movie-struck girl, 42–46; outward appearance of, 73–75; presentation of, 9; producing images of, 39–40; racial ambiguity of, 39; representing societal anxieties, 39; and variations of femininity, 40–41; visibility and desirability of, 46; as "woman of the street," 47–48
Melo Souza, José Inácio de, 88, 99, 192n42
Mendes, Gabus, 93–94, 113–14, 118–19
methodology, 23–26
Mexico, 31, 38, 72, 160, 164
microhierarchies (in movie theaters): appropriateness of women, 123–24; barriers between seating sections, 120; belittling cinema managers, 123; building cine-teatros, 119; and cultural constructions, 120; identifying "most distinguished families," 122; interviewees recalling, 125–26; pricing box seats, 120; private boxes, 122–23; social rules governing separate seating sections, 124; tiered seating, 119–20
middle class, 149–51, *150*, 160–61: as category, 147–48; cultural construction of, 120; defining, 30
Midnight Bar and Café (São Paulo), 89–90, 93
Miranda, Carmen, 54, 144
modern girl, archetype, 60–61. See also *melindrosa* (modern girl)
modernity: aspirational model for Brazilian film culture, 22; light-darkness dichotomy, 20–21; racial hierarchies, 21–22; relationship between film culture and, 19–20; urban space and, 22
moralism: bourgeois woman consumer, 149–50; and consumption habits, 147–48;

defining gender and family roles, 147–48; discourse on good/bad potential of cinema, 145; educating viewers, 146–47; finding God in film, 145–46; and growing consumer culture, 148; identifying mid-century "golden age," 143–45; middle-classness, 149–51, *150*

moviegoing, culture of, 3, 27, 51, 85, 107, 141; Black and immigrant communities of São Paulo, 126–37; Cinelândia constitution, 152–61; finding love in magazine ads, 137–40; geography, 111–19; historians looking at movie theaters, 14–15; house-street contrast, 46–50; microhierarchies, 119–26; moralism, 143–52; municipal regulation, 97–100; overview, 3–7, 175–80; polarized perspectives, 161–73; regional film production, 53–56; respectable womanhood, 93–97; rise and evolution, 16–23; sanitation movement, 87–93; sex-segregated bathrooms, 100–101; twenties moviegoing, 110–11; valuations of sexual morality and social status, 12

movie-struck girl: children faithfully mimicking love scenes, 43; concerns about family abandonment, 45; critics of, 42–43; and cultural imperialism, 45–46; overview, 42. See also *melindrosa* (modern girl)

movie theaters: advent of 3D films in, 154–55; associating with "darkness," 20–21; competing businesses, 89–90; as dark and enclosed space, 90–91; in the "dark" and the "light," 6–7; defining *senhoras* in public bathrooms, 101–6, *103*; as double-edged sword, 7; in early twentieth century, 108–9; exploitation films in, 85–87; fashioning modern nationhood, 55–56; fear of toxic air in, 90–91; fire hazards in, 89; gendered respectability in, 93–97; historians looking at, 14–15; identifying first "modern" cinemas, 152–53; indeterminacy of, 89; and local urban context, 56; microhierarchies in, 119–26; and middle-classness, 149–52; mitigating "darkness of the cinemas," 159–60; municipal regulation of, 97–100; "policing" of, 54–55; reflecting social differences in, 12; sanctioning flirtations in, 160–61; sex-segregated bathrooms, 100–101; shifting use of theaters in São Paulo, 161–73; social status of, 155–61; testing ideologies of hygiene in, 87–93

municipal regulation (of movie theaters), 97–100

national literacy rate in 1920s, 29–30
newspapers, audiences of, 29–30
newsreels, investing in, 144–45
Nil, Eva, 17
nitrate, film material containing, 89, 93
northeastern Brazilians (regional identity), 170–73

O Clarim da Alvorada, 28, 37, 130–31
O Correio Paulistano, 43, 151, 153
O Estado de S. Paulo, 107, *108*, 120, 122
O Homem do Povo, 45
O Progresso, 28, 38, 129–30
oral histories, 16, 25–26, 134, 162, 167, 170; contrasts and, 142–43; recalling social status through, 109, 155–61; silences and erasures, 127–28; and white-presenting women, 127. See also polarized perspectives
Otelo, Grande, 54, 144

Pagú. See Galvão, Patrícia
Palácio do Cinema, 172
Palcos e Telas, 18, 54
Para Todos, 51, 66, 133; deeming some cinemas better than others, 92; and gendered propriety, 93–95, *96*; and gendered respectability, 93–97; and modern girls, 33–36, *34*, *35*, 39–40, *40*; and movie-struck girl, *44*; popularizing *melindrosa* in, 53–54; and "unhygienic" cinemas, 101; victims and vamps, *47*, *48*, *49*. See also *Cinearte*
Pathé-Baby (product), 43–45

Penteado, Jacob, 89, 133
personal ads, themes of love and romance in, 137–40
places of amusement, cinemas and, 111–12
polarized perspectives: films produced in Boca do Lixo area, 165–66; mistrust of youth and counterculture, 170–73; peaks and valleys in film industry influencing, 164–65; rumors and urban legends of illicit behavior, 167–70; shifting use of São Paulo movie theaters, 166–67; shocking and violent use of Cine Marabá, 161–62; turbulent political and social changes influencing, 163–64; wider anxieties revealed by, 162–63
Polytheama, Brás, 93–94
population growth (in Brazil), shifts in, 8–9
pornochanchada (Brazilian sex comedy), 165–66
pornography, 164–66, 172
Praça República, 112–13
print culture (of Brazil): house-street contrast depicted in, 46–50; "modern girl" figure in, 28–42; movie-struck girl in, 42–46; overview, 27–28, 50
prostitution, specter of, 31, 36
public health officials, 22, 32, 87, 89, 91–92, 95
public space, 9, 25, 42, 50, 104, 147, 166, 179
public sphere, 13–14

"racial democracy," myth, 21, 57, 127, 132, 187n36, 201n79
racial hierarchies, 21–22
racial identity, honor and, 11
Rago, Margareth, 14, 31, 36
regional film cycles (of Brazil), 55–57
regional production (of silent cinema), 53–56
religious groups, appealing to, 134–35
Resende, Beatriz, 31–32, 58
respectability, gendering, 93–97, *98*
Revista Feminina, 31, 42, 54
Río, Dolores del, 22, 144
Rio de Janeiro, moviegoing in, 8, *10*, 113, 151; *Cinearte* emerging from, 53–55;

rationale for focusing on, 18–19; gendered respectability in, 93–97; inauguration of Cine Capitólio in, 154–55; movie theaters in, 17–18; print culture in, 28–30; producing *Lips Without Kisses* in, 66–76; sanitation movement in, 87; "select" cinemas in, 43; tiered seating in, 119. *See also* moviegoing, culture of; São Paulo (city), moviegoing in
Rolnik, Raquel, 97
Rossi, Gilberto, 76, 79, 82
Rubenstein, Anne, 104, 160

sanitation: defining *senhoras* in public bathrooms, 101–6, *103*; and gendered respectability, 93–97; glasses and, 154–55; movement, 25, 86, 92, 154; municipal regulation, 97–100; sex-segregated bathrooms, 100–101; testing ideologies of hygiene in, 87–93
São Paulo (city), moviegoing in, 3–5, 8, *171*; Black and immigrant communities, 126–37; Cinelândia constitution, 152–61; defining *senhoras* in public bathrooms, 101–6, *103*; expanding population, 110; exploitation films in, 85–87; finding love in magazine ads, 137–40; rationale for focusing on, 18–19; gendered respectability in, 93–97; geography of moviegoing, 111–19; map of cinemas in, *112*; microhierarchies, 119–26; moralism, 143–52; movie theaters in, 17–18; municipal regulation in, 97–100; newspapers and periodicals in, 18; overview, 107–10, 141–42, 175–80; polarized perspectives, 161–73; print culture in, 28–30; sanitation movement in, 87–93; sex-segregated bathrooms, 100–101; twenties moviegoing, 110–11; mid-to-late twentieth-century moviegoing, 141–73
São Paulo Modern Art Movement, 29
Scena Muda, 18, 54
"scientific" films, 86–88, 106–7. *See also* exploitation films
scientific motherhood, 32
Segreto, Paschoal, 111

Selecta, 18, 66
senhoras (ladies), 3, 12; defining in public bathrooms, 101–6, *103*; and gendered respectability, 93–97; and ideologies of hygiene in movie theaters, 87–93; and municipal regulation, 97–100; overview, 85–87; sex-segregated bathrooms, 100–101
Serrador, Francisco, 16–17, 95
Serrano, Jonathas, 20
Sewell, Jessica, Ellen, 183n43
sex-segregated bathrooms, 100–101
sexual morality, 5–7, 12, 15, 25–26; and middle class, 142; and sex comedy, 165; in silent cinema, 52–53, 59, 67
sexual norms, 7, 173, 179
sexual perversion. *See* illicit behavior, rumors and urban legends of
sex worker, 11, 36, 48, 116, 126, 172
silent cinema: overview, 51–53; regional production of, 53–56; restoring fatherhood and patriarchy in, 57–66; undressing *melindrosa* in, 66–76; urbanization and gender amid social change in, 76–84
Simões, Inimá, 152–53, 156, 162–63, 167, 170
Sluis, Ageeth, 14
social status, 5, 8, 12, 18, 105, 109; ascertaining, 26; Cinelândia and, 152–61; maintaining, 97; of "movie-struck" women, 50; precarity of, 25
sources, 23–26
Stamp, Shelley, 42
street cinemas, 152–53
Süssekind, Flora, 20

3D films, advent of, 154–55
"traditional" Brazilian family, defining, 5, 8, 52–53
Traffic (film), 111
trans-Atlantic slave trade, 8
tropicália (movement), 171

uniforms, gender and respectability in: sanitation workers, 154–55; usherettes, 95–97, *96*
United States, 8, 21, 86, 88. *See also* Hollywood
Unknown Brazil (film), 51–52, 54–55
urban environment: cinema as key to formation of, 22–23; defining *senhoras* in public bathrooms, 101–6, *103*; gender and, 13–16; gendered respectability in, 93–97; municipal regulation in, 97–100; reform, 87–91; sex-segregated bathrooms, 100–101; shifts in urbanization, 8–9; testing ideologies of hygiene in, 87–93
urban wonders, adulation of, 51–52
usherettes, 95–97, *96*

vagrants, depiction of, 80–81
Valentino, Rudolph, 4, 22, 130
Vargas, Darcy, 147
Vargas, Getúlio, 143–45, 179
Varieté (film), 135–37
Vaughan, Mary Kay, 15
Vera Cruz (film production company), 144, 164. *See also* Companhia Cinematográfica Vera Cruz
Vida Doméstica, 6

Weinstein, Barbara, 95, 97, 148, 166
"whitening," ideology, 21
women, moviegoing activities of, 3, 27, 51, 85, 107, 141; cultural imperialism, 45–46; defining *senhoras*, 101–6; and domestic sphere, 13, 30–31, 42, 46, 142; entering workforce, 9; fatherhood and patriarchy, 57–66; finding love in magazine ads, 137–40; house-street contrast, 46–50; increased spatial mobility, 13–16; microhierarchies, 119–26; moralism, 143–52; movie-struck girls, 42–46; overview, 3–7, 175–80; respectable womanhood, 93–97; sanitation movement, 87–93; sex-segregated bathrooms, 100–101; women in print culture, 27–50. See also *melindrosa* (modern girl); movie-struck girl
workforce, women entering, 9
working class, cultural construction of, 120

Xavier, Ismail, 21–22, 55

youth and counterculture, mistrust of, 170–73